The Alignment Economy

Rebuilding the Connection Between Effort and Stability

Christine Marletti

The Alignment Economy: Rebuilding the Connection Between Effort and Stability

Paperback ISBN: 979-8-9959221-0-0

Hardcover ISBN: 979-8-9959221-1-7

Audiobook ISBN: 979-8-9959221-2-4

E-Book ISBN: 979-8-9959221-3-1

First published 2026.

Printed in the United States of America.

For my children—
may you never know what it feels like to work hard and still wonder if stability will ever arrive.

For my father—
who always found a way to keep working, no matter how hard the economy pushed back.

For my sisters—
whose resilience reminds me every day that persistence often survives long after fairness does.

For my wife—
whose patience, love, and support made room for the countless hours spent chasing ideas like this, even when they stole time from us.

For everyone still waiting for the system to finally catch up with their effort—
this conversation was always for you.

...and to Ronnie, wherever you are—
I hope your story helped inspire something larger than any of us imagined.

With deep gratitude to my editors—Clara Keller, Brittany Vandegrift, and Andrew Appel—thank you for helping carry this work across the finish line.

Author's Note

I grew up poor. Not the kind of poor that gets romanticized in retrospect — the kind where your school clothes come from Goodwill and you eat meals like goulash or chili surprise, because your parents are quietly stretching whatever's left. You don't recognize it as poverty when you're living it. You recognize it later, when you understand what your parents were doing and why.

My father was a Teamster who drove a truck for forty-two years. My sisters built lives with their hands and their persistence. None of them lacked effort. None of them lacked diligence. What the system lacked was any mechanism to translate that effort into stability — and over time, despite everything they did right, the distance between what they earned and what things cost kept growing.

I have been incredibly fortunate. I went to school while working full time, pushed as hard as I could for as long as it took, and found a position in this economy where I am not behind. I am aware of what that cost and I'm aware that others who worked just as hard did not end up where I did. The difference between us wasn't effort. It was circumstance — the kind of circumstance that our current system was never designed to account for.

There is a saying I've carried for years, whose origin I can't trace with any certainty: if you finally make it to the top, the least you can do is send the elevator back down. That's what this book is. It's not a policy paper written from a distance. It's an attempt by someone who felt the weight of that shame — the public assistance, the thrift store clothes, the careful silences around money — to build something that might prevent the next family from feeling it too.

Regardless of title or position, we're all one unfortunate set of circumstances away from being left behind. I think about this often. This work exists because I have not forgotten that.

How to Read This Book

If you picked up this book, there is a good chance something about the economy already feels off. Maybe it feels harder to get ahead than it should. Maybe growth looks strong on paper while daily life feels increasingly unstable. Maybe you have watched people work harder, become more educated, take on more responsibility, and still struggle to build the kind of security previous generations often expected. Or maybe you simply suspect that something fundamental no longer fits.

This book was written for that instinct.

Because large systems are difficult to see while you are living inside them. Most of us experience the economy through symptoms. A paycheck that stretches less than it used to. Costs rising faster than confidence. Business decisions that make sense on paper but somehow produce instability anyway. Policies that promise correction but seem to require more correction later.

What we rarely see is the structure connecting those experiences. That is what this book attempts to make visible. Before a system can be criticized, defended, repaired, or redesigned, it must first be understood. And understanding large systems takes time. Which is why this book is intentionally built in sequence.

The early chapters focus on recognition: why the economy increasingly feels disconnected from effort, why instability often feels personal before it becomes visible as structural, and why growth and lived experience can feel increasingly disconnected.

The middle chapters focus on mechanism: how systems drift, how incentives compound, and what healthier alignment between productivity, participation, and stability could realistically require.

The later chapters focus on possibility—not as abstraction, but as something capable of existing in the real world. Why change is difficult. How trust is built. And what conditions would need to exist for something more durable to emerge.

You do not need to agree with every conclusion. And you do not need to fully understand every concept the first time it appears.

This book builds.

Some ideas may feel abstract before later chapters make them practical. Some arguments may feel incomplete before surrounding pieces reveal why they matter.

That is intentional.

Complex systems rarely become visible all at once. Sometimes understanding arrives gradually. Sometimes several disconnected ideas suddenly click into place. If that happens, let it. This is not a book designed to be rushed. It is a book designed to be considered.

Some readers will move straight through from beginning to end. Others may find themselves returning to earlier chapters after later sections reshape how they understand what came before.

Both are valid ways to read this work.

It is also worth saying clearly what this book is, and what it is not.

The Alignment Economy was written to explain the structure.

Its purpose is not to reproduce every fiscal assumption, simulate every economic condition, or contain the complete legislative and technical framework required to operationalize a system of this scale. Those questions matter. They deserve serious scrutiny. But they require different tools.

The purpose of this book is to explain:

- why the current system behaves the way it does;
- why instability can persist despite growth and productivity;
- what structural misalignment looks like;
- and what healthier alignment could realistically require.

Understanding comes before implementation. A system cannot be seriously evaluated until it can first be clearly seen.

For readers who wish to test assumptions more deeply, companion materials exist that examine the technical, operational, and legislative foundations behind the framework discussed here in greater detail.

They are intentionally separate because serious ideas should survive different forms of scrutiny. Some questions are philosophical. Some are technical. Some are legislative. And some are practical. This book begins with understanding. The rest exists for those who wish to test what understanding reveals.

So, before we begin, there is only one thing I would ask of you: Read with curiosity. Not agreement. Not skepticism. Curiosity. Because by the end of this book, the most important question may no longer be:

What is wrong with the economy?

But something more difficult, and perhaps more useful:

Why does the economy behave this way... and what would it take to build something that holds?

What This Book Argues

The economy is not failing in the way many people assume. In many ways, it is doing exactly what it was designed to do. Growth continues. Markets expand. Productivity rises.

Yet for millions of people, stability feels increasingly harder to reach. People work harder, become more educated, take on greater responsibility—and still struggle to build the kind of security previous generations often expected.

That disconnect matters. Because healthy systems should not require people to work harder every decade simply to stand still.

This book argues that the problem is not ambition. Not success. Not markets. And not capitalism itself. Healthy markets have created extraordinary prosperity. Innovation has improved lives. Businesses have expanded opportunity. Competition has driven progress. Those things matter.

The harder question is this: *What happens when the systems governing work, wages, taxation, productivity, and the cost of living gradually stop moving together?*

Over time, small misalignments compound. Wages rise, but purchasing power weakens. Productivity grows, while stability becomes harder to maintain. Growth continues, yet everyday life feels increasingly fragile. The result is not necessarily collapse, but something more subtle. A system that still functions but increasingly feels harder to trust.

This book explores the possibility that the issue is not effort, but structure.

That instability may not be the result of individual failure, poor choices, or isolated policy mistakes, but the predictable outcome of systems that drift out of alignment over time.

The purpose of *The Alignment Economy* is not to argue for tearing systems down.

It is to ask whether healthier alignment between effort, participation, productivity, and stability could still be possible. And if so: *What would it realistically take to build something that holds?*

You do not need to agree with every conclusion that follows. But this book asks that possibility be taken seriously. Because before systems can be improved, they must first be clearly seen.

THE ALIGNMENT ECONOMY · WAGES & PRODUCTIVITY · INDEXED GROWTH SINCE 1948

The Broken Link: Productivity and Pay Since 1948

Indexed growth (1948 = 100): net productivity vs. typical worker compensation — real, inflation-adjusted

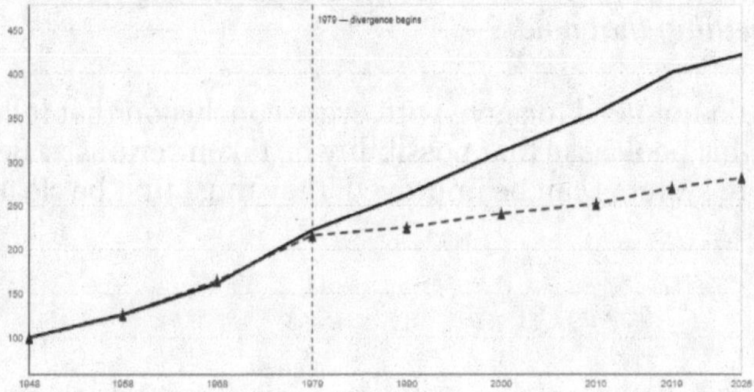

Net Productivity — Typical Worker Pay (real, inflation-adjusted)

PRODUCTIVITY GROWTH SINCE 1979	TYPICAL WORKER PAY GROWTH SINCE 1979	MISSING WAGES PER HOUR TODAY
+90.2%	**+33%**	**$16.40**
BLS/BEA via EPI Productivity-Pay Tracker, updated May 2025	Real, inflation-adjusted — one-third the rate of productivity	What the typical worker would earn if pay had tracked productivity since 1979

> *Forty-six years. A 90% rise in what the economy produced per worker. And the typical worker's real purchasing power rose only 33%. If pay had tracked productivity, the typical worker would earn $16.40 more per hour today.*
>
> ***That is not a political number. It is the arithmetic of a broken structural link — and it has been compounding since 1979. The design problem is fixable. The fix requires a design solution.***

Sources: EPI Productivity-Pay Tracker, updated May 2025. Underlying data: Bureau of Labor Statistics Labor Productivity and Costs program (total economy, unpublished); BLS Current Employment Statistics; BLS Employment Cost Trends; BLS Consumer Price Index; Bureau of Economic Analysis National Income and Product Accounts. Missing wages figure: EPI Wage Calculator, BLS Labor Productivity and Costs data and BLS Current Employment Statistics, updated 2025. All compensation figures are real (inflation-adjusted). Index base: 1948 = 100.

THE ALIGNMENT ECONOMY
Christine Marletti · July 2025
the-alignment-economy.com

Chapter 1 – The Original Promise of the System

How it Started

In 1994, I was a young middle manager walking the floor at McDonnell Douglas in Long Beach, California. I had a habit of stopping to talk to people — not to inspect, not to manage in the traditional sense, but because the floor is where you find out what is actually happening. That day I stopped at a small group and asked the question I always ask.

"How's everything going?"

One of the men — I'll call him Ronnie, maybe 23 or 24 years old — answered without hesitation. He had the kind of energy that makes you stop whatever you're thinking about and simply listen.

"Life is great. I've got a great girlfriend, a kick ass job building airplanes, and I own 22 pairs of jeans."

I've been thinking about that last sentence for thirty years.

The jeans were not about fashion. They were not even about money. They were *proof* — proof that what Ronnie was doing meant something. That the system was taking his effort and returning something tangible. Something he could see, feel, and count. He was 23 years old, building aircraft that would carry people across oceans, and the economy was keeping up with him. Not perfectly. Not extravagantly. But reliably.

That is what alignment looks like when it works.

This book is about what happened to it — and what it would take to rebuild it.

250 years ago, a new idea changed the world. The idea sounds simple now: if people are free to work, create, and trade, then effort will be rewarded and life will get better over time. Before that shift, most people lived in systems where position was fixed. Where you were born mattered more than what you did. Work guaranteed survival, not progress. So, when this new system took shape, it introduced something that had not existed at scale before — the possibility of mobility.

For the first time, people believed that if they did the right things, their lives would move forward. Not randomly. Not occasionally. Reliably. That belief changed behavior. People worked differently when effort mattered. They planned differently, built differently, and took risks they would not have taken before — because for the first time, there was a system behind them that made those risks worth taking. It was never written down, but everyone understood it: if you showed up, worked hard, and stayed the course, your life would move forward. Not perfectly. But reliably. That understanding was the contract. And people built their lives around it.

What the system was supposed to do

The system was not just about freedom. It was about conversion. Work into income. Income into stability. Stability into growth. Growth into opportunity. That chain is not just economic — it is personal. It is how people measure whether their lives are working. At the beginning, that chain held together. If you worked more, you earned more. If you earned more, your life improved. If your life improved, you could plan ahead. And if you could plan ahead, you could build something larger than your next paycheck.

The early system was not perfect. There were inequalities, gaps, and failures. But there was something more important than perfection: predictability. People could see a pattern. Work led to progress. Time produced improvement. Effort generated reward. That pattern created confidence, and confidence created participation. People showed up because they believed it would matter. When people believe something will matter, they give more of themselves to it. That belief is the real foundation of any economic system. Without it, participation becomes forced instead of voluntary, and when that happens, the system weakens.

Businesses were part of the same loop. A business hired workers, produced goods or services, and generated profit. That profit depended on workers being productive and customers being able to afford what was produced. That created a natural balance. If workers did better, they could spend more. If they could spend more, businesses could grow. If businesses grew, they could hire more workers. The loop reinforced itself, and the system sustained itself without constant correction.

It is important to be clear about something early: this is not an argument against markets, business, profit, or growth. Those things matter. They are part of what lifted living standards and created opportunity at a scale human history had never seen before. The problem is not that the system produced growth. The problem is that over time, the relationships underneath that growth became less connected to the people participating inside it. A system can be highly productive and still drift. Recognizing that difference matters, because fixing drift requires understanding what worked before deciding what must change.

Stability did not mean comfort for everyone. It meant something simpler: bills could be paid without constant stress, a setback did not immediately create crisis, planning for next year felt possible, and effort created forward movement. Stability is not luxury. It is the absence of constant instability. Families built their lives around that structure. One income could support a household. Savings accumulated. Homes were purchased. Children were raised in environments that felt predictable. Parents could pass stability forward. Children could start from a stronger position. That is how the system compounded across generations. Each generation didn't start over. They started slightly ahead. That was the quiet power of the system — not just that it worked, but that it kept working.

Think about what that actually looked like in practice — not in the abstract, but in a house, in a neighborhood, in a specific decade. In the 1950s and 1960s, a man who drove a truck, welded pipe, ran wire, or framed houses could buy a home, raise children, and retire with something to show for it. The job was physical. The hours were long. But the connection was clear: you put in the time, the system returned stability. Not wealth, stability. Which was the point.

None of this is meant to romanticize the past. That period of American life was far from perfect. Opportunity was unevenly distributed, many communities were excluded from prosperity, and structural barriers limited who benefited fully from growth.

But imperfect systems can still reveal important truths. For much of the twentieth century, the relationship between effort and stability, while flawed and incomplete, was more predictable than it feels for many working families today.

People were not guaranteed success. But work more reliably translated into progress.

The feeling Ronnie described did not disappear with his generation. It changed shape.

Sarah and Marcus live in a different economy than Ronnie did. Sarah is a public-school teacher and Marcus is a logistics supervisor. Their combined salaries would put them somewhere inside what most people would call the "middle class" of our economy. They are responsible, hardworking and rarely talk about the economy either. They talk about timing. Whether the roof can wait another year. Whether the deductible will reset before the next specialist visit. Whether the vacation was worth postponing again.

They had stable jobs.

Two incomes.

A life that looked responsible from the outside.

And yet increasingly, ordinary planning felt heavier than it once should have.

Not crisis.

Pressure.

The kind that quietly accumulates.

Different generation. Different circumstances. Strangely familiar feeling:

"Something feels harder than it should."

Then the 1970s arrived. Inflation hit 12 percent, then higher. A gallon of gas went from 36 cents in 1970 to over a dollar by 1980 — not because anyone chose it, but because the system had lost its anchor. Wages chased prices that chased wages that chased nothing stable. A plumber who locked in a mortgage in 1968 was fine. A plumber trying to buy that same house in 1979 was looking at an 18 percent interest rate and could not make the math work, no matter what he earned.

Many people who lived through that decade developed a lasting distrust of systems. Not because they were cynical, but because they watched a system they counted on stop holding, and nobody could tell them why or when it would come back. That distrust was earned. And it passed down to the next generation, and the one after that. The feeling that even when things look stable, the floor can drop out from under you. That the economy is something that happens to you, not something that works with you. That feeling is not wrong. It was accurate then. And for most working people, it has stayed accurate since.

What drift feels like

The system did not break in a way people could point to. There was no single moment where everything changed, no headline that said the system no longer works. Instead, something quieter happened. Things began to feel slightly off. Not enough to explain, but enough to feel. The earliest signs were easy to dismiss — a grocery bill that seemed a little higher, a rent increase that felt aggressive, a raise that did not go quite as far as expected. People told themselves prices go up sometimes, this is just a tough year, it will balance out. For a while, that explanation held.

Over time, those small adjustments stopped being temporary. People began watching spending more closely, delaying purchases, rethinking decisions that used to feel simple. At first this felt like being responsible – adapting to changing conditions. But there is a difference between adapting occasionally and adapting constantly. When adjustment becomes constant, something deeper is happening. Not because you changed. Because the system did.

Drift builds pressure slowly, like adding weight one pound at a time. People were still working, still earning, still moving forward on paper. But it felt heavier. Everything required more effort than it used to. The most common description people give is this: "I'm working harder, but I'm not getting ahead." That feeling is not emotional — it is structural. It means effort is no longer translating into progress at the same rate. Imagine walking on a moving walkway that slowly reverses direction. You are still walking. Still putting in effort. But you are no longer moving forward. Eventually you are working just to stay in the same place.

People started noticing that raises felt different. Not smaller in number, smaller in impact. A raise that used to create breathing room now only covered increased costs. A promotion that should have improved lifestyle now just stabilized it. Income was still increasing, but its power was not. At the same time, costs began to behave differently – not just increasing, but increasing without a clear pattern. Housing moved faster than wages. Healthcare became unpredictable. Everyday expenses rose in ways that felt disconnected from income. There was no anchor tying these costs back to what people earned, which meant there was no reliable way to stay ahead, no matter how well they did.

Margin is the space between what you earn and what you need. In a stable system, people have some margin — not always large, but enough to absorb normal life events. As drift progressed, that margin shrank, then disappeared. Without margin, every small disruption becomes a problem. A car repair becomes a financial event. A medical bill becomes a setback. A missed paycheck becomes a crisis. People began operating closer to the edge — not because they were irresponsible, but because the system no longer provided enough space. And when people stop feeling secure, they stop moving forward, even if they are still working just as hard.

Drift does not look the same for everyone, but it shows up everywhere. An hourly worker sees slight wage increases alongside faster increases in rent and food, and ends up working more hours just to maintain the same position. A middle-income household with two steady incomes watches rising childcare, housing, and healthcare costs eat the difference, leaving them able to maintain their lifestyle but unable to build forward. Even higher earners feel it — more comfortable, but less secure than they expected. The pressure is distributed unevenly, but nobody is exempt from it.

Drift is confusing because it does not match what people are told. They hear the economy is growing, productivity is increasing, opportunities exist — and all of that may be true. But their personal experience does not reflect it. When systems drift, people rarely blame the system first. They blame themselves. They think they need to work harder, make better decisions, be more disciplined. And for a while, that works. Until it does not. And when it stops working, it does not fail all at once. It fails quietly — in smaller margins, tighter months, delayed decisions. By the time people realize it is not temporary, they are already adjusting to something that was never supposed to be normal. There comes a point where increased effort no longer solves the issue — where people take on extra work, cut expenses further, optimize everything, and still feel stuck. That is the moment where drift becomes visible as something structural, not personal. But most people don't see it that way at first. They think they are falling behind. That they missed something, or didn't push hard enough. The system keeps moving, so the failure feels personal — even when it isn't.

When people stop feeling secure, they stop thinking long-term. In a stable system, people plan for the future — buying homes, saving for retirement, investing in growth. In a drifting system, they manage monthly costs, avoid immediate problems, and delay long-term decisions. That shift has consequences that extend far beyond any individual household. Long-term thinking drives investment, innovation, and growth. Without it, the system becomes reactive. And once instability feels normal, people stop expecting anything different — which means the system can continue drifting without resistance, because people no longer believe they are owed anything better.

Why wages, costs, and output split apart

In a stable system, three things move together: what the economy produces, what people earn, and what things cost. When those three stay connected, the system feels balanced. If production increases, wages follow. If wages increase, people can handle costs. Everything moves as part of the same structure. Over time, those three pieces stopped moving together. They did not break at the same moment — they separated gradually, the separation became noticeable, then it became normal, until today they operate almost independently. When the parts of a system move independently, the people inside it absorb the difference. That is the root of the problem.

Output — everything the economy creates, measured by GDP — has increased significantly. The economy produces more than ever before. Wages have also increased, but not at the same rate as output. As businesses became more efficient, they could produce more with fewer people, automate processes, and expand globally. This increased total output, and from a system perspective, that looks like success. But output measures production. It does not measure distribution. It tells us how much is created, not how that value is shared. Productivity gains did not flow directly to labor — more value was created, but it stayed within corporate structures and capital returns. Wages still benefited, just not proportionally. And over time, that gap becomes impossible to ignore.

Costs did not just increase — they became disconnected. Housing began to move independently, driven by supply constraints and investment demand rather than wage levels. Healthcare became difficult to predict and consistently rose faster than income. Essential costs — food, shelter, transportation, utilities — are not optional. People cannot stop eating or stop paying rent. When these costs rise without any coordination with wages, the pressure is immediate. The real issue is not that costs increased. It is that proportion was lost. In a stable system, costs scale with income. In a drifting system, costs move independently. That breaks the relationship. And when that relationship breaks, effort loses its direction.

Over the last several decades, productivity continued rising. Businesses became more efficient. Technology accelerated output. Markets expanded.

Yet for many households, the practical cost of participation moved faster than compensation.

Housing climbed.

Healthcare climbed.

Education climbed.

Childcare climbed.

For millions of families, the question slowly shifted from: "How do we get ahead?" to: "Can we stay ahead of what keeps rising?"

The economy continued growing.

But the lived experience of participation increasingly felt disconnected from that growth.

Policy tries to correct these issues, but it reacts, it does not lead. By the time policy adjusts, costs have already changed, wages have already lagged, and pressure has already built. Each adjustment was isolated: a minimum wage change here, a tax adjustment there, a subsidy for something else. Each one tried to fix part of the system. None fixed the structure. Instead of one aligned system, we now have wage systems, cost systems, and policy systems each operating independently. Wages adjust based on labor markets. Costs adjust based on supply and demand. Policy adjusts based on past data. Each part is reacting to something different, which means there is no synchronized movement, no shared direction, and no automatic correction.

This creates feedback loops that amplify the problem rather than correct it. If costs rise faster than wages, people reduce spending. When spending drops, businesses adjust. When businesses adjust, wage growth slows. When wage growth slows, the gap widens further. This is not a correcting system — it is a diverging system. And in a diverging system, doing more does not guarantee getting ahead. That is why this cannot fix itself. There is nothing inside the system that tells it where "aligned" actually is. To fix position, you need a reference point. The economy does not currently have one.

The National Productivity Unit

What is missing is a single unit that connects output, wages, and costs. Without it, alignment is impossible. Think about something simple: if a scale is off, you need a known weight to recalibrate it. If a map is off, you need a known location to reorient it. If a system is drifting, you need a fixed point to bring everything back into alignment. Instead of building that reference point, we tried to fix problems one at a time — adjusting minimum wage, tax brackets, subsidies, benefits. Each attempted to correct part of the system. None corrected the structure, because none were anchored to the same thing. An anchor does not control everything. It connects everything. It gives every part of the system a shared reference, so instead of guessing, wages know where they should be, costs know where they should be, and policy knows where to align.

If the feeling millions of people experience is structural, then the solution cannot simply be emotional, political, or temporary.

Structural problems rarely yield to isolated adjustments. They require missing relationships to be rebuilt. The challenge is not simply making wages higher, benefits stronger, or policies more generous.

The challenge is restoring a relationship between what the system produces and what participation inside that system actually requires. Without that connection, every improvement risks becoming temporary.

Which raises an uncomfortable question: What if the economy is not missing effort, ambition, or productivity?

What if it is missing an anchor?

Before going further, one distinction matters. An anchor is not the same thing as a replacement. The purpose here is not to replace markets, replace money, or redesign everyday economic life from scratch. It is to create a shared point of reference — a way to reconnect wages, costs, and productivity to one another so they stop drifting independently. People would still work, businesses would still compete, and the economy would still function through markets. The difference is that the relationships underneath those things would become more visible and more stable.

This is where the National Productivity Unit comes in. The NPU is a single number built from two things that must always be linked: what the economy produces, and what it costs to live inside that economy. These are represented as GDP per capita and the Essential Economic Basket Value — the actual cost of housing, food, healthcare, transportation, utilities and basic communication. Not luxury. Not excess. Just the essentials required to participate in daily life. The formula brings them together: $NPU = (\alpha \times GDP_{per\ capita}) + (\beta \times EEBV)$. Because it is defined mathematically, it does not depend on opinion or shift based on narrative. It reflects conditions as they actually exist. That is what allows it to be written into structure — not as guidance, but as enforceable logic.

One way to think about NPU is not as a price tag on life, but as a common ruler. It creates a shared way to understand whether effort, compensation, and the cost of participation are still moving together — or quietly drifting apart. Like any ruler, it does not determine the outcome. It helps reveal the relationship.

No modern economy is simple. No single measurement can perfectly capture the complexity of millions of businesses, workers, households, and institutions moving simultaneously.

The goal is not perfection. The goal is alignment. Not rigid control. Not engineered outcomes. But a more reliable relationship between effort, participation, and stability than many people experience today.

No serious system removes tradeoffs completely. Markets will still fluctuate. Industries will still change. Technology will still disrupt work faster than institutions adapt. Mistakes will still happen. The question is not whether instability disappears. The question is whether the relationship between effort and stability becomes more reliable than it feels today.

Building something like that is not simple. But ignoring the absence of that relationship has not made complexity disappear either.

The framework uses a fixed 50/50 weighting between productivity and participation cost. Half of the signal comes from GDP per capita, and half comes from the Essential Economic Basket Value. That balance is intentional. It prevents the system from being pushed too far toward output while ignoring lived participation costs, or too far toward costs while ignoring productive capacity. The constraints enforce that balance automatically, without requiring political intervention each time conditions shift. The operating baseline is fixed at 50/50. Future changes would require Congress, public justification, modeling, and guardrails.

Once the NPU exists, wages can be expressed in NPU units, tax systems can scale with NPU, benefits can be tied to NPU, and policy can anchor to NPU. Everything operates from the same reference point. The question changes from "what should minimum wage be?" to "what is 1.0 NPU?" – and that question has a calculated answer.

That does not mean every government program automatically converts into an NPU-based system. The purpose of the National Productivity Unit is to provide a common economic reference point that can be used where continuity, eligibility, contribution, or stabilization functions benefit from a shared measure of participation.

Some programs may continue operating substantially as they do today. Others may incorporate NPU-indexed thresholds, eligibility standards, contribution formulas, or continuity protections where authorized by law and supported by implementation requirements. The goal is not universal conversion. The goal is consistency. Wherever participation must be measured, protected, or stabilized, a common reference point allows those functions to operate within the same economic framework while preserving the flexibility necessary for different programs to serve different purposes.

What this looks like in practice

Throughout this book, examples use fifteen hundred annual work hours as the baseline for economic participation. That number was chosen intentionally.

The purpose of the National Productivity Unit is not to measure the maximum number of hours a person can work. It is to measure meaningful participation in the economy. People raise children, care for family members, pursue education, volunteer in their communities, recover from illness, and simply live their lives. A healthy economy should leave room for those things.

Fifteen hundred hours reflects a design choice: the belief that economic participation should support life, not consume it. Different societies may ultimately choose a different baseline. The exact number matters less than the principle behind it.

To make this real, assume the NPU equals $20 per hour. This number comes from economic output and cost of living—it represents the real value of one hour of participation in the economy.

At 1.0 NPU, a worker earning $20 per hour and working 1,500 hours earns $30,000 annually—enough to cover essential living costs and maintain basic participation in the economy. This is not luxury. This is the participation floor.

At 1.25 NPU, the worker earns $37,500 annually. That difference creates a financial buffer, the ability to absorb disruptions, and the capacity to plan ahead.

The difference between 1.0 and 1.25 NPU is not the difference between participation and non-participation. It is the difference between merely maintaining participation (participation floor) and achieving a measure of economic stability.

And unlike today's minimum wage — a number set politically and rarely updated — the NPU adjusts automatically as economic conditions change.

A skilled tradesperson earning 2.0 NPU earns $60,000 annually at 1,500 hours. An executive at 5.0 NPU is earning $150,000 annually. The system still rewards skill, experience, and output — strongly. There is no cap on success. What changes is that those rewards exist within a structure that keeps them tethered to reality. A business owner facing this system has clear incentives: invest in productivity and you are rewarded, expand sustainably and you are rewarded, extract excessively and you face constraints. The system rewards alignment rather than exploitation, not through moral instruction but through structural design.

The biggest change is not income level — it is predictability. People know what their income means, how it relates to costs, and how it will adjust over time. That changes behavior. Workers invest more in skill development, remain in the workforce longer, and take calculated risks instead of avoiding them. Businesses plan long-term instead of reacting short-term. They invest in productivity instead of cost avoidance. They expand based on real demand instead of speculative margins. Over time, this creates a different type of growth — not just expansion, but aligned expansion, where increases in output, income, and participation reinforce each other instead of pulling apart.

Why growth without stability is failure

For a long time, we believed the system was working because we measured the wrong thing. We measured growth, output, and expansion. Those numbers were strong, so we assumed the system was strong. But those measurements only tell part of the story. They tell us what the system produces. They do not tell us what the system delivers to people. And if a system does not deliver stability, it is not working — no matter what the numbers say. Production is what the economy creates. Outcome is what people experience. Those are not the same thing. A system can produce more every year and still deliver less stability. That is exactly what happened.

Growth is important. But growth is not the goal. The goal is stability through participation. Growth is supposed to support that goal, not replace it. When output becomes the target, efficiency increases, production expands, scale improves — all of which look positive — but the connection between output and people weakens at the same time. People hear that the economy is strong and growth is up. But their experience does not match. That creates frustration — not because people do not understand the numbers, but because the numbers do not reflect their reality. Growth creates the appearance of progress. But if output increases while stability does not, there is no real progress. There is only expansion without benefit. And expansion without benefit is drift by another name.

Stability allows people to plan, invest, build, and participate fully. Without it, everything becomes temporary. People think short-term, reduce risk, and delay decisions. That slows the entire system even if output remains high — because a system that produces without stabilizing will eventually weaken. Participation becomes cautious, investment becomes limited, innovation slows. Not immediately, but in stages. First, participation becomes cautious. Then, long-term investment slows. Then, trust weakens. Once trust weakens, the system begins to lose its ability to generate voluntary participation. At that point growth can still exist, but it becomes fragile — dependent on intervention rather than driven by engagement. That is the critical risk. Not that the system stops producing, but that it loses the ability to sustain itself.

We did not lose growth. We lost alignment — the connection between effort, reward, cost, and outcome. Adjusting wages, taxes, and benefits will not fix that, because those adjustments do not address the core issue. They do not reconnect the system. A real solution must reconnect output to wages, wages to cost of living, and cost of living back to the economy. It must restore the full chain. The National Productivity Unit does exactly that — it reconnects production, income, and cost into a single system. Not by slowing growth or limiting success, but by aligning the system so that growth supports stability.

We started this chapter with a simple idea: that effort should be rewarded. That idea still matters. The system no longer delivers on it consistently. That is what we are fixing — and everything that follows in this book builds on that foundation. The system must convert effort into stability. Consistently. Predictably. At scale. Once you see it that way, it becomes hard to unsee.

As far as I know, Ronnie never stopped working hard. Most people do not. That is part of what makes the growing disconnect so difficult to explain. People are not working less.

- Many are working more
- Learning more
- Managing more
- Adapting more

And yet for many households, stability feels harder to hold than it once did. That does not necessarily mean the system failed. But it may mean the relationship between effort and outcome quietly drifted farther apart than we realized.

If that relationship drifted, then understanding how, and whether it can be rebuilt, becomes one of the most important questions we can ask. Because for people like Ronnie, this conversation is not theoretical. It is daily life. And if effort no longer reliably leads to stability, then understanding why may be one of the most important economic questions of our time.

Chapter 2 – The Visible Cracks in the System

There is a point where people stop trusting what they are told. It does not happen all at once. It does not come from one event. It comes from a simple feeling: something about this does not add up anymore. You hear that the economy is strong. You hear that growth is up. You hear that opportunity is everywhere. But your experience does not match that story. You are working, earning, doing what you are supposed to do — and still, something feels off. Not broken in a dramatic way. Just not working the way it should. That is the first visible crack. It is a quiet realization at first — not that something is wrong with you, but that something may be wrong with the system itself.

For a long time, people could rely on a basic relationship: if you worked more, you moved forward. If you improved your skills, your life improved. That relationship created stability. Then something subtle changed. People started noticing that working more did not always mean getting ahead, that promotions did not feel like progress, that raises did not create relief. At first it felt like a bad year, a tough stretch, an exception. But then it kept happening. And eventually people stopped asking "Why is this happening right now?" and started asking "Why does this keep happening?" That question is where doubt begins.

Every month, Sarah and Marcus sit at the kitchen table with the same intention, stay ahead.

They had done most things the way they were told responsible adults should.

Stable jobs.

Two incomes.

A mortgage that once felt manageable.

Retirement accounts they contributed to consistently, even when it hurt.

Health insurance.

College savings for their daughter, even if the contributions sometimes felt painfully small.

On paper, they were doing fine. But increasingly, life felt less like building and more like balancing. The insurance deductible climbed again. Groceries cost more than they remembered. A minor HVAC repair became a budgeting event. Vacation discussions turned into calculations. Not because they were irresponsible. Not because they stopped working. But because more and more of life required defensive planning.

The question quietly changed. Less: "How do we move forward?" and more: "What breaks first if something goes wrong?"

This distinction matters more than it first appears. A household under pressure often feels like a household making mistakes. But when millions of people begin adjusting in similar ways — delaying purchases, postponing repairs, avoiding risk, and planning around uncertainty — it becomes harder to explain as individual failure alone. At some point, repeated personal strain starts to look less like coincidence and more like structure.

They rarely described this as economics. Like millions of households, they described it differently: "Why does everything feel harder than it should?"

When a system works, people do not overthink every decision. There is enough stability that life moves forward without constant analysis. But when cracks form, behavior changes. People start calculating everything. Can I afford this right now? What happens if something goes wrong? Should I wait? Life stops feeling like forward movement and starts feeling like risk management. For many families, life slowly becomes less about aspiration and more about contingency.

Emergency funds become survival calculations.

Career decisions become insurance decisions.

Relocation becomes risk exposure.

Having children becomes a financial equation.

Ordinary choices begin carrying disproportionate consequences.

This shift matters because systems influence behavior.

When people increasingly organize their lives around avoiding instability rather than pursuing opportunity, the economy itself begins changing shape.

Less risk-taking.

Less mobility.

Less long-term confidence.

Not because ambition disappeared.

Because predictability did.

And when people shift into constant risk management, they are no longer building. They are protecting. And once people shift from building to protecting, the system is no longer doing what it was designed to do.

One of the clearest signs of a healthy system is how often people can say yes without stress — yes to a small purchase, yes to a short trip, yes to investing in something new. These are not big decisions. They are normal decisions. But when the system cracks, those easy moments disappear. Everything becomes "let's think about it" or "maybe later." Progress is not just built on big decisions. It is built on thousands of small ones. When those small decisions slow down, the entire system slows down with them.

Another crack appears in how people absorb normal life events. In a stable system, a car repair is manageable, a medical bill is inconvenient but not destabilizing, a missed paycheck is stressful but not catastrophic. There is margin. When the system begins to crack, that space shrinks and then disappears. Suddenly a car repair becomes a financial problem, a medical bill becomes a setback, a missed paycheck becomes a crisis. Nothing about these events changed. What changed is the system's ability to absorb them.

Most people do not immediately understand what is happening, they feel it first. Pressure without a clear cause. Effort without clear reward. Movement without real progress. They may not use words like misalignment or structural drift. They just know: this feels harder than it should. And one of the most important and most dangerous parts of that shift is how personal it feels. People think they need to work harder, make better decisions, be more disciplined. They take on more work, cut expenses, optimize everything they can. For a while, that helps. Until it does not. Because the problem is not individual effort. It is structural. And no amount of individual adjustment can fix a structural problem.

Why institutions stopped coordinating

When people feel pressure, they often assume the system changed on its own. But systems do not move by themselves. They are shaped by institutions — the policies, markets, and business structures that decide how rules are written, how incentives are set, and how decisions get made. At their best, institutions act as stabilizers. Policy supports stability. Markets reflect real conditions. Businesses operate within a shared structure. In the original design, each part had a role, and those roles were connected.

The shift did not happen all at once. Gradually, each institution began responding to its own signals instead of the system as a whole. Policy responded to political pressure. Markets responded to price signals. Businesses responded to profit incentives. Individually, each response made sense. Collectively, they stopped moving together. They were connected by a common reference point — a shared sense of what balanced looks like — but over time, that reference point faded. Not because it was removed. Because it was never formally defined. And when institutions lose a shared reference, coordination turns into reaction.

Businesses are a core part of the system — they create jobs, produce goods and services, drive growth. But businesses respond to incentives, and over time those incentives shifted. Without alignment, the focus on efficiency, scale, and margin does not guarantee system balance. A business can increase productivity, reduce labor costs, and expand output while still contributing to system imbalance. Those improvements are not tied to wage growth, cost stability, or overall alignment. The reinforcing loop that once drove the system — workers earn, they spend, spending supports businesses, businesses hire — changed direction. Now costs rise, people reduce spending, reduced spending makes businesses adjust, adjustment slows wage growth, and the gap widens further.

This is not the fault of any one group. Policy did not fail intentionally. Markets did not break on their own. Businesses did not choose misalignment. Each part responded rationally to incomplete signals. The system is still active — policies are still created, markets are still moving, businesses are still operating — but activity is not the same as coordination. Coordination requires a shared reference, a shared direction, a shared structure. Without that, everything moves. Nothing aligns. And when nothing aligns, the burden of that misalignment does not disappear — it moves to the people inside the system.

This is also not an argument that institutions stopped trying or that government simply failed. Policy makers, businesses, and markets were often responding to real pressures with the tools they had available. The challenge is that even reasonable responses struggle when they are not connected to a shared reference point. Effort still exists. Coordination weakens.

Why policy responses did not hold

Once the cracks began to show, institutions did not sit still. Policies were introduced, programs were expanded, adjustments were made. This is important to understand: the system did not fail because nothing was done. It failed because what was done could not solve the problem. If you look at the major policy responses over time, they all make sense on their own. Wages too low? Raise wages. Costs too high? Provide relief. Instability rising? Add support. Each response targets a real issue, helps at least temporarily, and that is why they were accepted. Because individually, they worked just enough to feel like progress. That is what makes the problem hard to see — every fix looks like movement, even when the system itself is not moving toward stability.

But a pattern kept repeating. A problem appears, a policy is introduced, the pressure eases slightly, the problem returns in a new form. Relief solves immediate pressure. Resolution fixes underlying structure. Most policy responses delivered relief. Very few delivered resolution. The system would feel better for a moment, then drift again. This creates a false signal — it looks like progress, but it is not durable. Every policy change produces immediate visible effects, then the system adjusts around it. Costs rise again. Wage pressure returns. Gaps reopen. Not because the policy was wrong, but because the system was never anchored. The same forces that created the problem continued operating after the fix.

There is a deeper structural reason why this keeps happening. In a connected system, everything affects everything else. When one part is adjusted without alignment, pressure moves rather than disappears. Raise wages and costs adjust. Reduce costs and supply shifts. Add support and demand changes. Each decision helps one area and pressures another. Without a shared anchor, these adjustments do not stabilize the system — they redistribute imbalance. And that creates the common experience of every solution seeming to create a new problem.

The core limitation is this: policy cannot lead a system when it does not have a target to aim at. Every policy debate circles around similar questions — what should wages be, what should costs be, what level of support is enough — but without answering the deeper question: what should these be relative to? Without that answer, every number is an informed guess. And without a reference, the debate never resolves. One group argues for higher wages. Another argues for cost control. Another argues for reduced intervention. All of them are reacting to real problems, but they are not anchored to the same system. Tradeoffs replace structure. And when tradeoffs become the system, there is no stable outcome — only shifting pressure.

This helps explain something many people instinctively feel but struggle to articulate: why so many solutions seem to help for a while and then stop holding. Policies may ease pressure temporarily. Businesses adapt. Households adjust. Markets rebalance. But if the underlying relationships remain disconnected, the system slowly returns to the same tension in a different form. The symptoms change. The instability stays.

Misalignment does not always appear dramatically. Sometimes it appears through systems quietly compensating for one another. An employer struggles to absorb rising labor costs. Workers take second jobs. Public assistance fills gaps. Healthcare becomes employer-dependent. Housing costs absorb wage gains.

No single institution necessarily fails. Instead, institutions begin compensating for structural instability elsewhere. What appears disconnected often shares a common root, the absence of a reliable coordinating relationship.

For Sarah and Marcus, none of these pressures arrived dramatically. No single event signaled failure. No moment announced: "The system changed."

Instead, adjustments accumulated. One delayed repair. One insurance increase. One postponed vacation. One more conversation about what could wait another year.

Individually, each compromise seemed reasonable. Collectively, they slowly changed how the future felt.

There is also a dimension of this problem that policy has consistently failed to address. Some workers split their time across multiple employers, where no single employer meets the minimum wage thresholds on its own but the aggregate hours qualify as full time. When those workers rely on assistance programs because their wages do not cover essential costs, the burden falls to every taxpayer rather than the corporations whose business model depends on low-wage part-time labor. Those taxpayer-funded subsidies continue to burden the system, and nothing in the current policy framework has fixed it — because fixing it requires reconnecting labor cost to the companies that created it, which requires an anchor those companies are currently not held to.

For many years, debates about wages often focused on public assistance. If a large number of working people required food assistance, housing assistance, or other forms of support despite being employed, the conclusion seemed obvious: taxpayers were being asked to absorb costs that compensation alone was not covering.

But public assistance is not the problem. It is a signal.

The deeper issue is whether compensation remains sufficiently aligned with economic participation to allow workers to sustain themselves without requiring increasing external support. The Alignment Economy therefore does not penalize workers for receiving benefits, nor does it treat benefit usage itself as the measure of failure.

Instead, the framework measures compensation alignment directly. Where workforce compensation becomes materially disconnected from sustainable participation, corrective contribution mechanisms apply regardless of whether individual workers receive public assistance. The objective is to address the underlying compensation structure rather than the downstream symptoms that structure may produce.

In that sense, public assistance remains important as evidence that something may be wrong, but the system itself responds to the cause rather than the consequence.

The illusion of control

Through all of this, the system does not feel out of control. It feels like decisions are being made, adjustments are happening, leaders are responding. Which leads to a natural assumption: someone must be steering this. But here is the contradiction that has to be faced. The system looks controlled and behaves unstable at the same time. Both of these can be true. And that is what makes it so hard to see.

From the outside, the system shows all the signs of control. Interest rates are adjusted. Policies are debated and passed. Budgets are negotiated. Programs are expanded or reduced. There is constant activity, constant decision-making, constant movement. As humans, we associate motion with control — if something is being worked on and adjusted, we assume it is being managed. But activity is not the same as direction. To truly control a system you need a clear target, a way to measure progress toward it, and a mechanism to adjust toward alignment. Without those three things, you do not have control. You have response. And response, no matter how constant, is not the same as control.

The current system has data about what happened, signals about what is happening, and projections about what might happen. What it does not have is a defined state of alignment — a shared target. So decisions are made based on what looks off right now, not how to bring the system back to balance. There is a critical difference between steering toward a known destination and correcting deviation from one. The current system is built for correction. Not for steering. Because corrections happen constantly, it feels like steering. But without a destination, each correction is isolated.

This does not mean economists, policy makers, or institutions are unintelligent or indifferent. In many cases, they are solving incredibly difficult problems with incomplete information. The issue is less capability than structure. Even strong decisions become harder to sustain when the system lacks a consistent definition of alignment itself.

This is where it becomes personal. You experience it as inconsistency. Things improve, then reverse. Relief comes, then fades. Stability appears, then disappears. You hear that the economy is improving but your costs still feel high. You hear that wages are rising but your buying power does not change. You hear that support programs are expanding but access still feels limited. The system reports on movement — growth, output, employment — but it does not report on alignment. So you can have growth without stability, income without purchasing power, support without security, and all of it can look positive in the data.

People feel the gap between expectation and reality. Alignment is what closes that gap.

The more complex a system becomes, the easier it is to assume someone understands it better than you do. When things do not make sense, people often conclude there must be a reason, it is probably under control, they just do not see the full picture. But complexity does not guarantee control. It often hides the lack of it. Without an anchor, even the smartest analysis cannot create alignment, because the issue is not intelligence. It is structure. A system without an anchor defaults to reactive equilibrium — it constantly moves toward balance but never holds it. It feels like it is almost working. Close to stabilizing, close to solving the problem. But it never quite gets there, because it is missing the one thing that allows stability to hold.

The cost of staying unanchored

Drift is not passive — it has direction. Without an anchor, it moves away from alignment. And the changes compound. At first, they are almost invisible: a little more pressure, a little less margin, a little more uncertainty. But they build. You do not wake up one day and say the system has drifted 20 percent. You feel it differently. It takes longer to get ahead. It is harder to recover from setbacks. Stability requires more effort. That weight accumulates slowly until it becomes normal — and when something becomes the expected experience, people stop questioning it even when it is the source of the problem. At that point, the system no longer needs to hold itself together — people hold themselves in place inside it.

You adapt without realizing it. You delay decisions, reduce risk, hold more cash, avoid long-term commitments.

Individually, these are rational choices. Collectively, they change the system, because the system depends on participation — people spending, investing, taking risks, moving forward. When people shift into protection mode, the system loses momentum. And that creates a loop: instability leads people to protect, protection reduces participation, reduced participation slows the system, the slower system creates more instability. Growth without alignment cannot break that loop. It increases output without guaranteeing stability, so the system grows while people still feel pressure.

The biggest cost is not financial. It is behavioral. When people stop believing the system works, they stop fully participating in it. Planning becomes stressful. Risk feels dangerous. Confidence fades. Expectations quietly shrink. People stop believing that effort will reliably lead to progress, that stability will hold long-term, that the system will correct itself. They do not say it out loud, but they adjust their behavior around it. And when participation drops, there is less innovation, less investment, less growth that actually reaches people. That is the gap this book exists to close.

What the anchor must do

We already have things that look like anchors: inflation targets, wage benchmarks, interest rates, cost indexes. But none of them solve the problem, because they only see part of the system. They answer questions like what are prices doing and what are wages doing, but not the question that actually matters: are these things aligned with each other? A real anchor does not measure one part — it connects all parts. It links what people produce, what people earn, what things cost, and what the system can sustain, simultaneously. If even one of those is disconnected, drift returns.

The anchor must be system-wide, because if one part operates outside it, that part becomes the source of imbalance. It must scale automatically with the system, because if it does not move with productivity and output, it becomes outdated and drift starts again. It must be objective — defined by measurable reality, not opinion or negotiation — because people do not trust systems that change based on who is in power. And it must be usable at the level of daily decisions, not just at the policy level, because people live in decisions: can I afford this, should I take this job, does this raise actually matter. The anchor must show up in those moments clearly and consistently. If it does not, people go back to guessing. And guessing is exactly what created the instability.

At the beginning of this chapter, we started with a feeling: something does not add up. Now we understand why. The system is active but not aligned, managed but not anchored, growing but not stabilizing. That is why it feels the way it does. A way to anchor this system exists — not by controlling it, but by aligning it. A way to connect output, income, and stability into a single structure so that when the system grows, people move with it. That system has a name. We are going to build it next.

This is where most conversations about the economy begin separating into isolated debates. Raise wages. Lower healthcare costs. Fix housing. Reduce inflation. Expand tax credits. Strengthen labor protections.

Each proposal addresses something real. Each may even help temporarily. But over time, the same tension often reappears. Why? Because systems adapt. Housing costs adjust. Benefit structures shift. Compensation strategies evolve. Inflation absorbs gains. Labor markets rebalance.

The underlying relationships remain disconnected. This does not mean reforms are meaningless. It means fragmented systems rarely produce durable coordination.

If instability is structural, isolated interventions can only go so far. Which raises a more difficult question: What if the problem is not that we lack solutions, but that we lack a coordinating relationship capable of aligning them?

Sarah and Marcus are not unusual. That may be the most important part of the story. The growing pressure many households feel is not confined to one profession, one political belief, or one income bracket. It appears differently. But it appears widely.

And if millions of people are quietly adapting to the same instability, then the question becomes harder to avoid: What exactly are they adapting to?

If relationships inside the system have drifted apart, understanding how they reconnect becomes more than theory. It becomes necessity. Because if instability is structural, then eventually a harder question has to be faced: What exactly would a coordinating relationship strong enough to reconnect the system actually look like?

Chapter 3 – The Missing Anchor Has Shape

If you have ever felt like things were not adding up, you were not wrong. You were seeing the system without knowing what was missing. We have been talking about something you can feel even if you cannot name it yet — the difference between movement and progress, between growth and stability, between effort and outcome. Right now, those things are disconnected. But they should not be. And they do not have to stay that way.

Everything we covered in Chapters 1 and 2 points to the same root cause. The system has no anchor. Not a missing policy, not a missing program — a missing mechanism. The parts of the system are moving without a structure to hold them together. And when a system is missing its mechanism for staying aligned, no amount of adjustment can make it hold. Wages go up and costs follow. Costs stabilize and growth slows. Growth increases and stability does not follow. Every change helps something and breaks something else, because nothing is holding the whole system in place. That may not be a policy failure. It may be a design failure. And design failures do not correct themselves — they repeat until the structure changes.

David was exactly the kind of employee most companies say they want.

Reliable.

Skilled.

Hard to replace.

The person people called when systems failed because he understood how to make complicated things work again.

He had done well by most standards.

Steady work.

Good income.

A modest house.

Retirement savings he tried to contribute to consistently.

And yet, stability still felt strangely conditional.

Raises arrived, but rarely seemed to move life meaningfully forward.

Healthcare costs shifted.

Insurance changed.

Property taxes climbed.

Unexpected repairs erased careful planning.

The numbers always moved.

Just rarely in the same direction.

David was not struggling.

But he was constantly adjusting.

And increasingly, he found himself asking a question he never expected to ask after doing everything "right":

"Why does stability still feel this fragile?"

You already know what an anchor feels like, even if you have never used that word for it. Think about a time when things made sense — not perfect, not easy, but stable. Your income covered your life. Your decisions felt clear.

Progress felt real. You did not have to overthink everything or calculate every move. You moved forward and it held. That is what an anchor does. It does not remove effort. It removes confusion. It connects movement to meaning.

What NPU actually is

The structure that has been missing has a name: the National Productivity Unit, or NPU. Rather than layering another policy onto the system, NPU is designed to reconnect relationships that drifted apart over time. At first glance, this might sound like just another economic metric. It is something different. Every tool we have used before — wages, inflation indexes, GDP, interest rates — measures one part of the system. They describe movement. They do not create alignment. NPU does something different. It defines the relationship between the parts. Not what each piece is doing independently, but how they connect to each other in real time.

In plain terms, NPU represents one unit of real economic participation — what it actually costs to live inside the economy at the most basic level of stability. Not elaborate housing, not expensive meals, not luxury of any kind. The bare essentials: rent, food at recommended nutrition levels, prescribed maintenance medications, public transportation to get to work and back, electricity and heating, and minimal phone and internet access. That is 1.0 NPU. A modest addition of 0.25 — making 1.25 NPU — creates a buffer for saving, absorbing volatility, and participating in the economy at a level above "working poor." That is the livable wage. Not an estimate, not a political number — a calculated one.

It is worth pausing on what this does — and does not — mean. NPU is not an attempt to place a fixed price on human worth or prescribe one "correct" way to live. People will always choose differently, spend differently, and value different things. The role of an anchor is narrower and more practical: to establish a common reference for whether participation in the economy remains realistically connected to what the economy itself produces.

To make that connection real, it has to be measurable — not estimated, not debated, but calculated. The formula that produces it is: $NPU = (\alpha \times GDP_{per\ capita}) + (\beta \times Essential\ Economic\ Basket\ Value)$. Alpha represents the productivity-driven portion of the economy. Beta represents the stability foundation required for cost alignment. They must sum to 1.00, which means the system can never drift too far toward growth alone or cost alone — both are always present, always weighted, always held in relationship to each other. That formula is not there to make the system more complicated. It is there to prevent the system from pretending that growth and stability are separate questions. They are not. They have always been the same question.

No formula perfectly captures a modern economy.

No system eliminates friction.

Tradeoffs still exist.

Markets still move.

Technology still changes faster than institutions adapt.

Unexpected disruptions still happen.

The objective is not precision for its own sake.

Nor is it engineered equality.

The objective is directional alignment.

A stronger relationship between contribution, participation, and stability than millions of people experience today.

Because perfection has never been the standard by which economic systems survive.

Functionality is.

At first glance, a formula like this may feel overly simplified.

Or even arbitrary.

Why these variables?

Why not dozens of others?

Why not regional cost indexes, productivity curves, industry-specific adjustments, or labor market complexity?

Because an anchor has one primary responsibility:

It must reliably connect the system to the relationships that matter most.

At minimum, any durable economic anchor must answer two questions simultaneously:

What does the system produce?

And, what does participation inside the system require?

Remove production, and the system loses economic reality.

Remove participation costs, and prosperity becomes disconnected from lived experience.

Too many variables create instability.

Too few create distortion.

The goal is not to perfectly model every dimension of the economy.

The goal is to create a stable coordinating relationship strong enough to reduce drift.

This distinction matters.

Alignment is not the same thing as control.

The purpose of a coordinating system is not to determine outcomes.

Markets still compete.

Businesses still innovate.

Performance still matters.

People still make different choices and experience different results.

The goal is not engineered sameness.

The goal is preventing the relationships underneath the system from drifting so far apart that participation itself becomes unstable.

This governs relationships.

Not outcomes.

Why existing tools are not anchors

It is worth being specific about why the tools we already have cannot do this job, because the instinct is always to ask whether we could just improve what we have. We have tried that. Here is where each existing tool breaks.

Wages feel like they should be the anchor because they are personal – they show up in your life and determine what you can do. But wages are not anchored to system output, real productivity, or actual cost structure. They move, but they do not stay connected. That is why you can get a raise and find yourself asking where it went. The raise was real. The alignment was not.

Inflation is one of the most closely watched signals in the system, but it only tells you that something already happened. It does not explain why prices changed, whether income kept up, or whether the system is balanced. Policy reacts to it – rates change, programs adjust, markets shift – but none of that fixes alignment. You can stabilize inflation and still feel unstable, because costs may have leveled off while wages remain disconnected and output remains uneven. The signal improved. The system did not recover. Because nothing is holding it together.

GDP measures how much the economy is producing, and in one sense that matters. But it does not tell you who benefits from that growth, how it translates into stability, or whether it reaches people at all. The economy can expand while people feel more pressure. You feel that in small moments – standing in a store doing mental math, looking at a paycheck and wondering where it went, deciding to wait on a purchase just in case. GDP tracks size, not connection. It measures movement, not alignment.

Interest rates are among the most powerful tools in the system. They influence borrowing, spending, investment, and growth. But they create pressure, not alignment. When something is out of balance, rates change to correct behavior. Correcting behavior is not the same as fixing structure. It is like steering a car with a loose wheel – you can adjust constantly, but the underlying problem remains. The system ends up in a state of permanent correction, always being nudged and adjusted but never fully aligned. Because that is what these tools were built to do: measure and manage parts of the system. They were never designed to connect those parts. That is not a failure of effort. It is a failure of design.

A reasonable question emerges here: If something like this is possible, why has it not already happened?

Part of the answer is that modern economies became extraordinarily good at measuring growth while becoming far less effective at measuring alignment.

GDP tracks expansion.

Inflation tracks price movement.

Employment tracks participation.

Financial markets track confidence.

But no major mechanism consistently asks:

How connected are production, compensation, and participation actually becoming?

The challenge was never identifying economic activity.

The challenge was building a coordinating relationship strong enough to influence incentives without destabilizing markets.

That is considerably harder. And considerably more politically difficult.

There is another reason ideas like this rarely emerge. Large systems tend to optimize around what they already measure. Once institutions, incentives, politics, and markets become organized around existing metrics, changing the coordinating logic becomes extraordinarily difficult — even when the limitations become visible. Most systems persist longer than expected, not because they are fully working, but because replacing coordination is harder than tolerating drift.

How NPU works inside the system

Every system comes down to two things: what it produces, and who participates in producing it. Everything else — wages, prices, growth — is built on top of that. But we have been treating those things separately. NPU connects output to participation directly, not loosely and not indirectly. That connection is the mechanism that has been missing.

Here is how it works in practice. The system produces output — goods, services, technology, infrastructure. People participate in generating that output through labor, skill, time, and contribution. NPU binds those two things together so that as output increases, participation reflects that increase. Not eventually, not unevenly — consistently.

Consistency does not mean instant adjustment. Economies are too complex, and people's lives are too important, to be governed by abrupt year-to-year swings. The purpose of the framework is not to force immediate synchronization between economic output and participation, but to maintain a measurable connection between them over time.

Changes in productivity, participation costs, and economic conditions are evaluated through structured review periods, stabilization mechanisms, and gradual convergence processes designed to preserve continuity. The relationship remains visible and actionable, but adjustment occurs through measured implementation rather than sudden disruption.

In practice, that means the system responds to changing conditions predictably and transparently while avoiding the instability that would result from attempting to transmit every economic fluctuation directly into wages, benefits, prices, or obligations.

And critically, cost is pulled into the same structure. Because what something costs determines what people can access and what stability actually feels like. When output, participation, and cost are all tied to the same reference point, a raise no longer disappears the moment rent and food move. A business no longer has to guess whether wage growth and cost pressure are about to pull apart again. The system moves without leaving people behind. That is what alignment actually means — not a concept, but a condition.

The purpose of alignment is not to flatten outcomes. People will still build more, risk more, invent more, and achieve more. The system does not remove ambition. It removes the instability that slowly disconnects effort from progress in the first place. Success still exists. Innovation still matters. The difference is that growth no longer has to produce insecurity at the same time.

This is not redistribution. It is not about taking from one group and giving to another. It is about ensuring the system reflects the relationship between contribution and output — a relationship that has always existed but has never been formally defined. Workers and businesses do not negotiate wages in isolation under this system. They negotiate position within the economy's output. As the system grows, that position grows with it. The value does not drift. It scales. That is a fundamentally different kind of security than negotiating a wage and then hoping the economy does not outrun it.

Redistribution moves resources after instability already occurs. Alignment tries to reduce the instability in the first place. This difference is significant. A system that continually produces widening disconnection must repeatedly intervene to compensate for it. A system with stronger alignment underneath requires less correction because wages, participation, productivity, and cost are no longer drifting independently.

The system also stabilizes naturally rather than requiring constant intervention. Right now, the system is always being adjusted because nothing is holding it in place. When alignment exists, adjustments become less necessary — not because the system is controlled, but because the parts are already responding to the same signal. Trust does not come from promises or policies. It comes from consistency. When people can see how their effort connects, how growth translates, and how stability is maintained, they stop guessing. And when people stop guessing, they start participating again.

What this changes in real life

None of this matters if it does not show up in real decisions. So, let's be specific about what changes and for whom.

For a worker at 1.0 NPU, income covers essential living costs — not comfortably, but reliably. For a worker at 1.25 NPU, there is a buffer: the ability to save, to absorb a disruption, to plan more than a month ahead. For a skilled tradesperson at 2.0 NPU, skill and experience translate into a position the system will maintain as it grows. For an executive at 5.0 NPU, the system still rewards high output strongly — there is no cap on success — but those rewards exist within a structure that keeps them tethered to reality rather than drifting away from it.

What changes most is not the numbers — it is the questions people stop having to ask. Right now, a raise prompts: will costs rise with it, will this actually improve my position, will this still make sense in a year? In an aligned system, a raise carries meaning because it reflects participation in a system that is already connected. The question disappears because the answer is already built in. Planning changes in the same way — not because the future becomes predictable, but because the relationships stay consistent. You can commit to something without building in a hedge for the thing that always shifts. That alone changes behavior in ways that compound across the whole system. Because when people can trust that progress will hold, they stop bracing for reversal and start moving forward again.

Entrepreneurship becomes more important inside an aligned system, not less. When survival pressure stops consuming every margin, more people are able to build, experiment, and take productive risks. Innovation grows best in environments where failure is survivable and long-term effort still feels rational.

For businesses, especially smaller ones, this distinction matters. Most businesses do not fail because owners suddenly stop working hard or stop understanding their customers. They struggle under unpredictability — labor volatility, cost swings, turnover, healthcare pressure, and unstable demand. A stronger coordinating structure does not remove competition. It reduces unnecessary instability so businesses can compete on execution instead of constantly reacting to drift.

For businesses, the change is equally concrete. Right now, businesses manage instability — they build buffers into pricing, adjust labor reactively, hedge against cost volatility, and plan for breakdowns. Not because they want to, but because they have to. When the relationships between output, labor, and cost are stable, that burden reduces. Businesses can plan long-term instead of reacting short-term, invest in productivity instead of cost avoidance, and expand based on real demand instead of speculative margins. Growth without stability is not sustainable growth. Alignment is what makes it sustainable.

At the household level, the shift is the simplest and the most important. Households do not think in systems — they think in life. Can we afford this? Are we stable? Can we plan ahead? Right now, those answers are uncertain even when income increases. When income reflects participation, participation reflects output, and cost stays aligned within the same structure, those answers become clear. Not perfect — but reliable. And reliable is what changes behavior. When enough people can plan with confidence, invest with clarity, and take risks without catastrophic downside, the feedback loop that has been running in reverse — instability, hesitation, reduced participation, weaker system — begins running the other direction.

For someone like David, the change would not feel revolutionary.

That is partly the point.

He would still work hard.

Still compete.

Still pursue promotions.

Still build skills.

Still benefit from strong performance.

But the relationship between effort and planning would begin feeling more predictable.

Raises would hold meaning longer.

Financial planning would require fewer defensive assumptions.

Unexpected costs would still happen.

But the distance between contribution and stability would narrow.

Not perfectly.

More reliably.

This distinction matters.

Alignment is not the same thing as control.

The purpose of a coordinating system is not to determine outcomes.

Markets still compete.

Businesses still innovate.

Performance still matters.

People still make different choices and experience different results.

The goal is not engineered sameness.

The goal is preventing the relationships underneath the system from drifting so far apart that participation itself becomes unstable.

This governs relationships. Not outcomes.

No framework permanently removes tension between growth, innovation, stability, and adaptation. Tradeoffs remain. The question is whether those tradeoffs become more manageable when the system underneath them remains connected.

Why this has not been built yet

By this point, a fair question forms: if this works, why has it not already been done? Because the pieces have existed for a long time. We have had data, productivity measures, economic models, and policy tools for decades. What we did not have was a way to connect them. Every system we built treats parts of the economy separately — wages are negotiated, prices are adjusted, growth is measured, policy reacts — but nothing binds those pieces together. So even when we improve one part, another part drifts. We were solving around the problem rather than fixing the structure beneath it.

There is also the matter of complexity. Every adjustment added another rule, another policy, another layer. Over time, the system became harder to understand and harder to fix. When a system is too complex, people stop trusting it, leaders stop simplifying it, and solutions become harder to see. We ended up focused on outcomes — income levels, tax rates, spending priorities — rather than on the structure producing those outcomes. If the structure is misaligned, outcomes will always drift no matter how much you adjust them. You cannot fix results if the system generating them is broken.

There is also a perception barrier worth naming. When something touches wages, prices, and output simultaneously, it sounds complicated, even threatening. People assume it must be restrictive, must reduce flexibility, must interfere with how things work. But that is a misreading. Control limits movement. Structure allows movement to make sense. NPU does not set prices, dictate wages, or restrict growth. It defines relationships. And we have also been conditioned to expect trade-offs — stability versus growth, fairness versus efficiency, flexibility versus consistency — as if we cannot have both. Those trade-offs exist because the system is not aligned, not because they are unavoidable. When the parts move together, the choice disappears.

Perhaps most importantly, change at this level requires understanding before it can happen. Familiar instability feels safer than unknown stability — that is human nature, and it is not wrong. It means structural change has to be understood before it can be accepted. That is what this book is doing. Not pushing, not forcing — explaining, connecting, making something visible that has not been visible before. Because once you see it, you stop trying to fix the symptoms. You start asking how to fix the system that keeps producing them. And once that question becomes the right question, the answer — which already exists, already has a structure, already can be implemented — becomes impossible to ignore.

David would probably never describe what he wanted as economic reform.

Most people would not.

What they want is simpler.

To believe that hard work still connects to something stable.

That planning matters.

That effort still compounds.

That the future can feel more predictable than fragile.

The challenge is not whether people deserve stability.

The challenge is whether a system can be structured to support it without sacrificing ambition, innovation, competition, or growth.

By now, the right question is probably no longer whether instability exists or whether relationships drift. The harder question is operational: Could something structured this way actually work without disrupting everything already in place?

Could something like this actually function in the real world?

That question matters.

Because ideas survive criticism.

But systems survive implementation.

Chapter 4 – From Understanding to Construction

At this point, something has changed. You are no longer trying to understand the problem. You already see it. You are no longer asking if the system drifts. You know it does. And you are no longer wondering if there is a better way. You've seen one. So, the question shifts. Not: "What's wrong?" But: "What do we do about it?"

This is where most ideas fall apart

Understanding is easy compared to implementation. It's one thing to say that a system is misaligned or that the parts are disconnected or even that the outcomes don't hold.

It's another thing entirely to say: "Here's how we rebuild it." Because now, everything becomes real. Systems have to operate. People have to participate. Businesses have to function. Government has to administer.

Before moving further, one more point. Building structure is not the same thing as central planning. Markets would still set prices. Businesses would still compete. Workers would still negotiate, change jobs, and pursue opportunity. What changes is not freedom of movement. What changes is the reliability of the relationships underneath that movement. Structure governs coordination. It does not replace choice.

This is where many good ideas stop.

They diagnose.

They persuade.

But they never cross into construction.

We are not stopping here. Because a system only matters if it can be built. That means that whatever gets created has to be structured. It has to be scalable. It has to be enforceable. And it has to work inside the real world.

And "build" has to mean more than theory. It means payroll systems must be capable of administering it. Businesses must be able to operationalize it without constant confusion. Existing institutions must be able to transition into it rather than collapse under replacement. Courts must be able to interpret it consistently. If a system cannot survive contact with administration, it does not survive at all.

Now we move into structure, rules, and flow.

This is where resistance usually appears.

Not because people disagree, but because implementation suddenly becomes real.

These are not objections. They are necessary questions. And if we can't answer them clearly, the system doesn't hold. So, we're going to answer them. Not in pieces. As a system. Because that's the only way this works.

Elena never struggled to understand production.

Demand changed.

Customers changed.

Supply chains changed.

That was business.

What increasingly frustrated her was unpredictability.

Hiring became harder.

Retention became harder.

Wage planning felt reactive.

Healthcare costs shifted unexpectedly.

Turnover forced repeated training investments.

Strong employees quietly disappeared for marginally better offers elsewhere.

And even when business performed well, long-term planning increasingly felt uncertain.

Chris, her operations manager, spent more time than he wanted solving labor instability problems that had little to do with actual operations.

Scheduling gaps.

Hiring delays.

Compensation adjustments that never seemed to fully stabilize retention.

Productivity interruptions caused by staffing uncertainty.

Neither of them talked about this as economic philosophy.

They talked about it differently:

"Why does everything feel harder to stabilize than it used to?"

Start with a simple truth

Every functioning system needs three things:

- A unit of measure

- A structure for interaction
- A flow of movement

Without all three, the system breaks down.

We already have the first piece, that's NPU. It defines how output is measured, how participation is expressed, and how value connects.

That part holds. Now we need the structure. This is where things get real. Structure answers: "How do people engage with the system?" "How do businesses operate within it?" and "How are decisions made consistently?"

And then we need flow. Because a system isn't static, it moves. Income moves. Costs move. Contributions move. Resources move. If that flow isn't defined, the system drifts again.

So, now we start the construction phase

Not all at once. Step by step. So that by the end, you can see, not just what the system is but how it actually operates. Let's be clear about one thing. This is not about replacing everything overnight. It's about building something that can integrate, transition, and stabilize without breaking what already exists. Because that's where most systems fail. They try to tear down, replace, and restart. And that creates instability.

This system doesn't do that. It builds alongside. It aligns gradually. It absorbs over time. That's how stability is maintained during change. Not by forcing it. By structuring it.

So where do we start? Not with policy. Not with enforcement. With interaction. Because if people can't interact with the system. Nothing else matters.

This means we start with the interface. How individuals:

- Enter the system
- Participate in the system
- Move within the system

This is where NPU becomes real. Not as a concept. As something you use. Because the moment a system becomes usable, it becomes understandable. And once it's understandable, it becomes adoptable.

This is the first step toward implementation

Not complexity. Clarity. We are not building a system that needs to be explained constantly. We are building one that makes sense when you use it. So, as we move forward, keep this in mind.

Because that's what creates trust. Not promises. Structure that holds. This is where everything starts to come together. Up to now, you've seen the problem, you've understood the mechanism, and you've felt the impact

Now, we begin to build the system itself. And this is where many ideas fail. They sound right. They read well. They even persuade. But they cannot survive contact with real operation. That is the test now. Not whether this sounds good. Whether it holds.

And we start with the most important layer. The layer that connects people, work and output. Because if that layer holds, everything else can be built on top of it. This is where NPU stops being an idea. And becomes a functioning system.

The first layer: how people enter and operate within the system

A system only works if people can use it. Before policy. Before enforcement. Before distribution. A system has to answer one question: "How do I exist inside this?" Because if that answer isn't clear, nothing else matters. People won't trust it. Businesses won't adopt it. And the system will fail before it starts.

This is where a system can break. They are built from the top down. Policy first, rules second, people last. Which means the people inside the system have to do three key things. They have to interpret it, they have to translate it, and they have to navigate it. That's where confusion begins.

We're not building it that way. We're starting from the inside. From the individual. Because if the individual experience is clear, everything else becomes easier to build. So, let's start with the simplest interaction. You enter the system. Not as a number. Not as a category. As a participant. And that participation has to mean something. Right now, when you enter the economic system, you get a job, receive a wage, and pay costs. There is no clear connection between what you contribute, what the system produces, and what your position actually represents

So, you operate inside uncertainty. NPU changes that immediately. Because the moment you enter the system, your participation is expressed in NPU. Not abstractly. Directly.

This is where the system becomes tangible. Instead of asking: "What is my hourly rate?" "What is my salary?" You are positioned within the system based on your level of participation relative to total output.

This is not just a different unit

It's a different way of understanding value. Because your position in this system is no longer fixed in dollars, subject to drift, or disconnected from output. It is:

- Anchored
- Scaled
- Connected

This is where NPUX comes into play. This is also where people need reassurance. Because structure is often confused with flattening. That is not what is happening here. The system still rewards skill. It still rewards effort. It still rewards greater contribution.

What changes is that those rewards are no longer detached from the system that makes them possible. NPUX represents your individual position within the system's output.

NPUX is simply a way of expressing economic value relative to the National Productivity Unit.

The "X" is not a separate unit. It represents whatever multiple of the NPU applies to a particular wage, price, debt obligation, asset, or economic transaction.

A worker earning 1.5 times the National Productivity Unit has an NPUX of 1.5. A monthly rent equal to 0.8 times the National Productivity Unit has an NPUX of 0.8.

Throughout this book, NPUX serves as a shorthand for understanding relative economic position within the system. It does not replace negotiation, competition, investment, entrepreneurship, or market pricing. Rather, it provides a common reference point that allows those outcomes to be understood relative to a shared economic anchor.

Let's make that real - instead of negotiating $25 per hour or $80,000 per year, you negotiate your NPUX position. This NPUX position reflects skill, contribution, demand, and productivity.

And here's the key difference, that position moves with the system. So, when output increases or productivity improves, your position doesn't stay fixed while everything else shifts. It scales. This is what eliminates drift at the individual level. Because the relationship between your contribution and the system's output is no longer indirect. It's defined.

Traditional wage negotiation does not disappear. Workers, employers, markets, and industries still negotiate compensation. What changes is the reference point. Instead of evaluating value solely through nominal dollars, compensation can be understood relative to a shared economic anchor tied to productivity and participation.

This does not remove flexibility. People still change jobs, increase skills, and negotiate roles. Businesses still compete, hire, and differentiate

What changes is the foundation. The negotiation happens within a structured system. Not in isolation. So, two people can still earn different NPUX levels based on value, skill, and impact but both are anchored to the same system. This creates consistency without removing competition which is something the current system struggles to do.

Let's talk about entry-level participation

This is where the system proves itself. Right now, entry-level work often feels disconnected.

- Low wages
- Limited mobility
- Unclear path forward

With NPU, entry-level participation has defined meaning. Because even at the lowest level, participation is measured, contribution is recognized, and growth is structured

This changes the starting point entirely. Instead of: "I hope this leads somewhere" It becomes: "I know how this scales"

That clarity drives behavior. People invest more in skills, effort, and growth because the system reflects it.

Now let's move to mid-level and skilled workers

Skilled workers expect growth to matter.

Right now, that relationship often weakens over time.

Raises lag.

Costs rise.

Progress feels harder to hold.

With NPU, growth becomes structural because increased participation leads to higher NPUX and stronger system position.

Growth stops feeling fragile.

It holds.

Now let's look at high-value roles

Executives, specialists, and high output contributors still negotiate position. Nothing about that changes. But now, their position is visible. Their impact is measurable. Their scale is tied to system output. This closes a critical gap. Right now, high-end compensation can disconnect from system reality. This system keeps it anchored. Without removing incentive. This is important. Because incentive drives innovation.

Now let's talk about mobility

Because a system only works if people can move within it. Mobility exists at three levels:

- Role mobility — changing jobs
- Skill mobility — increasing capability
- Position mobility — increasing NPUX

In the current system, these are not always connected. You can gain skill without income. You can change roles without stability. You can improve output without proportional reward.

NPU connects all three. So, movement becomes predictable, measurable, and achievable. This is what restores trust in effort because effort leads somewhere.

Now let's address the question people will ask

"How do I actually get paid?" This matters. Because this is where systems become real. You still receive currency. Your income is still earned through your employment relationship, but that income now has a reference point — your NPUX position relative to the system's output. Which means your income is not arbitrary, static, or disconnected. It is anchored to output, scaled with the system, and protected from drift. This is where stability becomes tangible, not theoretical. Daily.

Now consider cost interaction

Because income only matters relative to cost. In this system, cost is not independent, it is tied to the same structure. So, income moves with output. Cost aligns within the same system

This Is What Eliminates the "Chase" where wages increase, costs rise faster, and stability disappears. Now the system holds together because all parts move within the same framework.

This is the first layer of construction. And it's the most important. Because if individuals can enter, operate, and understand their position, everything else becomes possible. Without this layer, nothing else works. Not policy. Not distribution. Not enforcement. With this layer, everything else has a foundation.

So, let's pause here for a moment. What we've built is not abstract. It's usable. It answers how you enter, how you participate, how you grow, and how you are compensated

The second layer: how businesses operate within the system

We just built the first layer. We defined "How people enter the system." "How participation is measured." and "How income connects to output."

That layer holds, but it's not enough. Because individuals don't operate in isolation. They operate inside businesses, organizations, and markets. So, the system has to work for them too. Not just conceptually, operationally. Because if businesses can't function inside the system, the system fails.

We're not making that mistake. This system must work for the small contractor, the mid-sized manufacturer, and the global enterprise because all of them are part of the same system.

Start with the core function of a business. Every business does three things. It transforms input into output. It employs participation. And it operates within cost constraints. That's it. Everything else builds on top of that.

Right now, those three things are not aligned. That's the problem. Labor cost moves independently. Output value fluctuates. Pricing reacts to pressure. So, businesses are constantly adjusting. Not because they want to, because they have to. This is why business feels like constant reaction. You're always managing cost swings, adjusting compensation, and responding to market pressure instead of operating inside a stable structure.

NPU changes that foundation because now labor (NPUX), output (system productivity), and cost (aligned structure) are connected. This is where business stops guessing and starts operating.

Let's Walk Through What Actually Changes

1. Hiring and compensation

Right now, hiring is disconnected. You try to answer: "What should this role pay?" and "What will the market accept?" and "What can we afford?" Those answers often conflict.

For Elena, hiring stops feeling like educated guesswork...Roles become easier to define and retention becomes easier to predict.

Chris spends less time solving instability and more time solving operations.

With NPU, hiring becomes structured. You don't guess compensation. You assign an NPUX position for that role which reflects the contribution to output, the skill level, and the system demand.

This does two things immediately. It creates clarity and it creates consistency. You know what the role represents. And the person entering that role understands it too.

Negotiation still exists. This is important. Businesses still compete for talent. Individuals still negotiate their position. But now negotiation happens inside structure. Not in isolation which means less distortion, less guesswork, and more transparency.

2. Labor cost becomes predictable

This is one of the biggest shifts. Right now, labor costs fluctuate unpredictably. Wage pressure builds unevenly. Businesses react instead of plan.

With NPU, labor cost is anchored because NPUX positions scale with system output, reflect real productivity, and stay aligned with cost structure. This doesn't freeze cost, it stabilizes it. Which means you can forecast, plan, and invest.

That changes business behavior. Instead of short-term adjustments, you move toward long-term strategy

3. Pricing becomes rational again

Right now, pricing is reactive. Costs go up and prices adjust. Demand shifts and prices adjust. Competition pressures and prices adjust. There is no anchor, which is why pricing feels unstable.

With NPU, pricing exists within structure because the input costs are aligned, the labor is structured, and the output value is connected.

This creates a range of stability. Not fixed prices, but predictable boundaries. Which means businesses still compete. But they do so within a system that holds relationships, reduces volatility, and prevents extreme distortion.

4. Profit is still earned but now it's understood

That means this system still embraces investment. It still rewards people who build wisely, allocate capital well, and create real value. It does not cap upside. It makes upside more durable by grounding it in a system that holds.

This system does not eliminate profit. It clarifies it. Right now, profit can disconnect. It can come from arbitrage, timing, and structural gaps.

Most business leaders are not looking for certainty. They are looking for predictability. They understand competition, market pressure, and risk. What becomes difficult to absorb is chronic instability – labor volatility, cost unpredictability, and shifting structural incentives. Alignment does not remove business difficulty. It makes difficulty more manageable.

With NPU, profit reflects real contribution because output is tied to system value, cost is aligned, and participation is structured. So, profit becomes a signal, not just a result. It tells you: "This is where value is being created."

5. Competition still exists but it becomes healthier.

Competition doesn't go away, it improves. Right now, competition is often distorted because businesses compete on labor suppression, cost shifting, and structural advantages.

With NPU, competition shifts to:

- Efficiency
- Innovation
- Quality
- Output

Because those are the things that actually create value.

6. Small businesses gain stability

This is one of the most important outcomes. Right now, small businesses are the most exposed. They face cost volatility, labor uncertainty, and thin margins.

With NPU, they gain structure because labor is predictable, costs are aligned, and participation is clear. This reduces fragility which allows growth, hiring, and investment.

7. Large businesses gain clarity

Large organizations already operate at scale. But they still deal with complexity, variability, and disconnection.

NPU simplifies their operating environment because the system itself holds relationships, reduces distortion, and aligns inputs and outputs. This improves efficiency at scale.

Let's Look at the Core Concern: "Does this restrict business?" Simply no. It removes instability. Businesses still make decisions, compete, grow, and fail or succeed.

What changes is the environment. Instead of constant uncertainty, they operate within structured alignment. That is not restriction, that is stability.

Let's connect this back to individuals

Because this is where the system locks together. Individuals operate within businesses. Businesses operate within the system. If both layers are aligned then participation connects to output. Output connects to value. Value connects to cost. That is a fully connected system.

It is the second layer of construction and it answers "How businesses hire." "How they compensate." "How they price." and "How they compete." Without this layer, the system breaks at scale. With this layer, the system becomes operational.

As we know, individuals and businesses are not the whole system. Government, policy, distribution, and stability mechanisms still exist. So, the next question becomes: How does the system manage flow at the national level?

The third layer: flow, governance, and system stability

A system that doesn't control flow will fail. So far, we've built two layers: Individuals → how people participate and Businesses → how organizations operate. Both are necessary, but neither is sufficient because systems don't just exist, they move. Money moves, value moves, contribution moves, and risk moves. If that movement, that flow, is not defined, the system will drift again.

This is where systems can break at scale. They define participation, rules, and incentives, but they don't define how everything moves together. So, over time, imbalances grow, gaps widen and instability returns. This is why the third layer matters most. Because this is where the system either holds or collapses.

The third layer has one responsibility; to maintain alignment across the entire system as it moves. That means managing flow, maintaining stability, absorbing disruption, and enforcing structure.

Let's be clear, this is not about control. This is not central planning or overregulation or restricting movement. This is about ensuring that movement stays aligned. Because movement without structure creates drift.

This distinction matters because it is easy to misunderstand what coordination actually means.

The purpose of alignment is not to determine outcomes. No institution decides who succeeds. No administrator determines wages. No central authority allocates ambition, innovation, or opportunity.

Businesses still compete. Workers still negotiate. Markets still reward performance.

People still make different decisions and experience different outcomes.

What changes is the reliability of the relationships underneath those decisions. This governs relationships, not outcomes.

The stability system – the core mechanism

At the center of this layer is one concept: The Stability Fund. This is not a program, it is the system's balancing mechanism. The Stability Fund performs three critical functions:

1. Absorbs system variability

Economic systems are not static. They experience growth, slowdowns, shocks, and disruptions. Without a buffer, those shocks transfer directly to people. That is when a system stops feeling like a structure and starts feeling like a threat. Because normal life becomes fragile. A slowdown becomes a household problem. A disruption becomes a family problem. A policy delay becomes a paycheck problem.

The Stability Fund exists to stop that transfer. Income becomes unstable, costs spike, or businesses contract, then the Stability Fund absorbs that variability. So, instead of shocks hitting individuals, they are smoothed across the system.

2. Maintains baseline participation

Every system must ensure that participation remains viable. That entry remains accessible. That stability exists at the foundation.

This is where the EEBV (Essential Economic Basket Value) operates. It defines the baseline level of participation required for system stability. The Stability Fund ensures that baseline holds even when output fluctuates or demand shifts or conditions change.

3. Aligns distribution across the system

Because the system produces unevenly, some sectors grow faster and/or generate more value while others lag, stabilize, and support. Without alignment, this creates imbalance. The Stability Fund redistributes structurally, not arbitrarily. Not as a discretionary policy choice, but as a system function.

Where the Stability Fund gets its resources is a critical piece of this. The Stability Fund is not funded randomly. It draws from the total system output and participation flows which includes individual participation contributions, business output participation, corporate allocation structures, and system-level economic activity.

This is not a separate system. It is embedded within the same structure as NPU. This is where the system becomes closed-loop. Everything connects: participation leads to output, output leads to contribution, contribution leads to stability and stability leads to participation. That loop is what helps keep the system aligned. Because the major components operate from a common economic reference point, drift is no longer hidden for decades at a time. It becomes visible earlier, measurable more clearly, and correctable before it grows into a structural failure.

For Elena, alignment would not eliminate difficult business decisions.

Competition would still exist. Margins would still matter. Customers would still delay purchases. Bad quarters would still happen. But compensation planning becomes more predictable. Retention improves. Hiring volatility decreases. Employees spend less energy reacting to instability. And long-term planning becomes less dependent on guessing where costs will unexpectedly spike next.

For Chris, operations begin looking more like operations again.

Less reaction.

More execution.

Now let's address governance, because this is where people get skeptical. "Who controls this?" The answer is different than expected. No one controls outcomes. The system governs relationships. Governance exists to enforce structure, not dictate behavior. That means ensuring NPU alignment holds, ensuring flows remain consistent, and ensuring rules are followed.

This is not discretionary power, it is structural enforcement because people do not want a system that micromanages their choices. They want a system that stops punishing ordinary participation. This is about integrity of the framework, not control over daily life.

This system requires administration. But administration is not the same thing as centralized control. The role of governance is narrower: maintain system integrity, monitor alignment, administer stabilization mechanisms, and ensure the rules operate consistently. In practice, this would likely exist within existing institutional structures rather than as a standalone authority disconnected from democratic oversight. Its responsibility is not to direct outcomes, but to preserve the reliability of the framework itself.

It does NOT set wages, control prices, or direct business decisions. It ensures the system holds.

More accurately, it establishes participation floors and alignment rules rather than attempting to manage every outcome directly. The framework creates a common economic reference point, defines minimum participation standards, and provides mechanisms for maintaining alignment between productive output and economic participation over time.

What it does not do is dictate every wage, control prices, determine job structures, prescribe business models, assign occupations, or direct private operating decisions. Employers still compete, workers still negotiate, entrepreneurs still innovate, and markets still function. The difference is that those activities occur within a framework designed to keep participation connected to the productive capacity of the economy rather than allowing the two to drift indefinitely apart.

To be clear, no system removes tradeoffs. No structure permanently eliminates friction. Economic shocks still happen. Technology still disrupts industries. Markets still overcorrect. Policies still require adjustment.

The objective is not perfect equilibrium. The objective is greater resilience. A stronger ability for people, businesses, and institutions to adapt without chronic instability becoming the norm.

Failsafe mechanisms – the system's self-correction

No system is perfect so this one must be self-correcting. This is where the failsafe governor comes in. It operates automatically, not politically. It monitors two key variables:

X — System Output Health

Y — Participation Stability

When X or Y moves outside defined thresholds, the system adjusts. Stability Fund allocation increases. Contribution ratios adjust. Flow dynamics rebalance. This is not reactive policy, this is built-in system behavior.

Example 1 - mild disruption

Output slows slightly. Participation remains stable. System response is minor Stability Fund deployment with no structural adjustment.

Example 2 – severe disruption

Output declines significantly. Participation destabilizes. System response is increased Stability Fund deployment, activation of the system's built-in stabilization governors, and temporary reinforcement of baseline participation continuity mechanisms.

Rather than relying on emergency intervention, the framework uses pre-established stabilization structures designed to moderate disruption, preserve continuity, and support recovery during periods of economic stress.

This prevents system collapse because adjustment happens early, response is automatic, and stability is preserved

Now let's address the biggest structural integration, program consolidation. Right now, the current system includes:

- Social Security
- Welfare programs
- Assistance systems
- Disaster relief structures

All fragmented. All managed separately. That fragmentation creates inefficiency and instability.

In this system, those programs are unified into the Stability Fund. This does not remove support it integrates support into system structure.

Social Security Transition (critical mechanism)

This is one area where precision matters because trust matters.

For people currently retired — or nearing retirement — continuity would be essential. Benefits already earned would not simply disappear or reset. The purpose of alignment is stability, not disruption.

Over time, as legacy obligations and demographic pressures increasingly strain the current system, retirement support would transition into a more sustainable structure connected to the Stability Fund. Existing commitments would be preserved while future participation gradually aligns to a system designed to remain solvent long-term.

The goal is not to remove retirement security.

The goal is to protect it from instability.

This must be precise. Current system remains intact until insolvency trigger.

Retirement continuity does not depend upon eliminating existing commitments. Current beneficiaries continue receiving earned obligations, and implementation occurs through coordinated transition mechanisms designed to preserve stability throughout the process.

As the Stability Fund demonstrates sustained capacity to support retirement obligations, future retirement participation may increasingly transition toward Stability Fund administration. Existing commitments remain protected, continuity remains the governing principle, and implementation occurs in coordination with the Social Security Administration and related institutions.

The objective is not abrupt replacement. The objective is long-term retirement stability that remains sustainable regardless of demographic shifts, labor-force changes, or structural economic transition.

Corporate participation – completing the loop

Businesses participate but corporations operate at scale. They must contribute proportionally to system stability.

Markets still compete inside this system. Businesses still fail or succeed based on execution, efficiency, trust, and innovation. Alignment does not eliminate competition. It changes the conditions underneath competition so that firms are rewarded for creating real value rather than adapting fastest to structural instability.

Corporate contribution is based on total output contribution, labor utilization, and system integration level. This ensures high-output entities contribute proportionally and that system stability scales with system growth.

Global markets create enormous advantages. Investment moves faster. Innovation scales faster. Businesses access opportunity across borders. None of that changes.

The challenge emerges when value creation increasingly disconnects from the communities, labor, and productive systems responsible for sustaining it. The purpose of alignment is not to punish capital movement. It is to reduce structural disconnection between economic participation and economic reward.

That distinction matters.

Offshore capital integration

This is critical for real-world function. Capital leaving the system must remain connected to the system.

Mechanism: offshore participation remains connected to domestic NPU participation through graduated alignment incentives. Re-entry pathways are encouraged, while increasing disconnection receives progressively adjusted participation treatment designed to preserve long-term alignment between productive activity and domestic economic participation.

This prevents value extraction without participation, system leakage, and structural imbalance.

This is the complete third layer. We now have 3 of the 4 layers:

Where layer 1 covers Individuals and their Entry into the economy, their participation within the economy and their compensation for their efforts.

Where layer 2 covers Businesses and their hiring from within the economy, pricing within the economy and their overall operation within the economy.

And finally, where layer 3 covers System Flow around stability, governance, allocation and enforcement across the entire economy.

This is a fully connected system. Nothing operates independently. Everything is measured, connected, and stabilized. And this is what prevents drift permanently. Because one question still remains: How does this system transition from what exists today? That critical process is where this system succeeds or fail completely.

The fourth layer: transition without disruption

Every system fails or succeeds at one point. Not in theory, not in design, but in transition. Because it's one thing to build a system that works, it's another to move from what exists to what should exist without breaking everything in between.

This is where many new systems collapse. They try to replace everything at once, reset structure overnight, and force alignment. That creates instability, resistance, and failure.

This system does not replace, it aligns. We are not tearing down the current system. We are building alignment into it until the old structure becomes unnecessary.

Before we go further, we need to address the core concern because it's already forming in the reader's mind. "Does this system limit success?" "Does this reduce upside?" "Does this flatten outcomes?"

The answer is no. This system does not reduce merit. It does not suppress performance. It does not cap success. It does something far more important, it ensures that success is connected to real contribution. This is still a merit-based system. Higher contribution leads to higher NPUX. Higher NPUX leads to greater position. Greater position leads to greater reward. Nothing about that changes. What does change is that relationship now holds consistently.

And this system still rewards investment because investment is what drives innovation, expansion, and risk-taking.

In this system, investment becomes more powerful, not less, because it operates inside stability. Right Now, Investment carries hidden risk, not just business risk but system risk, cost instability, demand swings, and structural drift.

With NPU alignment, that risk reduces because labor is stable, cost is structured, and output is connected. So, investment becomes clearer. Not easier, but more predictable. Which means capital flows more efficiently. Not away from opportunity, toward it.

Before moving forward, one concern deserves direct attention:

Does this system limit success?

No.

Performance still matters.

Investment still matters.

Risk still matters.

Higher contribution still leads to higher reward.

What changes is not opportunity, but reliability.

Success remains possible.

It simply becomes more connected to real contribution and less dependent on structural instability.

Now that we've addressed incentives, let's build the transition.

Step One – parallel system introduction

The system does not begin by replacing wages or pricing. It begins by introducing NPU alongside the existing system. This means individuals still earn income, businesses still operate normally, markets still function.

But now there is a second layer, a reference layer where participation is measured in NPU. Output is tracked structurally. Alignment begins forming.

Nothing breaks because nothing is removed.

Step Two – dual visibility phase

This is where the system becomes visible. Individuals begin to see their NPUX position and how it connects to output and how it compares over time.

Businesses begin to see role-based NPUX structures, labor alignment, and cost stability emerging

This phase builds understanding without forcing change. Large systems rarely change all at once. Nor should they.

Transitions at this scale are rarely linear. Some elements would likely work immediately. Others would require adjustment. Unexpected friction would emerge. Incentives would need refinement. Administrative complexity would reveal weak points that theory alone cannot predict. That is not evidence the system failed. It is how serious systems mature. Stability comes from adaptation, not perfection on the first attempt.

Most durable reforms emerge gradually. Tested, adjusted, improved through real-world friction rather than theoretical confidence.

Any serious implementation of alignment would likely involve phased adoption, measured transition periods, institutional safeguards, and repeated evaluation.

That is not weakness. That is how resilient systems are built.

Step Three – partial integration

Now the system begins to matter. Certain elements begin to tie to NPU:

- Compensation adjustments
- Pricing frameworks
- Contribution flows

But not completely, because the system must earn trust before it takes control That is why the transition matters as much as the destination. A stable system cannot be built through destabilizing change. If the path to alignment creates panic, the public will reject the structure before it has a chance to prove itself. So, the transition has to demonstrate the same principle as the system itself hold first, then scale.

Step Four – stability fund activation

This is the first major structural shift. The Stability Fund begins receiving contributions, managing flow, and absorbing variability. Existing programs begin aligning, not ending, aligning.

Step Five – structural shift

Now the system becomes primary. NPU becomes the dominant reference. Compensation fully aligns. Flow is governed structurally. Legacy systems phase out naturally not by force, by redundancy.

Let's answer a hard question: "What happens during disruption?" Disruption is not avoided, it is managed because the Stability Fund is active early. This Means variability is absorbed and participation remains stable. Transition does not destabilize households.

Now let's reinforce what matters most. Because at this point, the reader needs to feel this clearly. This is not a controlled system. It is not rigid. It is not restrictive. It is structured. And structure does not remove freedom, it makes freedom meaningful. Because in an unstructured system effort can disconnect. Growth can disappear. Success can drift.

In a structured system effort holds, growth scales, and success sustains. This is the difference between opportunity and illusion and this system chooses opportunity

Now step back and look at what we've built

We now have:

Layer 1 – Individuals with clear participation and growth

Layer 2 – Businesses with operational stability and alignment

Layer 3 – System Flow for stability, governance, enforcement

Layer 4 – Transition for real-world implementation without disruption.

This is no longer a concept, this is a system that can exist. And more importantly, a system that can be adopted. Which brings us to a closing question, not: "Does this work?" but: "What happens when this system is fully in place?"

At this point, the question is no longer whether a system like this can be imagined. The harder question becomes what happens when aligned relationships begin operating at scale — not in theory, but in everyday life.

Because that's where everything we've built becomes reality.

When the system is fully alive

The first thing you notice is calm. Not silence, not stagnation, calm. Because the constant tension disappears. The tension of "Is this enough?" "Will this hold?" "What happens next?"

And if you're paying attention, there's probably something else happening right now. Not just a question about what comes next. A quiet evaluation. You're not just asking whether this works. You're asking something more personal: "Where does this fit into my world?" "What would this change for me?" "Is this something I would actually trust?"

Those questions matter more than understanding because they are the point where ideas stop being observed and start being tested. That tension has been part of everyday life for so long most people don't even recognize it anymore. Until it's gone.

This is what stability actually feels like. Not dramatic, consistent. Predictable. Understandable.

Work starts to feel different. Not because work changes, but because what work means changes. Right now, work often feels disconnected. You put in effort, you get paid. But the relationship between those two things is unclear.

In a fully aligned system, that relationship is visible. You understand what your participation represents and how it connects to output and how it scales over time. That changes motivation. Not artificially, but naturally. Because people move toward systems that make sense.

Businesses start operating instead of reacting. This is one of the biggest shifts. Right now, businesses spend enormous energy reacting. Adjusting pricing, managing cost volatility, navigating uncertainty.

In this system, that pressure reduces. Not completely, but structurally. So, businesses shift from reaction to construction, building, expanding, and investing, because they trust the environment they're operating in.

Now let's talk about money flow, because this is where people often misunderstand systems. Right now, money doesn't move cleanly. Money pools, stalls, and concentrates.

Not always because of intent, but because of structure. In an aligned system, flow improves. Not forced, enabled. Because participation at every level is connected. So, when value enters the system it moves through it.

Money has a way of going where it's needed most and then continuing on. Healthy systems are not defined by how money accumulates, they are defined by how it moves. Healthy systems are not defined by how quickly money concentrates, they are defined by how well value circulates through real participation. That is what keeps businesses alive, households stable, and opportunity real or as Will Rogers put it:

"Give it to the people at the bottom and the people at the top will have it before night, anyhow. But it will at least have passed through the poor fellow's hands."

That's not redistribution, That's flow. And flow is what creates a healthy system. Because value doesn't sit, it moves. This system doesn't force that movement, it allows it by ensuring that participation exists at every level. Stability exists at the base. Contribution remains connected.

This is what a healthy economic system looks like. Not one where value concentrates instantly or is artificially pushed but one where value moves through participation.

Now focus a little on inequality

Because this is where the conversation usually goes. This system does not eliminate differences, it does not make outcomes equal, it makes outcomes connected. High performers still rise. Investors still gain. Builders still scale. But the system ensures that the floor is stable, the ladder is real and the ceiling is not artificial.

This is the balance we've been missing, not equality, alignment.

Now let's talk about risk

Because risk never disappears. And it shouldn't. Risk is what drives innovation. It's what creates:

- New businesses
- New technologies
- New opportunities

This system does not remove risk, it removes unnecessary instability so risk becomes productive again, not destructive. This is where investment changes, not in amount but in quality. Because investors now operate in a system that holds structure, reduces distortion, and maintains alignment. That means capital flows toward real opportunity, not temporary advantage.

Now step back and look at the whole system

When everything is connected:

- Individuals understand their position
- Businesses operate with clarity
- Value flows through participation
- Stability absorbs disruption
- The system begins to reinforce itself
- Confidence increases participation
- Participation strengthens output
- Output reinforces stability
- Stability increases confidence

This is a positive feedback loop and it's the opposite of what we have today. Today, instability creates hesitation. Hesitation reduces participation. Reduced participation weakens the system. That loop is broken here.

This is the system we were trying to build all along, we just didn't know what was missing. Now we do and once you see it you can't go back to not seeing it. Because the difference is clear between a system that moves and a system that holds.

Elena and Chris would still have difficult days.

That would not change.

Business remains difficult.

Competition remains real.

Uncertainty never disappears entirely.

But instability would become less dominant than it feels today.

Planning becomes more credible.

Retention becomes more predictable.

Investment decisions become less defensive.

The system would still reward strong businesses and strong performance.

It would simply ask a harder question beneath them:

How sustainable is success when the relationship between participation and stability continues drifting farther apart?

If alignment is possible—not perfectly, but meaningfully—then the question is no longer whether complexity exists.

The question becomes whether complexity is a reason to avoid coordination—

Or a reason to build it more thoughtfully.

Final thought of this section

This system does not promise perfect outcomes or equal results or risk-free growth. It promises something far more important, that the system will make sense. And when a system makes sense, people trust it. People use it. People build inside it. And that's how systems change. Not all at once, but permanently.

We've now built the full picture. At this point, something important has happened. We didn't just describe a better system, we built one that:

- Connects participation to output
- Aligns cost with reality
- Preserves incentive
- Rewards investment
- Supports stability
- Transitions without collapse

That matters because most proposals solve one problem.

Some solve two.

Very few solve the system.

This one does.

Because once a system can be seen clearly, once a better structure exists, it does not go away.

It waits to be built.

Chapter 5 – What Happens When the Economy Breaks

Most people don't think about the structure of the economy when things are working. They think about their job, their bills, their plans. What they can afford and what they can't. The system is invisible when it behaves. It only becomes visible when it stops behaving predictably. And when that happens, pressure rarely appears all at once. It accumulates until the system can no longer hide it.

There is a moment, sometimes slow, sometimes sudden, when people begin to feel that something is off. It doesn't start with a headline. It starts with small shifts. Prices move faster than expected. Hours get cut instead of expanded. Hiring slows without explanation. Raises don't stretch as far as they should. Nothing looks broken, but nothing feels stable either. That is the beginning.

Then comes the second phase. Decisions start changing. A business that planned to expand pauses. A household that planned to spend pulls back. A manager who was ready to hire decides to wait.

No one calls it a crisis yet, but behavior starts tightening. This is where most systems should respond. Most don't. Instead, the system keeps moving forward as if nothing has changed. Wages continue on their path. Costs continue on theirs. Production continues. Consumption continues. But underneath, something important has already broken, the connection between them. When that connection breaks, pressure doesn't disappear. It moves. Sometimes it moves to workers.

Sometimes to small businesses.

Sometimes to public systems.

Sometimes to debt.

Sometimes to families quietly absorbing more than they should for longer than they can sustain.

The pressure never vanishes.

It simply relocates to wherever resistance is weakest.

That is what makes structural instability difficult to recognize.

It rarely announces itself all at once.

It distributes itself gradually.

And it moves toward the places least able to absorb it. Workers feel it first. Not because they caused it, but because they are closest to the edge. A shift in hours becomes a shift in income. A shift in prices becomes a shift in survival. A delay in adjustment becomes a gap in reality. This is where instability becomes personal.

This is important because the argument being made here is not that markets fail, competition fails, or that businesses are somehow acting irrationally. In many ways, the opposite is true. Most participants inside the economy are responding logically to the incentives and pressures in front of them. Businesses protect themselves. Workers adapt. Families compensate. Investors reduce uncertainty where they can. None of that behavior is unreasonable. The problem emerges when individually rational decisions begin producing collectively unstable outcomes. When that happens repeatedly, the question stops being whether participants are behaving correctly and becomes whether the structure connecting them is behaving correctly. Markets matter. Incentives matter. Competition matters.

But even strong systems drift when the relationships underneath them stop holding together.

Take someone specific. Call him a plumber — though it could just as easily be an electrician, a welder, a contractor, or anyone who runs a small crew and bids jobs for a living.

He's been at this for eighteen years. He knows his trade cold. He's good enough that people call him by name, not just by his company. He clears somewhere around $80,000 to $90,000 in a good year. He has two guys who depend on him for work. He carries the insurance, the truck payments, the equipment. He bids commercial jobs that take months to close and residential jobs that can turn in a week.

Here is what his relationship with the economy actually looks like.

Material costs move without warning. Copper pipe that cost him one number when he bid the job costs something different when he buys it to do the work.

He can't absorb a slow winter the way a large company absorbs a slow quarter. When the phones stop ringing for six weeks, the overhead doesn't pause.

He watches inflation the way a weather forecaster watches a storm system — not because he has time to think abstractly about economic theory, but because it hits his margin directly and immediately. When his costs go up, he has to decide: raise his prices and risk losing bids, or hold his prices and watch his margin shrink.

He's not behind. He's not failing. By any reasonable measure, he's doing it right. But the system he's working inside makes doing it right feel fragile in a way it shouldn't.

That fragility is not a personal problem. It is a structural one. And it is exactly what this chapter is about.

Economic pressure is not new.

Every generation experiences downturns.

Markets cool.

Industries change.

Recessions happen.

That is not the argument being made here.

Cyclical disruptions are normal.

They come and go.

Structural fragility is different.

Structural fragility accumulates.

It quietly compounds underneath periods of growth, expansion, and even optimism until pressure begins surfacing in places that should otherwise be stable.

The concern is not that economies experience stress. The concern is what repeated stress reveals about the relationships underneath them.

Businesses feel it next. Not always immediately. But inevitably. Demand becomes less predictable. Costs become harder to manage. Planning becomes less reliable.

So, they do what rational systems tell them to do, they protect themselves. They slow hiring. They delay investment. They reduce exposure. None of those decisions are irrational. They are responses to instability. But taken together, they amplify it.

This is where the system begins to turn against itself. Each participant is acting reasonably. But the structure is no longer holding those actions together. So instead of stabilizing, the system begins to compound its own pressure. At this point, the third phase begins. The one most people recognize. Layoffs. Sharp price movements. Policy response. Public concern.

Now it has a name. Now it is visible. Now it is being addressed. But this is where tempo matters. Because by the time instability becomes visible, it has already been building. By the time response begins, behavior has already shifted. By the time intervention arrives, damage has already been distributed. This is the core problem. Not that systems respond. But that they respond too late. And when they do respond, they do so bluntly. Interest rates move. Spending increases or contracts. Programs expand or tighten.

These are large tools. They operate at scale. But instability does not begin at scale. It begins at the point of connection. So, the system tries to correct a structural problem with directional tools. Push here. Pull there. Slow this. Stimulate that.

None of this means current tools are useless. Monetary policy matters. Fiscal policy matters. Emergency intervention matters. The issue is not whether these mechanisms work at all. It is whether they are capable of responding at the point where instability actually begins. Most existing tools respond after conditions become visible at scale. They react to inflation after prices move. Employment weakness after participation falls. Demand weakness after spending slows. That timing matters because systems are shaped long before headlines recognize them. By the time intervention arrives, households have already adjusted, businesses have already delayed decisions, and defensive behavior has already spread. Existing tools can slow instability. Sometimes they can reverse it. But repeatedly needing large corrections raises a harder question: why is the system repeatedly reaching those conditions in the first place?

Sometimes it works for a while. But it doesn't hold. Because the underlying problem has not been resolved. The system is still unanchored. So even when it stabilizes temporarily, it remains vulnerable. And when the next disruption arrives, the cycle repeats. This is why economic instability feels familiar. Not because the events are identical, but because the pattern is. There is always a buildup. A period where things feel slightly off. A delay in response. A sudden shift. A correction. A recovery. And then, eventually, another cycle.

For people living inside the system, this does not feel like a cycle. It feels like uncertainty. It feels like trying to plan in a system that does not hold still long enough to be trusted. That uncertainty changes behavior in ways that are not always visible. People become more cautious. Less willing to take risk. Less able to plan long term.

Even when the system appears to be growing, businesses behave the same way. They optimize for flexibility instead of stability. They hedge instead of build. They react instead of lead. Not because they want to, but because the system rewards it.

This is the hidden cost of instability. It is not just the downturn. It is the behavior it creates long before and long after. And that behavior has consequences. Innovation slows. Investment becomes selective. Opportunity narrows.

Not because capability disappears, but because confidence does.

At this point, most discussions about the economy focus on outcomes. Growth rates. Employment levels. Inflation numbers. But those are surface indicators. They tell you what happened, not why it keeps happening. To understand that, you have to look at structure. You have to look at how the system behaves when it is under pressure. Because that is when its design is revealed. Not in stability, in stress. A well-structured system absorbs pressure. It redistributes it. It prevents localized stress from becoming systemic failure.

A poorly structured system does the opposite. It transfers pressure. It concentrates it. It amplifies it. That is the difference. And that is the point. The system we have today does not fail because people are making bad decisions. It fails because it requires good decisions to operate inside a structure that does not hold them together. That is why smart policy is not enough. That is why effort is not enough. That is why adjustment is not enough. Because none of those change the structure.

So, when the economy breaks, it is not a surprise, it is the expected outcome of a system that was never designed to hold under pressure. And until that structure changes, the pattern will not change. That brings us to the real question. Not whether instability can be managed, but whether it can be designed out of the system itself. Because if it can, then the goal is no longer to respond better, it is to build differently.

Why the current system fails under pressure

By the time most people recognize that something is wrong in the economy, the system has already made a series of decisions. Those decisions were not coordinated. They were not guided by a shared structure. They were not aligned. They were responses.

Each part of the system responds to pressure in the only way it can. Individually. A worker sees prices rising faster than income and adjusts spending. A business sees costs rising or demand weakening and adjusts hiring. A lender sees risk increasing and adjusts access to capital. A policymaker sees instability and adjusts policy tools.

Each of those responses makes sense on its own. None of them are irrational, but they are not connected. This is where the first structural weakness appears. The system does not move as one. It moves as a collection of reactions.

When pressure enters the system, there is no shared mechanism to absorb it. So instead of being distributed, it is passed along. And it always moves in the same direction. Toward the parts of the system with the least ability to resist it. This is why workers feel instability first. Not because they caused it, but because their position in the system is the most exposed.

Wages do not adjust in real time, costs do. When prices rise quickly, income does not automatically follow. When demand drops, hours are reduced before prices stabilize. When uncertainty increases, job security becomes flexible.

The system does not stabilize income, it tests it. That creates the first major imbalance, costs move faster than wages. And when that happens, the gap is not theoretical. It is immediate.

A household does not experience inflation as a percentage. It experiences it as a constraint. Food becomes tighter. Housing becomes heavier. Transportation becomes a calculation. The system does not adjust to protect the household. The household adjusts to survive the system. That is not stability. That is adaptation under pressure.

Businesses face a different version of the same problem. They are not reacting to one variable, they are reacting to all of them at once. Costs may be rising. Demand may be weakening. Labor may be uncertain. Capital may be tightening. And none of those variables move in coordination. So, businesses do what rational systems teach them to do. They protect flexibility. They delay hiring. They pause expansion. They reduce long-term commitments. They shift risk off their balance sheet.

These are not failures of leadership, they are rational responses to a system that does not hold steady. But those responses create the second major imbalance. They reduce participation. Fewer people are hired. Fewer hours are worked. Fewer investments are made. And when participation drops, output follows.

Now the system has two problems, costs that moved too fast and participation that moved too slow. There is no mechanism connecting them. So, the gap widens.

At this point, policymakers enter the cycle. They do not see the system at the level of individual decisions. They see it at the level of outcomes. Inflation is high. Employment is weakening. Growth is slowing.

So, they use the tools available to them. Interest rates are adjusted. Spending is increased or reduced. Programs are expanded or constrained. These tools are powerful, but they are not precise. They do not operate at the point where the system broke. They operate at the level where the system is visible.

This is where another weakness appears. The system is corrected at the wrong level. If instability begins at the connection between wages, costs, and output, then correcting it at the level of aggregate demand or aggregate supply will always lag behind. It may slow the problem. It may shift the timing. It may change the severity. But it does not remove the underlying condition. So, the system enters a loop. Pressure builds. Participants react. Imbalances form. Policy responds. Conditions shift. Then it begins again. This loop creates a pattern that is easy to recognize but difficult to stop. Because each part of the system is doing its job. Workers are adjusting. Businesses are adapting. Policymakers are responding.

Nothing appears broken in isolation, but the system as a whole is not holding. This is where most explanations fall short. They focus on one part of the system and try to fix it. Raise wages. Or lower costs, or stimulate demand or control inflation.

Each of those can help, temporarily, but none of them change the structure. They do not create a shared mechanism that keeps the system aligned under pressure. So even when one part improves, another part drifts. That is why solutions often feel incomplete. Because they are. They are solving symptoms inside a system that is still misaligned. And as long as the system is misaligned, pressure will continue to move instead of being absorbed.

That movement is not random. It follows a predictable path. From uncertainty to reduced participation to reduced output to reactive correction to temporary stabilization to renewed drift. That path is the system. And that is why the system fails under pressure. Not because it stops working, but because it continues working in a way that transfers instability instead of containing it. It means the problem is not failure of effort, it is failure of structure. And once a problem is structural, it cannot be solved with adjustment alone.

It requires a system that behaves differently when pressure enters it. A system that does not transfer instability. A system that absorbs it. That is the shift.

And that is what we build next.

How the NPU system absorbs shock

If the problem with the current system is that pressure moves unchecked, then the solution is not to eliminate pressure. That is not possible. Economic systems will always experience disruption. They will always experience change. They will always experience periods of imbalance.

It is worth saying plainly: no economic system eliminates hardship, uncertainty, or failure. There will still be downturns. Industries will still change. Companies will still make bad decisions. Technology will still disrupt labor. Individual outcomes will still vary. Stability is not the promise of perfection. Stability means pressure is less likely to compound into collapse. It means setbacks are less likely to become permanent disruption. It means the system absorbs more strain before ordinary participants are forced into defensive survival. A stable system still experiences change. It simply behaves differently when change arrives.

The goal is not to remove shock. The goal is to change what happens when shock enters the system. In the current system, shock moves. In a stable system, shock is absorbed. That difference does not come from better decisions. It comes from better structure.

A system that absorbs shock must have three things:

- a way to detect pressure early
- a way to distribute that pressure across the system
- a way to prevent that pressure from concentrating in one place

Without those three elements, instability will always cascade. The NPU-based system introduces all three. Not as separate programs, as a single, connected mechanism. This system does not control decisions. It does not tell businesses what to produce. It does not tell workers where to work. It does not direct capital toward specific outcomes. It creates conditions where those decisions can be made inside a stable structure. That is not restriction. That is function.

Before going further, an important clarification is necessary. A system designed to absorb pressure is not the same thing as a system designed to eliminate consequences. Markets still move. Businesses still succeed or fail. Demand still rises and falls. Poor decisions still carry cost. The purpose of stabilization is not to override reality. It is to prevent normal pressure from cascading into avoidable instability. In the same way infrastructure prevents ordinary disruption from becoming systemic failure, an economic system must have mechanisms that preserve function under stress. Roads do not eliminate accidents. Electrical grids do not eliminate outages. But both reduce the chance that isolated disruption spreads into widespread failure. Economic systems require the same logic. The question is not whether disruption exists. The question is whether disruption remains contained or compounds into instability that spreads farther than it should.

At the center of that mechanism is the Stability Fund. This is not a reserve in the traditional sense. It is not a temporary pool of money that appears only during crisis. It is a continuous part of the system's operation. In stable periods, the system builds capacity. In unstable periods, the system uses it. That may sound simple. But it represents a fundamental shift. Because in the current system, stabilization is a decision. In this system, stabilization is a function. That changes everything.

When stabilization is a decision, it depends on cadence. It depends on understanding. It depends on agreement. It depends on execution. All of those introduce interruption. And interruption is what allows instability to spread.

In the NPU system, the response does not wait. It is triggered by the same conditions that signal imbalance. When participation slows, the system responds. When output weakens, the system responds. When cost pressure begins to separate from income, the system responds. Not through external intervention, through internal adjustment. Where current systems respond after instability becomes visible, this system responds at the point where instability begins. That difference in timing reduces the need for large, disruptive corrections later.

This is where the structure begins to matter. Because the Stability Fund is not separate from the economy. It is integrated into it. It collects during periods of strength. It distributes during periods of weakness. And it does so based on system conditions, not discretionary judgment.

This creates the first major difference, pressure is absorbed at the point where it appears. When participation begins to decline, the system supports continuity. When income begins to weaken, the system stabilizes flow. When uncertainty begins to rise, the system reduces the need for defensive behavior. This does not eliminate risk, but it prevents risk from turning into instability.

For many families, life slowly becomes less about aspiration and more about contingency. Emergency funds become survival calculations. Career decisions become insurance decisions. Relocation becomes risk exposure. Having children becomes a financial equation. Ordinary choices begin carrying disproportionate consequences. This shift matters because systems influence behavior.

When people increasingly organize their lives around avoiding instability rather than pursuing opportunity, the economy itself begins changing shape. Less risk-taking. Less mobility. Less long-term confidence. Not because ambition disappeared. Because predictability did.

The second difference is distribution. In the current system, pressure moves toward the weakest point. In the NPU system, pressure is spread across the entire system. That is what the Stability Fund does. It does not protect one group at the expense of another. It protects the function of participation itself. Because participation is what drives output. And output is what sustains the system. When participation is preserved, the system continues to function even under stress. This is why the structure matters more than the individual components. You can increase wages. You can reduce costs. You can even stimulate demand. But if participation breaks, the system still destabilizes. The NPU system is designed to keep participation intact. That is its primary function under pressure.

The third difference is timing. In the current system, reaction follows acknowledgement. In the NPU system, reaction follows condition. That may seem like a small shift. It is not. Because acknowledgement takes time. Condition does not.

When a system is built around recognition, it reacts. When a system is built around condition, it adjusts. That is how instability is contained before it becomes visible. This is where the concept of flow becomes critical. In the current system, flow is inconsistent. Income moves one way, costs move another. Support arrives later. There is no continuous relationship between them.

In the NPU system, flow is structured. Income, cost, and participation are linked through a shared framework. That framework is anchored in NPU. Which means the system is not trying to coordinate separate parts. It is operating through a single relationship. When that relationship holds, the system holds. When that relationship begins to stretch, the system adjusts. This is not theoretical, it is mechanical. The system monitors its own condition through measurable inputs. It adjusts its own behavior through predefined responses. It maintains its own balance through continuous flow. This is what allows it to absorb shock. Not by stopping movement, but by preventing that movement from becoming separation.

At this point, an important question emerges. If the system is absorbing pressure, where does that pressure go? It does not disappear. It is redistributed. Across time. Across participants. Across the system as a whole.

Instead of being concentrated in one moment or one group, it is spread in a way that maintains function. That is what stability actually means. Not the absence of change, but the ability to continue operating through it.

This is also where the question of contribution becomes important. Because absorbing shock requires capacity and capacity must be built. In the current system, that capacity is inconsistent. It depends on savings, policy timing, and external intervention. In the NPU system, that capacity is structural. It is built continuously through participation in the system itself. Which means that during periods of strength, the system is preparing for periods of stress. Not through prediction. Through design.

Before answering that question, another one deserves equal attention: what is instability already costing? Lost investment. Delayed hiring. Workforce disruption. Emergency intervention. Business closures. Household debt. Slower recovery cycles. These costs already exist. The difference is that they are rarely experienced as one system-wide burden. They are distributed unevenly and often absorbed privately. Families absorb them through instability. Businesses absorb them through uncertainty. Governments absorb them through reactive spending. The issue is not whether systems carry cost. Every system does. The issue is whether those costs are paid reactively through disruption or structurally through prevention.

This is where some participants will ask a fair question: Does this mean contributing more? The answer is not as simple as yes or no. It means contributing differently. In the current system, contributions are often disconnected from outcomes. They are fragmented across programs, taxes, and reactive measures.

In the NPU system, contributions are integrated into a single structure that serves a clear purpose, maintaining system stability. That creates a different kind of relationship. Participants are not contributing into uncertainty. They are contributing into a system that directly supports the conditions they rely on. For workers, that means more stable income. For businesses, that means more predictable demand. For investors, that means more durable growth.

In some cases, contributions may increase, but those increases are not arbitrary. They are tied to the value of a system that no longer breaks under pressure. And that value is measurable. Reduced volatility. Reduced disruption. Reduced need for emergency intervention.

Those are not abstract benefits. They are operational improvements. Which means the system is not asking for more without return. It is aligning contribution with outcome. That alignment is what allows the system to sustain itself. Because a system that holds under pressure does not need to be constantly repaired. It continues. It adapts. It absorbs.

And that changes the entire experience of participating in it. At this point, we have moved from understanding failure to understanding function.

The next step is to see how that function behaves in real conditions. Not in theory, in practice. Because the true test of any system is not how it is described. It is how it performs when the world around it changes.

How the system behaves in the real world

Up to this point, we have described how the system is built. Now we need to see how it behaves. Because no system is defined by its design alone. It is defined by what it does when conditions change. The easiest way to understand that is to walk through three types of environments:

- a normal year
- a mild downturn
- a severe contraction

These are not rare scenarios. They are the conditions every economic system cycles through over time. In the current system, instability creates hidden costs that are rarely measured directly. Interrupted production. Delayed investment. Emergency intervention. Long recovery cycles.

Those costs are distributed unevenly and often exceed what a stable system would require to prevent them. So, the question is not whether the system requires contribution, it is whether it reduces the total cost of instability. The difference is not whether they happen, the difference is how the system responds when they do.

The system does not respond to every downturn through a single mechanism. During periods of economic contraction, multiple stabilization layers operate together. Measurements are smoothed to reduce the influence of short-term volatility. Scheduled convergence adjustments can be slowed or temporarily paused when conditions warrant. Participation continuity remains anchored to stable reference values rather than reacting immediately to every fluctuation in economic output.

Where disruption exceeds normal adjustment capacity, temporary Stability Fund support provides an additional layer of continuity protection. The objective is not to prevent recessions from occurring, but to reduce the likelihood that temporary economic shocks become long-term participation failures.

1. A normal year – stability builds capacity

In a normal year, the economy is expanding at a steady pace. Participation is stable. Employment is consistent. Businesses are investing. Households are spending within predictable ranges. Nothing feels strained. Nothing feels urgent. This is when most systems relax.

The NPU system does not, because stability is not a signal to disengage. It is a signal to prepare. During a normal year, the system does three things continuously:

- It aligns
- It circulates
- It builds capacity

Alignment means that income, cost, and output continue to move together, because they are anchored to the same structure, they do not drift apart. Circulation means that value continues to move through participation. Wages are earned. Goods and services are produced. Demand remains active.

Nothing stalls. Nothing pools excessively, but the most important function in a normal year is capacity building. A portion of system activity flows into the Stability Fund. Not as a reactive measure. As a continuous function. This is where the system prepares for pressure it has not yet experienced. The contribution is not arbitrary. It is tied to the scale of the system itself. As output grows, capacity grows. As participation expands, resilience expands. This is the first major difference from the current system. Preparation is not dependent on forecasting. It is embedded in operation.

That means when the system is strong, it becomes more stable, not more exposed. No emergency measures are needed. No sudden interventions are required. The system is already doing what it needs to do. And because the

Stability Fund is being built during strength, it is not extracting value from the system. It is preserving it for continuity.

This is also where contribution logic becomes visible. Some participants will contribute more during periods of strength. Not because they are being penalized, but because they are participating more fully in a system that is generating more value.

Contribution scales with participation, not vulnerability.

It allows the system to build strength without creating imbalance.

At the end of a normal year, nothing dramatic has happened. Which is exactly the point. The system has grown. The system has remained aligned. And the system has quietly built the capacity it will need when conditions change.

2. A mild downturn – stability engages

Early in a mild downturn, the shift is subtle at first. Demand begins to soften. Growth slows. Some sectors feel pressure before others. In the current system, this is where instability begins to build unnoticed. In the NPU system, this is where stabilization begins. Because the system is not waiting for collapse. It is responding to condition.

As participation begins to slow, the system adjusts. The Stability Fund begins to engage. Not as a full deployment, but as a controlled release, because the goal is not to override the system. It is to prevent drift from becoming separation. Income flow is supported where it begins to weaken. Participation is maintained where it begins to decline.

This reduces the need for defensive behavior. Businesses are less likely to freeze hiring. Households are less likely to sharply reduce spending. The system does not eliminate caution. But it prevents panic. That is the difference between a slowdown and a cascade. Because when behavior stabilizes, the system stabilizes.

The Stability Fund acts as a buffer. It absorbs the early pressure. It redistributes it across the system. Instead of allowing the slowdown to concentrate, it smooths the transition. This is where timing matters most. Because early stabilization requires less force. If pressure is addressed at the point where it begins, it does not need to be corrected at the point where it becomes visible. That reduces disruption. It also reduces cost, because the system is not trying to repair damage, it is preventing it.

This is another place where contribution logic becomes clear. The capacity built during stable periods is now being used. Not all at once. Not indiscriminately, but precisely where it is needed to maintain participation. That means the system is not asking for new contributions during stress. It is using what was already structured during strength. That is a fundamental shift.

In the current system, downturns often require emergency measures. In this system, downturns activate existing structure. As a result, the economy does not stop. It slows, but it holds.

3. A severe contraction – stability protects the system

In a severe contraction, pressure is no longer subtle. Demand drops sharply. Employment is at risk. Entire sectors may experience disruption.

This is where many systems break because the level of pressure exceeds the system's ability to respond incrementally. So, the response becomes reactive. Large-scale interventions. Emergency programs. Rapid adjustments. And even then, the damage is often unevenly distributed.

In the NPU system, this is where the full structure activates. The Stability Fund transitions from buffering to protection. This is not a gradual adjustment. It is a full system response. Participation is preserved as the primary objective. Income flow is maintained to prevent collapse in demand. Businesses are supported in maintaining operations rather than shutting down activity. The goal is not to prevent contraction. The goal is to prevent collapse. Because contraction is part of any dynamic system. Collapse is structural failure.

The NPU system is designed to prevent that failure. The Stability Fund provides the capacity to sustain participation during extreme conditions. This reduces the need for sudden, disruptive policy measures. It also reduces the uneven distribution of impact because the system is not reacting after damage occurs. It is maintaining function as pressure increases.

This is where contribution philosophy becomes most important. Some participants may look at this level of support and ask whether the system requires more from them. The answer is grounded in structure. Those who benefit most from a stable system, through scale, participation, and output, are also those most capable of contributing to its stability. This is not a penalty. It is alignment. Because instability is not free. It carries costs. Lost output. Disrupted investment. Emergency intervention. Long recovery cycles.

Those costs are often higher than the contributions required to prevent them. Which means the system is not increasing burden. It is reducing total cost. The question is not whether contribution exists. It is whether the system reduces the total cost of instability. When disruption, contraction, and recovery cycles are reduced, the overall burden on the system decreases—even if contributions are structured differently. And it is doing so in a way that maintains participation for everyone. This is the core outcome.

Even in severe contraction, the system continues to function. Not perfectly. Not without pressure, but without breaking.

The difference across all three conditions

Across all three environments, normal, mild, and severe, the structure behaves consistently. It builds during strength. It stabilizes during early pressure. It protects during extreme conditions. At no point does the system rely on delayed recognition. At no point does it require reactive reconstruction. It operates continuously. That continuity is what creates trust. Because people do not need to guess how the system will behave. They can see it. They can experience it. And over time, they can rely on it.

That is what separates a system that functions from a system that holds. And once a system proves that it holds under pressure, the question changes. It is no longer whether the system works. It is whether there is any reason to return to one that doesn't. Systems like this are not difficult to understand once they are seen. They are difficult to build because they require coordination across parts of the economy that have historically been managed separately.

That fragmentation is what allowed instability to persist. Not lack of capability. That brings us to another question: What this actually feels like to live and operate inside a system that no longer breaks.

For the plumber, none of this appears as policy.

It appears as hesitation.

A commercial bid he would have confidently accepted three years earlier suddenly feels risky.

Replacing equipment gets delayed.

Hiring another apprentice gets postponed.

One bad month starts carrying more weight than it used to.

Not because demand disappeared.

Not because effort changed.

Because predictability changed.

And when predictability weakens, even competent people begin organizing around defense instead of growth.

What this feels like for people and businesses

The framework does not attempt to centrally manage every price, wage, or decision inside the economy. Most decisions still emerge from individuals, businesses, markets, and local conditions. Alignment works differently. Instead of controlling every outcome, it creates a shared reference point that allows the system to coordinate around reality more consistently.

If a system is stable, people do not spend their time thinking about the system. They spend their time living inside it. That is the first sign something has changed. Not that people understand the system better, but that they no longer have to think about it as often.

In an unstable system, the economy is always present. It shows up in small decisions. "Can I afford this?" "Should I wait?" "What if something changes?"

Those questions are not occasional. They are constant. Even during periods of growth. Because growth without stability does not remove uncertainty. It hides it.

So, people learn to operate cautiously. They delay decisions. They limit risk. They adjust expectations. Not because they lack ambition, but because the system does not reward confidence. It rewards caution. That is what instability feels like over time. It is not just disruption during downturns. It is hesitation during normal conditions. And that hesitation has a cost. It reduces opportunity. It reduces mobility. It reduces the willingness to invest in the future.

That is what changes first in a stable system. The hesitation begins to disappear. Not all at once. But steadily. Because the system is no longer sending mixed signals. Income behaves more predictably. Costs do not move independently of participation. Shocks do not immediately translate into personal disruption.

So, people begin to make different decisions. They plan further ahead. They commit more confidently. They take risks that are calculated, not defensive. This is not optimism. It is the absence of constant uncertainty.

And that changes behavior in ways that are not always visible in data. A worker is more willing to pursue a better role. A family is more willing to make long-term decisions. A student is more willing to invest in education. Because the system no longer feels fragile. That is what stability creates. Not just protection, but participation.

Businesses experience a similar shift. In an unstable system, businesses are constantly managing risk. Not strategic risk but system risk. "Will demand hold?" "Will costs spike?" "Will labor remain available?" "Will conditions change unexpectedly?" Those questions drive behavior.

So, businesses optimize for flexibility. They keep operations lean. They delay expansion. They avoid commitments that rely on stability. Again, not because they lack vision, but because the system punishes exposure. That changes in a stable system. When participation holds, demand becomes more predictable. When cost and income remain connected, planning becomes more reliable. When shocks are absorbed, risk becomes manageable.

That does not mean every loss, every bad quarter, every failed investment, or every market consequence is absorbed by the system. Economic activity still involves risk. Businesses can still fail. Industries can still contract. Individuals and organizations still make decisions that produce different outcomes.

The role of the Stability Fund is narrower and more specific. It exists to respond to defined continuity events and stabilization conditions through pre-established triggers designed to preserve participation during periods of disruption. The objective is not to eliminate normal economic consequences, but to prevent temporary shocks from cascading into long-term structural instability when continuity can reasonably be preserved.

So, businesses begin to operate differently. They invest earlier. They hire with more confidence. They expand with clearer expectations. They shift from protecting themselves against the system to building within it.

That is a fundamental change. Because growth driven by confidence behaves differently than growth driven by reaction. It is more consistent. More durable. Less volatile.

This is also where the role of contribution becomes clearer. In a stable system, businesses may contribute differently than they do today. In some cases, that contribution may be higher. But it is not disconnected from outcome. It is tied directly to the stability that allows the business to operate with less disruption, less volatility, and more predictability.

That changes the calculation. Because businesses are not simply paying into a system. They are participating in one that reduces the cost of instability. Fewer sudden contractions. Fewer reactive decisions. Fewer lost opportunities.

Those are real economic benefits. Which means contribution is not a transfer. It is an investment in system function. In most discussions, stability and growth are treated as tradeoffs. They are not. Growth comes from participation. Participation depends on stable flow. When flow breaks, participation drops. When participation drops, growth slows. So, stability is not limiting growth. It is what allows growth to continue.

Workers experience this in a parallel way. They are not just receiving stability. They are participating in it. Their contribution supports the system that supports their income. And because that relationship is visible, it changes how participation feels, it is no longer passive. It is connected.

This is where the idea of fairness begins to shift. In an unstable system, fairness is often debated in terms of distribution. Who gets what. Who pays more. Who benefits.

In a stable system, fairness is experienced through function. "Does the system hold?" "Does it respond?" "Does it support participation?" If the answer is yes, the question of fairness becomes less abstract, because people can see the relationship between what they contribute and what they receive.

This does not eliminate disagreement, but it changes the foundation of it. It grounds it in structure rather than perception. That is a critical difference. Because a system that holds under pressure does not just reduce instability. It reduces friction. And that friction is what often drives conflict inside economic systems.

When outcomes feel disconnected from effort, frustration grows. When instability feels arbitrary, trust declines. But when the system behaves consistently, trust builds. Not because people are told to trust it, but because it proves itself over time.

This is what changes most in a stable system. Not the existence of risk. Not the presence of change. But the relationship people have with both. Risk becomes something that can be evaluated. Change becomes something that can be planned for. Instead of something that must be constantly feared.

This also affects investment. In an unstable system, investment carries an additional layer of uncertainty. Not just whether a decision is sound. But whether the environment will remain stable enough for that decision to play out. That uncertainty raises the threshold for action.

So fewer investments are made. Or they are made more cautiously.

In a stable system, that layer is reduced. Not eliminated. But reduced. Which means more capital is deployed into productive activity. More ideas are tested. More businesses are built. Because the system is not working against the act of building. It is supporting it.

This is where the idea of merit becomes clearer. A stable system does not flatten outcomes. It makes them more meaningful. Because success is less dependent on navigating instability and more dependent on creating value. That benefits everyone in the system. In an unstable system, outcomes are often shaped by timing and exposure to disruption. In a stable system, outcomes are shaped more consistently by contribution and value creation. Stability does not reduce merit, it allows it to matter more.

Workers, businesses, and investors all operate within a structure that rewards contribution more consistently. That is what makes growth real. Not just the ability to expand. But the ability to sustain that expansion. At this point, the system begins to feel different in a way that is difficult to measure but easy to recognize. It is less reactive. More steady. Less fragile. More durable.

People do not need to constantly adjust to the system. The system adjusts to maintain them. That is the shift. And once that shift happens, something else follows. People begin to expect stability. Not as a guarantee. But as a characteristic.

And when that expectation is met consistently, it changes the baseline. Instability becomes the exception, not the norm. That is when a system moves from functioning to trusted. And that is what makes the final step possible.

Understanding why a system like this does not just improve outcomes, but changes the foundation of how the economy operates.

Chris had seen this happen before.

What looked like caution from the outside often looked very different inside operations.

Hiring freezes rarely begin with certainty.

They begin with hesitation.

A role waits another month.

Capital spending gets pushed to next quarter.

Expansion plans pause—not because leadership lacks confidence, but because uncertainty quietly begins outpacing predictability.

Eventually, organizations begin optimizing for flexibility instead of growth.

And when enough businesses make that shift at the same time, the economy begins slowing long before anyone officially calls it trouble.

Why this changes everything

At this point, something important has happened. We did not just describe a better outcome. We described a different kind of structure. One that behaves differently under pressure. One that holds when conditions change. One that does not rely on timing, reaction, or correction to remain stable.

That distinction is what changes everything. Because most economic discussions focus on results. Growth rates.

Employment levels. Inflation targets. Those matter, but they are not the foundation. They are the result of how the system behaves. If the structure underneath those outcomes is unstable, the outcomes will be unstable. No matter how strong they appear in the moment.

That is what we have seen repeatedly. Periods of growth followed by disruption. Periods of stability followed by correction. Moments of progress that do not hold. Not because growth is flawed, but because the system supporting it is incomplete.

What changes here is not the goal of growth. It is the condition that makes growth real. Stability is not the opposite of growth. It is what allows growth to last. Without stability, growth expands into fragility. With stability, growth expands into strength. That is the shift. And it changes how every part of the system behaves.

Workers are no longer operating inside uncertainty. They are operating inside structure. Businesses are no longer reacting to instability. They are building within stability. Investors are no longer pricing in constant disruption. They are participating in more predictable systems of return.

That does not remove risk. But it changes the nature of it. Risk becomes something that can be understood and managed. Not something that must be constantly defended against. That nuance affects everything. It affects how decisions are made. It affects how capital is deployed. It affects how opportunity is created. Because when a system holds, people move differently inside it. They plan further ahead. They invest more confidently. They build more consistently.

The behaviors that sustain stability are the same behaviors that produce growth. Participation drives flow. Flow sustains confidence. Confidence drives investment. And investment drives expansion. When those behaviors are aligned, stability and growth are no longer separate goals, they are the same process.

The current system cannot fully replicate this behavior because its mechanisms are reactive and fragmented. Without a unified structure connecting participation, output, and cost, stability will always depend on timing and intervention rather than continuous alignment.

This is where the idea of contribution becomes fully visible. In a system like this, contribution is not an abstract obligation. It is part of the structure that makes stability possible. Some participants will contribute more than they do today. That is true. But the reason matters. They are not contributing more into uncertainty. They are contributing into a system that reduces the cost of instability for everyone, including themselves. That is not redistribution. It is alignment. Because instability has a cost. Lost productivity. Disrupted investment. Emergency intervention. Extended recovery.

Those costs are real. And they are often higher than the contributions required to prevent them. So, the system is not increasing burden. It is reducing total system cost. And it is doing so in a way that preserves participation across all levels. That is why the structure holds. Because it is not asking one part of the system to carry the weight, it is distributing that responsibility in proportion to participation and capacity. That creates balance. And balance is what allows the system to sustain itself.

The important thing to understand is that systems rarely break because people stop trying.

Most people continue adapting long after the strain becomes obvious.

Families adjust.

Businesses compensate.

Managers improvise.

Workers absorb more pressure than should reasonably be expected.

Which is precisely why fragility can become difficult to see.

The system still appears functional.

Stores remain open.

Jobs still exist.

Growth still appears in reports.

And yet beneath that appearance, more and more energy gets spent simply holding things together.

Because once enough effort goes toward managing instability rather than creating opportunity, the question quietly changes.

The issue is no longer whether people are resilient enough.

The issue becomes whether the system itself is.

And that is where understanding why systems resist change becomes unavoidable.

At this point, the system is no longer defined by how it performs during stability. It is defined by how it performs during change. And that is where the difference becomes undeniable. A system that only works when conditions are favorable is not stable. It is conditional.

A system that continues to function when conditions shift is stable. It is reliable. That reliability is what builds trust. Not promises, not projections, but performance. Repeated over time. That is how expectations change. People begin to assume the system will hold. Businesses begin to operate with that assumption. Investors begin to price that assumption into their decisions. And once that happens, the system becomes more than stable. It becomes self-reinforcing. Because behavior aligns with structure. And when behavior and structure move together, the system strengthens itself.

This is where the final shift occurs. The question is no longer: How do we respond when the system breaks? It becomes: Why would we accept a system that breaks at all? Because once a system is designed to hold, once it has been shown to absorb pressure, maintain participation, and support growth, the limitations of the previous system become clear. Not as a matter of opinion, but as a matter of structure. And that is what makes this different from every adjustment that came before.

This is still a market system.

Competition remains.

Businesses still innovate.

Individuals still choose where and how to work.

Capital is still invested in pursuit of return.

What changes is not whether the market exists. What changes is whether the market is operating inside a system that holds.

One that aligns participation with output.

One that stabilizes flow.

One that preserves incentive while reducing fragility.

One that holds.

And when a system holds, everything built inside it becomes more real. Opportunity becomes more accessible. Growth becomes more durable. Effort becomes more meaningful. That is not a marginal improvement. That is a transformation.

The same forces that keep the system stable are the ones that drive it forward. And once that transformation is understood, the path forward becomes clearer. Not because it is easy, but because it is visible. And once something is visible, it becomes a choice. A system that prevents collapse is not a safety net, it is infrastructure.

But understanding a system is different from changing one. Systems rarely remain in place because no alternatives exist. More often, they remain because people, institutions, and incentives adapt around instability until the instability itself begins to feel normal. Even systems under pressure can survive for long periods if enough participants learn how to compensate for their weaknesses. That creates another question—one that matters just as much as understanding the structure itself: if better systems are possible, why are systems so difficult to change once people have organized their lives around the current one? That is where we go next.

Chapter 6 – Why Systems Don't Change (Even If They Should)

Most systems do not fail all at once. They continue, they adjust, they compensate. That is why they last as long as they do. An unstable system does not collapse immediately, it bends. It shifts pressure. It creates workarounds.

Chris had learned something about instability that rarely appears in reports.

Most problems never arrive dramatically. They accumulate.

A hiring delay here.

An overtime increase there.

One experienced employee leaving unexpectedly.

A supplier issue that forces constant schedule adjustments.

None of it looked catastrophic.

In fact, from the outside, operations still looked successful.

Orders shipped.

Production continued.

Targets mostly held.

But inside the system, more and more energy was being spent compensating for pressure rather than improving performance.

The work still got done.

It just took more effort to hold the same ground.

Chris rarely described this as economic instability.

He described it differently: "Everything works... but it feels harder than it should."

Because systems rarely collapse when pressure first appears.

They adapt.

Systems that adapt can look healthy long after underlying relationships begin weakening. In fact, adaptation is often what delays recognition. People compensate. Businesses absorb pressure. Institutions create workarounds. Because the system continues functioning, the hidden cost becomes difficult to see. Effort quietly increases while outcomes become harder to sustain. The result is a strange kind of contradiction: the system still works, but it increasingly depends on compensation to keep working. Over time, that compensation starts feeling normal. And once instability feels normal, questioning the structure itself becomes harder.

From the outside, that can look like resilience. From the inside, it feels like constant adjustment. That difference is important. Because systems rarely change when they are working perfectly.

They also rarely change when they are clearly broken. They resist change the most when they are doing both at the same time, working enough to continue but broken enough to create pressure. That is where most economic systems live. They produce growth. They support participation. They enable investment But they also create instability. They require constant intervention. They produce outcomes that do not always hold. So, the system continues, not because it is optimal, but because it is functional.

The first challenge emerges here. A system that works "well enough" is harder to replace than a system that fails completely because failure creates urgency. Partial function creates hesitation. People adapt. Institutions adjust. Policies evolve. Each adjustment reduces pressure just enough to avoid collapse, but not enough to fix the structure. So, the system continues in a state of managed instability.

A second problem develops over time. Systems that are adjusted instead of rebuilt begin to divide into parts. Programs are added to address specific problems. Policies are layered to manage specific outcomes. Agencies are created to oversee specific functions. Each addition makes sense on its own. But they are not designed together. They are responses to different moments in time, different pressures, different priorities.

So, instead of one system, you end up with many. Each managing a piece of the problem. None managing the structure as a whole. That fragmentation creates complexity. Not complexity as a feature, complexity as a byproduct. Multiple flows of funding. Multiple eligibility systems. Multiple definitions of need, contribution, and outcome.

All operating at the same time. This makes the system harder to understand, harder to coordinate, harder to change. Because any meaningful change now requires alignment across all of those parts.

Then, coordination becomes difficult. Even when a better structure becomes visible, implementing it requires moving multiple parts at once. Programs must align.

Funding flows must integrate. Responsibilities must shift. And those changes cannot happen independently. Because each part of the system is connected to the others. Changing one part without adjusting the others creates new instability. So, change slows. Not because the solution is unclear, but because the system is interconnected in a way that resists coordinated movement. This creates a pattern. People will recognize problems. They will propose improvements. They will implement adjustments. But those adjustments happen within the existing structure. So, the structure remains and the cycle continues.

Eventually, transition itself becomes the risk. Not theoretical risk, operational risk. What happens if the change disrupts income? What happens if it interrupts benefits? What happens if it destabilizes businesses during transition? These are not small concerns. They are the reason systems are preserved even when they are imperfect. Because the cost of disruption can feel more immediate than the cost of instability.

Even if the long-term cost of instability is higher. This is where most proposals fail. They identify a better system. But they cannot show a path to it that does not create new instability along the way. So, the proposal is set aside. Not because it is wrong, but because it is risky. This is the critical point. A system is not replaced because it is better, it is replaced when it is both better and safer to implement than what exists. That is a higher bar. And it is the bar most ideas do not meet. Because they focus on the destination, not the transition. They describe what the system should become. But not how it gets there without disruption. That is what makes this different.

This system is not built on the assumption of immediate replacement. It is built on the assumption of continuity.

Nothing that people depend on disappears first. Nothing is removed before something stronger is in place. The system does not begin by taking control, it begins by aligning. It operates alongside what exists. It builds structure without interrupting function. Over time, as that structure proves itself, the system begins to shift. Not through force, through function. Participation flows into the new structure. Stability begins to come from the new mechanism. Fragmented systems begin to consolidate naturally. Because the new system is not imposed, it is adopted.

That does not mean transition would be frictionless. Large systems rarely change without resistance, confusion, or unexpected pressure. Administrative challenges would emerge. Some mechanisms would work better than expected while others would require adjustment. Businesses would adapt at different speeds. Institutions would learn in real time. None of that should be surprising. The question is not whether transition creates difficulty. The question is whether the transition creates less instability than the system already producing it. That is the actual comparison. Perfect implementation is not the threshold. Safer implementation is.

At this point, the question changes. It is no longer: Why hasn't this been done? It becomes: What would prevent it from being done now? Because once a system can be introduced without destabilizing what people rely on, once it can operate alongside the existing structure, once it can prove itself before it replaces anything, the primary barriers begin to fall. Not all at once, but steadily. And that is how systems actually change. Not through sudden replacement, through controlled transition. That is where we go next.

What cannot be disrupted

Before any system can change, one condition has to be met. People must not lose what they depend on. That is not a political statement, it is a structural requirement. If a transition introduces instability into the lives of the people it is meant to support, the system will not be accepted. Not because it is wrong, but because it is unsafe.

Most proposals fail at transition.

They describe a better destination without showing how people get there safely.

That assumption does not hold because for most people, the system is not abstract. It is income. It is housing. It is healthcare. It is survival

Anything that puts those at risk, even temporarily, will be resisted. So, the first rule of transition is simple. Nothing that people rely on can be disrupted. That includes:

- Income
- Existing benefits
- Business continuity
- Access to essential services

If any of those are destabilized during transition, the system fails before it begins. This is why the transition cannot be built around replacement. It must be built around continuity.

Continuity does not mean every legacy program remains structurally identical forever. It means that lawful participants are not destabilized, interrupted, or deprived of earned protections merely because the system modernizes. The objective is continuity of function and stability of participation, not permanent preservation of every administrative structure exactly as it exists today.

The system does not begin by removing what exists, it begins by supporting it. Existing income continues. Existing programs continue. Existing structures remain in place. Not as a permanent condition, but as a protected one. This creates the first layer of stability.

People do not have to adjust immediately. They do not have to requalify. They do not have to navigate a new system overnight. This is especially important for those who are already dependent on existing systems. Retirees, individuals receiving long-term support, households operating at the edge of stability – for these groups, disruption is not an inconvenience, it is a risk. So, the system does not ask them to move first, it protects them first. Existing support continues without interruption. Not as a temporary bridge, but as a guaranteed condition.

At the same time, something new begins to operate alongside it. The Stability Fund begins to function. Not as a replacement, but as a parallel structure. It starts collecting. It starts distributing. It starts proving its ability to maintain flow. But it does not yet replace anything. This is where the system begins to earn trust. Not through explanation, through performance.

People begin to see that the system can stabilize conditions without removing what they already depend on. That changes perception because the transition is no longer something that might happen to them. It is something they can observe.

Nothing in this framework depends on forcing people into identical outcomes or identical lives. People will still make different choices, take different risks, and value different things. Alignment is not about making everyone the same. It is about making the structure predictable enough that those choices can actually mean something over time.

Businesses operate under the same principle. They cannot be asked to absorb instability during transition. They must remain operational. Supply chains must continue. Employment must continue. Investment decisions must remain viable. If transition introduces uncertainty into business operations, the system creates the very instability it is trying to eliminate.

So, the structure avoids that. There are no sudden changes to operating conditions. No abrupt shifts in obligations. No immediate restructuring of how businesses function. Instead, the system begins to integrate gradually. Flows begin to align. Participation begins to stabilize. Predictability begins to improve without forcing businesses to adjust before the system itself has proven stability. This is the second layer of protection. The system does not demand adaptation, it enables it. Because adaptation driven by stability is sustainable. Adaptation driven by pressure is reactive. The goal is not to force behavior, it is to allow behavior to shift naturally as conditions improve.

This is where systems become difficult to change.

Because over time, adaptation becomes infrastructure.

Policies get written around instability.

Benefits evolve to compensate for gaps elsewhere.

Business models assume volatility.

Households organize around uncertainty.

Institutions slowly begin optimizing around the system as it exists rather than the system people wish existed.

Eventually, compensation becomes so normal that people stop recognizing it as compensation at all.

It simply starts feeling like reality.

And once something feels like reality, changing it begins looking disruptive, even when the current structure quietly carries enormous hidden cost.

Chris had seen this happen slowly.

At first, every adjustment felt temporary.

A staffing shortage solved with overtime.

A supplier issue solved with contingency planning.

A retention problem solved with incentives.

Each fix worked.

Until the fixes themselves became part of normal operations.

Over time, more energy went into compensating for instability than improving performance.

The organization adapted.

But adaptation quietly became infrastructure.

And once compensation becomes infrastructure, instability stops looking temporary.

It starts looking normal.

This applies to funding as well. The system does not immediately restructure all contributions, it begins by integrating flow where it can do so without disruption. Existing obligations remain intact during early transition. New structure builds alongside them. Over time, as the Stability Fund proves its capacity, flows begin to consolidate. Not abruptly, but as a result of demonstrated function.

This avoids one of the most common transition failures, forcing a new structure before it has proven it can hold. That is what creates instability. This system reverses that sequence. It proves first, then it integrates, then it replaces.

This is also where one of the most sensitive areas must be addressed, long-term income systems. Programs that people have paid into, programs that people depend on, programs that are tied to retirement and long-term planning cannot be disrupted. They must be preserved until the system itself provides a stronger foundation. That is why the transition is tied to condition, not to timing.

This point deserves unusual clarity because trust matters here more than almost anywhere else. People already receiving retirement benefits—or nearing retirement—would not suddenly find themselves navigating an unfamiliar system. Earned expectations remain protected. Existing obligations continue. The transition occurs underneath the structure people experience, not against it. The objective is continuity, not interruption. Over time, the source of support may gradually become more aligned and financially durable, but the experience for the individual remains stable. Security is preserved first. Structure evolves second.

Existing systems continue to operate as they are. They are funded. They are administered. They continue to serve those already relying on them.

At the same time, the Stability Fund begins to support those flows. Not by replacing them, but by reinforcing them. This continues until a clear threshold is reached. A point where the existing system can no longer sustain itself independently. At that point, the transition occurs. Not as a sudden change, but as a continuation of support through a different structure.

The individual does not experience a break, they experience continuity. The source changes but the support does not. That is how disruption is avoided. The system changes underneath the experience, not within it. This is the third layer of protection. No one is required to navigate instability in order to reach stability. That principle applies across the entire transition. Workers continue to earn. Businesses continue to operate. Programs continue to function. All while the new system builds the capacity to support all of them. This is what makes the transition viable. Not just the design of the final system, but the protection of the system people are already living inside. Because a system that cannot transition safely cannot be implemented. And a system that cannot be implemented does not matter, no matter how well it is designed. That is why this step is not optional, it is foundational.

Once continuity is protected, something important happens. The system no longer feels like a risk. It begins to feel like a replacement. And once that shift occurs, the next step becomes possible. Not forcing change, allowing it.

The bridge: layering instead of replacing

Most system changes are imagined as replacement. One structure ends, another begins. That is how change is often described. It is not how change actually works. Because replacement requires interruption. Something has to stop before something else can start. And in systems people depend on, interruption creates instability. That is why replacement is rarely successful at scale. It introduces the very risk people are trying to avoid.

So, the question becomes: If the system cannot be replaced all at once, how does it change? The answer is not replacement, it is layering. The new system does not begin by removing the old one, it begins by operating alongside it. This is the bridge. Not a moment, a structure.

The stability fund is introduced first. Not as a full system, but as a functioning component. It begins collecting. It begins distributing. It begins interacting with the existing system

At first, interaction is limited.

The Stability Fund supports areas where pressure is highest and disruption is lowest.

It reinforces stability where improvement can be measured clearly.

But it does not replace existing structures.

That restraint matters.

Because systems earn trust through performance, not explanation.

As the Stability Fund begins to function, something changes. Not immediately, but gradually. Flow begins to align. Instead of separate streams operating independently, connections begin to form. Income, support, and participation start to move through a shared structure. Not fully, but enough to create consistency.

This is the beginning of integration and it happens without forcing any part of the system to shut down. That is the key. Because integration driven by performance is stable. Integration driven by mandate is not.

As the system continues to operate, the Stability Fund grows, not just in size, but also in function. It begins to take on a larger role in maintaining participation. More of the system's stability comes from this structure. Less is dependent on fragmented responses. At this point, the system has not replaced anything but it has changed how the system behaves. That is the signal. When behavior changes before structure is replaced, transition is working.

This is where consolidation begins. Not as a directive, as a result. Programs that were previously operating independently begin to align with the Stability Fund. Their function is not removed, it is absorbed. Their purpose remains, but their operation becomes part of a unified flow. This is a critical distinction. The system is not eliminating support, it is removing fragmentation.

Instead of multiple pathways delivering partial stability, a single structure delivers consistent stability. That simplifies the system. Not by reducing what it does, but by aligning how it does it. Over time, this alignment reduces the need for separate structures. Not because they are forced out, but because they become redundant. The Stability Fund is already performing their function more consistently. This is how replacement occurs without disruption. Not through removal, through absorption.

This also changes how contribution flows through the system. At the beginning, contributions remain largely where they are. Existing structures continue to collect and distribute. The Stability Fund builds alongside them, but as integration increases, flows begin to shift. Not abruptly, gradually. More contribution is routed through the unified structure and less remains fragmented. This is not a sudden change in obligation, it is a change in alignment. Participants are not asked to navigate a new system, they are moved into it through function.

This is how coordination is achieved. Not by requiring all parts of the system to change at once, but by allowing them to align as the new structure proves itself. Each part connects when it is ready. Each function transitions when the system can support it. That removes the need for perfect timing and it removes the risk of misalignment during transition.

At this point, something important has happened, the system is no longer operating as two separate structures, it is operating as one system with a dominant core. The Stability Fund is that core. Existing structures still exist, but they no longer define how the system behaves. They operate within it. This is the turning point. Because once the system is operating through a unified structure, the final phase becomes possible. Full consolidation. Not forced, not immediate, but inevitable. Because the system that holds replaces the system that doesn't.

That is how the bridge works. It does not ask people to step into uncertainty, it builds stability underneath them. And once that stability is proven, the system does not need to be forced into place - It becomes the place.

That is the difference between designing a system and implementing one. Design can be immediate. Implementation must be earned. And this structure is built to earn it. That is what makes it viable. And that is what allows the next step to happen. Not just alignment, but full integration of how the system operates.

What prevents this from being controlled

Every system that touches money eventually faces the same question, who controls it? Not in theory, in practice. Because if a system can be controlled, it can be distorted. And if it can be distorted, it will be. That is not cynicism, it is history. Every system that influences income, cost, or participation becomes a target for influence. That influence could be political, institutional, or even individual and not always with bad intent, but with incentives. And incentives, over time, reshape systems.

So, if this system depends on trust, it cannot rely on trust. It must be structured so that control is limited by design, not by promise. This is where many systems fail. They assume good behavior. They build oversight. They create rules. And over time, those rules are interpreted, adjusted, expanded. Until the system no longer behaves the way it was designed.

This system cannot allow that. Because if the anchor can be moved, the system will drift again. So, the question is not: "Who runs the system?" the question is: "What prevents anyone from controlling it?" That is a different problem. And it requires a different kind of solution.

The first principle is simple.

The system must be governed by structure, not discretion. That means the core mechanism cannot be adjusted based on preference. It cannot be tuned for short-term outcomes. It cannot be influenced by pressure. It must operate based on defined relationships, not decisions.

This concern is reasonable because history gives people good reason to ask it. Systems tied to money, incentives, and public trust often become vulnerable to short-term pressure. That is exactly why the structure matters more than the promise. A system dependent on restraint eventually fails under incentives. A system constrained by calculation behaves differently. The question becomes less about trusting individuals and more about limiting what individuals can influence in the first place. That distinction matters because trust built on personality is temporary. Trust built on visible rules is durable.

NPU is not set, it is calculated. That matters more than anything else in this chapter. Because a value that is set can be changed but a value that is calculated must follow rules. Those rules become the guardrails. They define how output is measured, how participation is accounted for, and how cost alignment is maintained

And they do so consistently. Not when it is convenient, not when it is politically acceptable, always. This removes the most common point of control, the ability to "adjust the number." Because there is no number to adjust, only a relationship to calculate.

The second principle builds on this.

Transparency must be structural, not optional. In many systems, transparency is something that can be increased or reduced. Reports are published. Data is released. Oversight is provided. But access to that information can change. That creates asymmetry. Some people understand the system and others do not. That gap creates influence. Because those who understand the system can shape how others interact with it.

This system removes that gap. The calculation of NPU is not hidden, it is visible. Not just to experts, to everyone. The inputs are known. The relationships are defined. The outcomes can be verified. This does not require interpretation, it requires observation. Anyone can see how the system is performing, how the unit is moving, and how alignment is being maintained

That visibility creates a different kind of accountability. Not external, internal. Because when a system is visible, deviation cannot be hidden. And when deviation cannot be hidden, it cannot persist.

The third principle is independence.

Not independence in name, independence in function. The structure that calculates and maintains NPU cannot be tied to short-term political cycles, institutional incentives, or market pressures. If it is, it will be influenced by them.

So, its role must be narrowly defined. It does not set policy. It does not allocate resources. It does not make decisions about outcomes. It performs one function, it maintains the relationship that holds the system together

Nothing more. This limits its power and that is intentional. Because power is where control enters. By narrowing the function, the system reduces the opportunity for influence.

The fourth principle is constraint through interaction.

No single part of the system operates in isolation. The calculation of NPU depends on output data, participation data, and cost structures. These inputs come from different parts of the system. No single entity controls all of them. That creates a natural constraint. Because influencing the system would require coordinated manipulation across multiple independent inputs which becomes increasingly difficult as transparency increases. This is how structural integrity is maintained. Not by preventing change, but by making distortion visible and difficult.

The fifth principle is continuity of rule.

The system cannot change its own logic easily. Because if it can, it can be reshaped. So, changes to the structure itself must be rare, deliberate, and highly visible. Not because change is bad, but because structural change is powerful. And power must be constrained. This creates stability at the deepest level. Not just in outcomes, but in the rules that produce those outcomes.

Now, there is an important clarification here. This does not mean the system is rigid. It still adapts, because inputs change. Output grows. Participation shifts. Cost structures evolve.

The system reflects those changes automatically, through calculation, not intervention. This is what allows flexibility without control. Movement without manipulation. And that is the balance that has never been achieved before. Most systems choose either control with stability or freedom with drift. This system achieves both, freedom with alignment.

It should be pointed out again, alignment does not limit choice. It ensures that choices are made within a system that holds. Participants remain free to act, but the system no longer amplifies instability when they do. And when the structure holds, behavior can remain free.

This is where trust begins to solidify. Not because people believe in the system, but because they can see that it cannot be easily altered. That it behaves consistently. That it responds predictably.

Over time, that consistency becomes expectation and expectation becomes trust. This is what makes the system durable. Not just in implementation, but in time. Because systems do not fail immediately, they fail gradually. This happens through small adjustments, small exceptions, and small compromises, until the structure no longer holds. This system is designed to resist that process. Not by preventing change, but by protecting the relationships that define it. That is what keeps it aligned. And that is what allows the final step to happen. Not just transition, but permanence.

Innovation still matters. Markets still matter. Adaptation still matters. Technology, leadership, and productivity improvements will continue making systems more efficient. But efficiency and alignment are not the same thing.

Systems often become better at surviving instability without ever correcting the instability itself.

Why this holds over time

Most systems don't fail all at once, they drift. Slowly, quietly, almost invisibly at first. A small adjustment here. A temporary exception there. A change made for a good reason. Each one makes sense in the moment, but over time, they add up until the system no longer behaves the way it was designed to.

That is how alignment is lost. Not through collapse through erosion. This is what has happened before. Not because the systems were poorly intended. but because they were not built to hold under pressure. And pressure is inevitable. Whether it is economic pressure, political pressure, or social pressure. Every system experiences it. The question is not whether pressure will exist, it is whether the system can withstand it. That is what determines durability.

So, if this system is going to work, it must be built to hold. Not just when conditions are stable, but when they are not. That requirement changes how everything must be designed. Because durability does not come from strength alone, it comes from structure.

The first layer of durability is automatic adjustment. The system does not wait for correction. It responds as conditions change. When output increases, the system reflects it. When participation shifts, the system reflects it. When cost structures move, the system reflects it. Not after a delay, not through policy response immediately. Because the relationships are built into the system itself.

This eliminates one of the primary causes of drift, lag. Most systems fail because they react too slowly. By the time adjustments are made, conditions have already changed. That creates imbalance which requires further adjustment, which creates more lag. And the cycle continues. This system breaks that cycle because it does not rely on reaction. It operates through alignment in real time.

The second layer of durability is balance between growth and stability. Most systems lean too far in one direction. They prioritize growth, or they prioritize control. And in doing so, they sacrifice the other. This is where instability begins. Because growth without stability creates volatility. And stability without growth creates stagnation.

This system does not choose between them, it binds them together. NPU is structured to reflect both. Not as competing forces, as connected ones. This means the system does not have to correct for imbalance later, because imbalance is less likely to occur in the first place. Growth moves with stability, not against it.

The third layer of durability is behavioral alignment. This is where most systems are misunderstood. They assume that if the structure is correct, behavior will follow. But behavior does not follow structure, it responds to incentives. And if incentives are misaligned, behavior will drift. Even inside a well-designed system.

This system addresses that directly. Because when participation is consistently connected to output, the incentives align naturally. Effort leads somewhere. Contribution has meaning. Stability is reinforced.

So, people do not have to be forced into alignment, they move toward it. Because it benefits them to do so. This is what makes the system self-reinforcing. Not through enforcement, but through behavior.

The fourth layer of durability is simplicity at the core. This may seem counterintuitive. The system itself is comprehensive. But the mechanism holding it together is not. It is a relationship. Not a set of rules. Not a collection of policies. A relationship between output, participation, and cost.

That simplicity matters because overly complex systems often become fragile. They require constant management. They are difficult to understand. And over time, they become difficult to maintain.

Simple structures are different. They are easier to observe, easier to verify, and harder to distort. This is what allows the system to remain stable even as conditions evolve.

The fifth layer of durability is visibility over time. Not just in moments, but across cycles. Short-term fluctuations will always exist, that is part of any dynamic system, but what matters is how the system behaves over time. "Does it return to alignment?" "Does it maintain consistency?" "Does it hold under stress?" Because the system is visible, these questions can be answered, Not assumed, observed.

This creates a different relationship between the system and the people inside it. People are not waiting for explanations, they are watching performance. And performance builds confidence in a way that explanation cannot.

The sixth layer of durability is resistance to incremental erosion. This is one of the most important and least visible features. Most systems do not fail because of large changes, they fail because of small ones. Exceptions, adjustments, temporary measures, to name a few. Each one justified, each one reasonable but together, they change the system.

This system resists that process because the core mechanism cannot be easily modified. It is defined by relationship, not by adjustable parameters. So small changes do not accumulate in the same way. They cannot shift the foundation, only the inputs. And when inputs change, the system responds automatically, without altering the structure itself. This preserves integrity over time.

Understanding why systems resist change matters for an important reason. Resistance is not permanence. This resistance does not come from bad intent. It comes from incentives. Institutions optimize around the systems they inherit. Businesses build models around predictable rules. Agencies organize around defined responsibilities. Households make decisions based on familiar conditions. Political systems adapt to what people already understand.

Even when problems become visible, uncertainty creates hesitation. Because replacing a system introduces risk. And risk is often easier to fear than instability people already know. That hesitation is not irrational. It is structural.

Which is exactly why transition must feel safer than drift. History is full of systems that lasted longer than people expected—until recognition reached a threshold. Not because collapse suddenly arrived. But because enough people finally understood the underlying problem clearly enough to stop compensating around it.

Change rarely begins with consensus. It begins with recognition. The moment enough people stop confusing adaptation for function. That moment matters. Because systems rarely transform while the problem remains invisible. They transform when invisibility ends.

Now step back and look at the full picture. This system holds because it adjusts automatically. It balances growth and stability. It aligns behavior. It simplifies the core mechanism. It remains visible. It resists erosion.

Each of these layers reinforces the others. Not independently, together. That is what creates durability, not a single feature but rather a structure that holds from multiple directions.

This is also where something important becomes clear, the system does not need to be constantly defended. It does not require continuous intervention. Because it is not dependent on external management to remain aligned, it holds itself. Not perfectly, but consistently. And consistency is what matters. Because over time, consistency becomes expectation. And expectation becomes trust. This is how the system becomes stable not just in structure.

There is a second-order effect to this. When a system holds itself, it no longer requires constant intervention. Right now, a significant portion of government activity exists to manage instability by adjusting, correcting, responding, and rebalancing. That activity is not the goal, it is the cost of misalignment.

When alignment exists, that activity decreases. Not because it is eliminated by policy but because it is no longer necessary. This reduces operational workload, administrative staffing pressure, and ongoing policy intervention.

Over time, the system requires less effort to maintain, not more. That is what makes it sustainable at scale. But in perception, people begin to rely on it. Not because they are told to, but because it works. And that is the final test, not whether a system can be designed, but whether it can endure. This one is built to endure. And once durability is established, the final question becomes possible. Not "Will this work?" But: "How does this become real at scale?"

There is another effect happening at the same time. And it matters just as much. As the system aligns, it simplifies, because alignment removes the need for duplication. Right now, the system maintains stability through layers. Programs that overlap. Agencies that coordinate the same outcomes. Policies designed to correct other policies. Each one exists for a reason, but together, they create administrative weight, financial weight, and/or operational complexity.

This is how spending is reduced. Much of what is currently spent is not creating value, it is compensating for misalignment. When alignment is built into the system, that compensatory spending declines. The system requires less intervention, fewer corrective programs, and less administrative oversight.

This system does not add to that, it removes it. Not by cutting support but by eliminating redundancy. When multiple systems are trying to stabilize the same problem, you don't need all of them. You just need one that works. That is what consolidation does. It replaces fragmented effort with unified function. And when that happens, administrative layers shrink. Program overlap disappears. Coordination costs drop.

Not because of mandate, but because they are no longer needed. Not by removing support, but by removing inefficiency. This is where an important misconception needs to be addressed. At first glance, a system like this can appear larger because it touches more of the economy. But reach is not the same as size.

The current system is large because it is fragmented. It requires multiple agencies, layered programs, ongoing corrections, and administrative coordination.

This system replaces that structure with a single aligned framework which means fewer moving parts, fewer decision layers, and fewer administrative functions.

This is not an expansion of government function. The system becomes smaller in operation. It is a consolidation of it. Fewer systems are required to achieve the same outcomes, and over time, fewer resources are required to manage them even as it becomes more effective in outcome. That is the difference. Not expansion, consolidation. This system is not heavier, it is cleaner.

It is understandable why a framework touching multiple parts of the economy might initially appear larger. But complexity and size are not the same thing. The current system often requires multiple overlapping programs, separate administrative pathways, reactive interventions, and fragmented coordination to stabilize the same underlying problems. Alignment changes the structure underneath those efforts. The objective is not adding another layer. It is reducing how many layers are necessary at all. Over time, the expectation is not more administration. It is less correction, less duplication, and less effort spent compensating for instability that no longer needs management.

Fragmented systems require more oversight, more administration, more correction, and more compensation.

Aligned systems reduce the need for intervention because fewer failures require management.

The objective is not expanding structure.

It is reducing the amount of structure required to maintain stability.

How this becomes real

At this point, the system is no longer theoretical. You've seen what's broken, what's missing, what holds it together, how it transitions safely, why it can't be controlled, why it holds over time.

So, the final question is no longer: "Does this work?" It becomes: "How does this actually happen?" Not in theory, in reality. Because a system can be perfectly designed and still never be implemented. That is the gap we have to close now.

The first thing to understand is this, systems like this are not adopted all at once, they are not switched on, they are entered. This matters because large-scale systems do not change through a single moment, they change through accumulation. Participation increases. Confidence builds. Adoption expands. Until the system reaches a point where it becomes the default.

That is how scale is achieved. Not through mandate, through inevitability. The process begins where resistance is lowest. Not where the system is weakest, but where the value is easiest to see. Early implementation focuses on areas where stability improvements are immediate, where disruption is minimal, and where outcomes are visible.

This creates the first layer of adoption. Not universal, but real. And that matters more. Because once the system is operating in any capacity, it is no longer hypothetical, it is observable. And observation changes everything. People do not have to believe in the system. They can see it. They can compare it. They can evaluate it against what they are already experiencing.

This is how adoption spreads. Not through persuasion, but through contrast. When one part of the system begins to feel more stable, more predictable, more aligned, it becomes a reference point. Others begin to ask: "Why does this work better?" and that question drives expansion. Not policy, not pressure, but curiosity.

That is the second phase, expansion through demonstrated value. As more participants engage with the system, something important happens. The network strengthens. Because this system is not static, it becomes more effective as participation increases. Alignment improves. Stability deepens. Predictability increases.

This creates a reinforcing loop: More participation leads to stronger system. Stronger system leads to more participation. This is how scale accelerates. Not linearly, exponentially.

At a certain point, the system crosses a threshold. Not defined by policy but defined by behavior. When enough of the system is operating through alignment, the remaining parts begin to shift naturally. Because operating outside the system becomes less efficient, less predictable, less stable. This is the tipping point. Not forced adoption, functional necessity. At that point, the system does not need to be pushed forward. It pulls the rest of the system into it. This is how full-scale integration happens. Not through replacement, but through convergence.

Now, there is an important question here. What role does government play in this process? Because large systems do not exist in isolation, they operate within existing structures. The answer is precise. Government does not force adoption It enables structure. It establishes the framework that allows the system to operate. It ensures consistency of inputs. It supports transparency. But it does not dictate outcomes. Because the system itself is designed to function through alignment, not control.

This changes the role of policy. From directing behavior to enabling structure. That is a fundamental shift. Because it reduces the need for constant intervention and it allows the system to scale through function, not enforcement. This also reduces resistance. Because people are not being required to adopt something unfamiliar, they are moving toward something that works. That is a completely different experience.

Systems that deliver more consistent outcomes do not need to replace existing ones by force. Over time, they replace them through preference. And once that preference becomes widespread, the transition is no longer driven by policy. It is driven by behavior.

This is why the system must work at every stage, not just at full scale. Because each stage builds the next. If it fails early, it never reaches scale. If it holds early, scale becomes inevitable. That is why everything that has been built so far matters. Protection, continuity, layering, independence, and durability. Each of these is not just a feature, it is a requirement for scale. Because scale does not come from design, it comes from trust. And trust comes from performance.

Early implementations would not begin at full scale. They would begin in contained environments, specific sectors, regions, or economic layers, where stability improvements can be measured clearly. From there, expansion follows demonstrated results.

That sequencing matters because large systems are rarely proven through immediate national adoption. They are tested, measured, adjusted, and expanded. Real-world implementation would almost certainly involve phased environments where outcomes can be observed clearly, weaknesses can be identified early, and trust can be earned through performance rather than assumption. Serious systems mature through evidence. They do not demand belief first.

Now step back and look at the full arc.

At the beginning of this book, the question was: "Why doesn't the system feel like it works anymore?" Now the question has changed. "Why hasn't this been built yet?" And the answer is no longer unclear. Because now you can see what the system is and how it works, how it transitions, why it holds, and how it scales.

Chris had seen this pattern for years without fully naming it.

Every adjustment solved something.

But every adjustment also seemed to create another layer of complexity somewhere else.

The organization became better at compensation.

Not necessarily better at stability.

That realization changed the question.

The issue was no longer "How do we work harder inside the system?" The issue became "Why does the system require this much compensation to function at all?"

That is the question institutions eventually have to confront.

Even when they would rather not.

The system is no longer an idea, it is a structure that can be built. And once something can be built, the only remaining question is: Who chooses to build it?

Because once structure becomes possible, the next question is no longer philosophical. It becomes practical. What changes first? How are incentives aligned? How does participation move through the system in everyday life? Those questions matter because systems are not experienced as theory. They are experienced through work, contribution, taxes, savings, and stability. If alignment is going to become real, it has to show up there.

Chapter 7 – Where Change Actually Starts

Most people assume that systems change from the top. A new policy is introduced. A law is passed. A directive is issued. And from that moment forward, the system is expected to behave differently. That is how change is often described. It is not how change begins.

Large systems, especially economic ones, do not shift because they are told to, they shift because behavior inside them begins to change. Quietly at first, not everywhere, not all at once, and not in a way that immediately draws attention. Change begins at the edges. Not because the center is unimportant, but because the center is the most constrained. It carries the most responsibility. The most dependency. The most risk. Which means it is the last place that can move.

The edges are different. They are smaller, less interconnected. More exposed to instability. And because of that exposure, they feel pressure earlier. They are the first to notice when something stops working. And they are the first to try something that works better. Not because they are trying to change the system, but because they are trying to operate inside it.

This does not mean policy, institutions, or legislation become irrelevant. Large systems still require rules, coordination, and structure. The point is narrower: policy rarely succeeds when behavior inside the system remains unchanged. Laws can create conditions. Institutions can establish frameworks. But systems move when participants begin responding differently inside those frameworks. Durable change usually comes from the interaction between structure and behavior, not from either operating alone.

This is where real change begins.

A business facing unpredictable demand does not wait for a system-wide solution, it looks for a way to stabilize its own operations.

A worker facing inconsistent income does not wait for policy reform, they look for a way to make their situation more predictable.

An investor facing volatility does not wait for structural redesign, they look for environments where risk is better managed.

None of these decisions are coordinated. None of them are ideological. They are responses. But when enough of those responses begin to point in the same direction, something shifts. A pattern forms. And patterns are what systems follow. This is the part most people miss. They look for the moment when change is declared. But by the time change is declared, it has already begun. It has been tested, refined, observed. It has already proven that it can work, at least somewhere. That is the threshold that matters. Because once something works in one place, under real conditions, it stops being theoretical. It becomes an option. And options change behavior.

At first, only a few participants move toward it. Those closest to the pressure. Those most exposed to instability. Those who benefit most from improvement. They are not taking a risk. They are reducing one. That distinction is important. Because adoption at this stage is not driven by belief. It is driven by function. Something works better. So, it is used.

Early adoption does not depend on moral persuasion alone. Healthy systems make desired behavior visible, measurable, and economically rational. As organizations begin demonstrating stronger alignment between productive success and economic participation, those outcomes can be recognized through transparent qualification standards and incentive structures designed to reward sustained participation performance.

The objective is not to compel participation through mandates. It is to create conditions where alignment becomes increasingly visible, increasingly measurable, and increasingly advantageous over time. When incentives reinforce the same behaviors that strengthen system stability, adoption becomes less dependent on promises and more dependent on results.

As that usage increases, something else happens; visibility. Other participants begin to see the difference. Not in theory, in outcome. More stable income, more predictable demand, and more consistent planning.

These are not abstract improvements. They are operational ones. And operational improvements spread. Not because they are promoted, but because they are observed. This is how the system begins to move. Not through instruction, but through demonstration.

It is important to say this plainly: some implementations would likely fail. Some environments would misapply the structure. Some pilots would reveal weaknesses no theory anticipated. That is not evidence the system cannot work. It is how serious systems improve. Large-scale systems rarely emerge fully formed. They mature through experimentation, adjustment, and evidence. The relevant question is not whether every attempt succeeds. It is whether successful approaches become more repeatable over time than unsuccessful ones.

Most meaningful systems evolve through uneven experimentation.

What matters is not whether every attempt works.

What matters is whether successful patterns become visible, repeatable, and easier to adopt over time.

Because systems rarely spread through perfection.

They spread through demonstrated advantage.

At this stage, nothing has replaced the existing system. It still operates. It still supports the majority of activity. It still defines the baseline. But it is no longer the only way things can function. There is now an alternative path. Small at first, partial, incomplete, but real. And that is enough. Because once a better structure exists, even in a limited form, the system is no longer fixed. It is flexible. Participants begin to choose where and how they engage. Not all at once, but gradually.

They allocate more of their activity toward what works better. They reduce exposure to what does not. This is not a coordinated shift. It is an accumulation of decisions. Each one small, rational, local. But together, they begin to change the system.

The system does not start because it is declared. It starts because it is used. And once it is used, it becomes visible. Once it becomes visible, it becomes comparable. And once it becomes comparable, it becomes chosen. That is where change actually starts.

The first places this works

If change begins at the edges, the next question is simple. Where are those edges? Not in theory, in reality. Where does a system like this first prove itself, not because it is introduced, but because it is needed? The answer is not everywhere at once. It is where instability is already shaping behavior. Because those are the environments where improvement is easiest to see. And where adoption requires the least persuasion.

The first places this works are not defined by ideology, they are defined by pressure. Environments where participation is already inconsistent. Where planning is already difficult. Where outcomes are already unpredictable. Not broken systems, stressed ones. Because stressed systems reveal structure. They show where alignment is missing. Where flow is disrupted. Where small changes have large effects. That is where a system built on stability has the clearest advantage.

One of the first environments where this becomes visible is in sectors with variable demand. Industries where activity does not move in a straight line. Industries like construction, logistics, seasonal production, or project-based work.

These environments matter not because they are uniquely important, but because they reveal instability earlier and more visibly. Success here does not mean the system remains limited to them. It means pressure makes improvement easier to observe. Once outcomes become visible, adoption spreads into environments where instability is less obvious but still present. Early participation reveals value. Broader participation follows demonstrated reliability.

These are not edge cases, they are early indicators. Places where misalignment is easiest to see and where alignment, even in partial form, begins to change outcomes. Not perfectly, but enough to notice.

In these environments, instability is not occasional. It is expected. Demand rises and falls. Labor expands and contracts. Income moves with cycles that are difficult to predict and even harder to manage. Participants in these systems are already compensating. Businesses adjust staffing constantly. Workers move between periods of high activity and low income. Planning is short-term because conditions are uncertain. These systems function, but they do not hold.

Chris had spent years solving problems that never seemed to stop returning. Production pressure. Staffing pressure. Escalating overtime. Delayed investments. Budget constraints.

Every adjustment seemed to help for a while. Then something new surfaced somewhere else.

For years, he treated each issue as separate. A hiring problem. A labor issue. A cost issue. A market issue. Until eventually, a different possibility began to surface:

What if these were not separate problems at all?

What if the system itself had slowly stopped reinforcing the outcomes it was designed to create? Nothing dramatic happened. No crisis. No revelation. Just the quiet realization that working harder inside the same structure no longer felt like enough.

That moment matters.

Because systems rarely begin changing when people become angry.

They begin changing when enough people stop believing the old explanation still explains what they are seeing.

This is where stabilization begins to show immediate value. When income becomes more consistent, workers remain engaged. When participation holds, businesses can plan further ahead. When planning improves, output becomes more predictable. Nothing about the work itself changes. What changes is the stability around it. That difference is visible quickly. Not as a theory, as a result.

Another place this system takes hold early is in supply chains. Not at the center where large systems are already optimized, but at the points where coordination breaks down. Smaller suppliers. Regional distributors. Intermediary layers that connect production to delivery. These are the parts of the system most exposed to disruption. A delay in one area creates pressure in another. A cost shift upstream becomes a constraint downstream. Information does not always move as fast as conditions change.

So, participants in these environments operate defensively. They hold excess inventory when they can. They limit commitments when they cannot predict demand. They build buffers. Not because it is efficient, but because it is necessary. That is a signal.

Frustration alone rarely changes systems.

People can tolerate a surprising amount of pressure for a very long time. They adapt. Compensate. Wait for conditions to improve. Assume next year will feel different.

Recognition is different. Recognition begins when people stop treating instability as temporary and start seeing it as structural.

That shift matters. Because once people recognize a problem as structural, they stop asking: "How do I work around this?" and start asking: "Why does this keep happening?"

That question changes everything.

Another early entry point is in regions where economic activity is already uneven. Not necessarily low activity, but inconsistent activity. Areas where employment fluctuates. Where income does not move evenly across time. Where local economies experience cycles more intensely than national averages. These regions are often treated as problems to be managed but they are also environments where structural improvement is easier to detect. Because the baseline is not stable. When stability increases in these environments, the effect is not subtle. Participation rises. Local demand becomes more consistent. Businesses experience less volatility.

The system does not need to be explained, it can be seen. And that matters because visible improvement is what drives adoption. Not arguments, not models, but outcomes.

There is another category that matters just as much, emerging structures. New business models. New forms of work. New ways of organizing production. These are not constrained by legacy systems in the same way. They are already adapting, already experimenting, already looking for structures that allow them to operate more effectively. These environments do not need to be convinced to change, they are already changing. Because the decision isn't ideological, it's operational. "Does this reduce friction?" "Does this make outcomes more predictable?" "Does this hold under pressure?" If the answer is yes, then adoption doesn't require agreement, it requires use. Which makes them natural entry points.

They can integrate new structure more easily. They can test it more quickly. They can demonstrate it more clearly. And because they are growing, their influence expands over time. This is important. Because the system does not need to replace existing structures immediately. It can grow through new ones.

Now step back and look at what all of these environments have in common. They are not defined by size, or by geography, or by industry alone. They are defined by exposure to instability. That is the unifying factor. And that is what determines where the system begins. Not where it is easiest politically, not where it is simplest administratively, where it is most useful. That is the key. Because usefulness drives adoption.

When a system improves outcomes in a way that is visible and immediate, it does not need to be promoted, it is chosen. At first, that choice is limited. A business applies it to part of its operation. A region adopts it within a specific economic layer. A network of participants begins to align around it

Nothing changes at scale yet, but something important has happened. The system is no longer theoretical. It is operating. And once it is operating, it begins to generate something that no proposal can create on its own, evidence. Not controlled, not modeled, observed.

This is what changes the conversation. Because once evidence exists, skepticism shifts, it no longer asks, "Would this work?" It begins to ask, "Where else could this work?" That question is what drives expansion. And it does not require coordination to answer. Each participant can answer it independently. Each environment can test it locally. Each result adds to the pattern

And over time, the pattern becomes clear. This system does not need to start everywhere. It needs to start where it works first. Because where it works first is where it proves itself. And once it proves itself, everything that follows becomes easier. Adoption requires less explanation. Integration requires less resistance. Expansion requires less force. Because the system is no longer being introduced, it is being observed. And what is observed, and works, does not remain isolated, it spreads. That is where the next phase begins.

Why early adoption is rational (not idealistic)

Major systems rarely change because everyone suddenly agrees.

They change gradually.

Messily.

Often after long periods where the old system continues functioning well enough to survive but poorly enough to frustrate.

None appeared overnight.

None arrived through perfect consensus.

They became possible once enough people recognized that continuing the old structure carried more cost than changing it.

Change rarely begins with certainty.

It begins when the current explanation stops feeling sufficient.

At this stage, something important needs to be clarified. Early adoption does not happen because people believe in a system. It happens because it works. It matters because belief requires agreement. Agreement takes time. And large systems do not change on agreement. They change on behavior.

The first participants in any system shift are not the most convinced. They are the most exposed. They are the ones for whom the current system creates the most friction. The most uncertainty. The most cost. So, when a structure appears that reduces those conditions, even partially, it is not seen as a theory. It is seen as an improvement. And improvement is enough.

A business does not adopt a new approach because it aligns with a philosophy. It adopts it because it improves predictability with more consistent demand, more stable labor participation, and/or more reliable planning. These are not abstract benefits, they affect operations directly. Hiring decisions become clearer. Inventory becomes easier to manage. Investment becomes less speculative.

Because the system does not ask businesses to change how they compete. It improves the environment in which they compete. Markets still function. Prices still move. Efficiency still matters. But the volatility that forces defensive behavior begins to decline. So, businesses do not adopt the system because they are required to. They adopt it because it allows them to operate more effectively.

Workers follow a similar pattern. They are not evaluating systems at a theoretical level. They are responding to conditions. Income stability, consistency of opportunity, the ability to plan beyond the immediate. When those conditions improve, even slightly, behavior changes. A worker is more willing to stay engaged. More willing to pursue advancement. More willing to commit to longer-term decisions. Not because they have been persuaded, but because the environment supports it. This is where participation begins to strengthen. Not through policy, but through confidence. And confidence is not created by explanation, it is created by experience.

Investors approach the system differently, but for the same reason. They are not looking for certainty, they are looking for risk that can be understood. In an unstable system, risk includes variables that are difficult to price. Sudden demand shifts. Unpredictable labor participation. Policy-driven corrections that arrive after conditions have already changed. These factors increase uncertainty. Not because they are large, but because they are inconsistent.

That inconsistency raises the threshold for investment. So, capital becomes more selective, more cautious, and more reactive.

In a system where participation holds and flow remains aligned, that layer of uncertainty begins to narrow. Risk does not disappear, but it becomes more measurable. And when risk is more measurable, capital moves more consistently. That is the key. Investment is not driven by the absence of risk. It is driven by the ability to evaluate it. This system improves that evaluation. Not by controlling outcomes, but by stabilizing the conditions that influence them.

That distinction is critical because it reinforces something that must remain clear. This is still a market system. Businesses still compete. Workers still choose where and how to participate. Investors still allocate capital based on return. Nothing in this structure removes those dynamics. What changes is the environment they operate in. Less distortion and more consistency. Better alignment between effort and outcome. That is what makes early adoption rational. It does not require participants to think differently. It allows them to operate more effectively within the same incentives. And that is why adoption does not need to be coordinated.

Competition remains. Profit remains. Failure remains. Businesses still succeed or fail based on execution. Workers still choose where to participate. Investors still allocate capital according to opportunity and risk. What changes is not freedom of movement. What changes is the level of instability participants must constantly compensate around. The system does not eliminate competition. It makes participation inside competition more durable.

Each group – businesses, workers, investors – arrives at the same conclusion independently. Not at the same time, not in the same way, but in the same direction. Because the system improves the conditions they all depend on. This is where something subtle but important happens. The system begins to reinforce itself before it reaches scale.

A business that operates in a more stable environment creates more consistent demand. That demand supports more stable income. That income supports continued participation. Each part strengthens the others. Not by design alone, but by interaction.

This is how early systems grow. Not because they are pushed forward, but because they become easier to operate inside. And once that happens, the nature of adoption changes. It is no longer a question of whether the system works, it becomes a question of where it works best. And that question leads directly to the next phase. Not isolated adoption, but expansion through connection. Because once participants begin to experience stability, they begin to seek it elsewhere. Across operations. Across regions. Across networks. And that is when the system begins to move beyond the edges. Not through intention. Through demand.

The tipping point

At the beginning, the system exists alongside everything else. It is partial. It is limited. It is one option among many. Participants can choose whether to engage with it or not. And for a time, that choice does not carry much weight. The system is useful in certain environments. Helpful in specific conditions. But not yet necessary.

This is where most people misunderstand how systems scale. They expect growth to be gradual, linear, predictable. But large systems do not expand that way. They build slowly, then they shift quickly. Not because something changes in the design, but because something changes in behavior. That change is the tipping point.

Most major shifts begin the same way. The old answers stop resolving the pressure. "Work harder." "Spend less." "Wait it out." "Adjust around it." "Optimize more." For a while, these responses feel responsible. Sometimes they even work temporarily. Until eventually, people begin noticing something uncomfortable; the effort keeps increasing, the relief keeps shrinking, and the explanation that once made sense no longer fully explains reality.

That is the moment false alternatives begin collapsing.

Not because people suddenly agree on the answer.

Because they stop believing the old answer still works.

Before that point, adoption is optional. Participants engage because it improves their situation. But they can still operate outside of it. After that point, the dynamic reverses. Operating outside the system becomes the harder choice. Not impossible, but less efficient, less predictable, and more exposed. That is when the system stops spreading and starts pulling. To understand why, you have to look at what happens as participation increases. Each new participant does not just benefit from the system, they strengthen it.

None of this suggests a tipping point arrives cleanly or predictably. History rarely moves that way. Systems often linger in tension longer than expected. False starts happen. Resistance reappears. Progress stalls and resumes. Recognition spreads unevenly. Some participants move quickly while others remain cautious for long periods. What matters is not speed. What matters is whether the direction of behavior begins shifting consistently enough that the old structure no longer resolves pressure as effectively as the emerging one.

A business operating within a more stable structure creates more consistent demand.

That demand supports more stable income for workers. That income sustains participation across other businesses. Each connection reinforces the others. At small scale, this effect is limited. At larger scale, it compounds. More stability leads to more participation. More participation leads to stronger flow. Stronger flow leads to greater predictability. And predictability changes behavior. Businesses begin to rely on it. Workers begin to expect it. Investors begin to factor it into decisions.

This is where the shift begins. Not in the system itself, but in how people interact with it. At a certain point, the system reaches a threshold. Not defined by size alone, but defined by influence.

When enough activity is flowing through a stable structure, that structure begins to shape the broader environment. Even participants outside the system start to feel the difference. They see more consistent demand in connected markets. They see more stable labor participation in aligned sectors. They see more predictable outcomes in adjacent operations

At first, this creates comparison and then it creates pressure. Because participants operating outside the system begin to experience something new. Not instability, relative instability.

They are no longer comparing their conditions to the past. They are comparing them to something better that exists now. That comparison changes decision-making. A business sees that competitors operating within the system can plan further ahead. A worker sees that participation inside the system leads to more consistent income. An investor sees that capital deployed within aligned structures behaves more predictably. These are not theoretical advantages, they are operational ones. And operational advantages do not stay isolated they spread.

At this stage, adoption is no longer driven by curiosity. It is driven by necessity. Not because anyone is forcing it.

Because the alternative becomes less effective. This is the tipping point. The moment when the system no longer needs to prove itself. It has already done that. Now it begins to define the conditions others must respond to. This is where scale accelerates. Not through expansion alone, but through convergence.

Participants who were previously independent begin to align. Not all at once, but consistently. Each decision moves in the same direction – toward stability, toward predictability, toward alignment. And because those decisions are being made across the system at the same time, the effect compounds. What was once a localized improvement becomes a system-wide shift. This is why the transition does not feel dramatic.

There is no single moment where everything changes. There is no announcement that marks the shift. From the outside, it looks gradual. From the inside, it feels inevitable. Because once the system reaches this point, the direction is set. Not by design, by behavior. And behavior, once aligned with a structure that works, does not easily reverse. That is what makes this different from previous attempts at change. It does not rely on maintaining momentum through effort. It sustains momentum through advantage.

As long as the system continues to produce more stable, more predictable outcomes, participants will continue to move toward it. Not because they are committed to it but because it works better. And systems that work better do not need to compete for adoption, they become the default.

This is the point where the system stops being one option among many, it becomes the environment. Not fully, not immediately, but functionally. Because enough of the system is now operating within it so that everything else begins to adjust around it. That is what a tipping point looks like. Not a sudden change in structure but a shift in what is normal. And once that shift happens, the final barriers begin to fall. Not through force, but through irrelevance. Because what remains outside the system is no longer defended as better, only as familiar. And familiarity does not hold against consistent advantage. That is what carries the system forward from here. Not expansion alone, adoption that no longer needs to be argued – only followed.

Why resistance fades

This is where most attempts at change fail. They treat resistance as something to overcome, something to argue against or disprove or even defeat. But resistance at this level is not ideological, it is practical. "What happens to income?" "What happens to existing support?" "What happens to businesses during transition?" These are not abstract concerns, they are grounded in real risk. And if those risks are not addressed, resistance does not fade, it hardens.

That is why the structure of this transition matters more than the argument for it. Because this system does not ask people to step into uncertainty, it removes the need to. Nothing is taken away first. Nothing is disrupted before something stronger is in place. The system begins by stabilizing conditions, not replacing them.

That changes how resistance behaves. Instead of confronting a new system, participants begin to experience it. At first, indirectly. Through improved conditions in parts of the system that they are connected to. More stable demand. More consistent participation. More predictable outcomes. These changes do not require belief, they require observation. And observation changes perception. The system is no longer something unknown. It becomes something visible. That visibility is what begins to soften resistance. Because the question shifts from: "Why should this be trusted?" to: "What is actually changing?" That is a different question. It is grounded in experience, not assumption.

As the system continues to operate, something else happens. The risks people were concerned about do not appear. Income is not disrupted. Support is not removed. Businesses are not destabilized. Instead, conditions begin to improve. Not everywhere, not immediately, but consistently enough to be noticed. This is where resistance begins to weaken. Not because it has been disproven, but because it has not been validated. The expected problems do not occur. And when expected problems fail to appear, concern begins to lose its foundation.

At the same time, another force begins to emerge, comparison. Participants start to see the difference between operating inside the system and outside of it. They observe more consistent income in aligned environments. They see more predictable business conditions in connected networks. They witness more stable planning where the system is active. These differences are not theoretical, they are experienced. And experience is difficult to argue against.

This is where resistance changes form. It is no longer focused on preventing change. It becomes focused on understanding it. "How does this work?" "Where is it being applied?" "What would it take to participate?" That shift is subtle, but it is decisive. Because once resistance becomes inquiry, the direction has already changed.

From that point forward, the system does not need to defend itself. It needs to continue performing. Because performance does what argument cannot. It builds trust. Not immediately, not completely, but steadily. Each cycle where the system holds reinforces that trust. Each instance where instability is reduced strengthens it. Each example of improved outcomes expands it.

Over time, resistance does not disappear, it becomes less relevant. Because the system is no longer being evaluated as an idea, it is being evaluated as a functioning structure. And functioning structures are judged differently. Not on what they promise, on what they produce.

There is another layer to this, institutional resistance. Organizations built around the current system. Structures designed to manage its complexity. Processes that depend on its fragmentation. At first, these systems resist change as well. Not out of opposition, but out of alignment. They are built to operate within the current structure.

This concern is reasonable because institutions are rarely neutral to structural change. Existing systems create responsibilities, budgets, incentives, and expertise that naturally orient around the current structure. Resistance, in many cases, is not malicious. It is adaptive. Organizations built to manage instability will understandably question systems designed to reduce the instability they currently administer. That reality should be expected rather than ignored.

Change introduces uncertainty into their function. But the same pattern applies, as the system begins to consolidate function, as fragmentation decreases, as coordination becomes simpler, something happens: the complexity these institutions are designed to manage begins to shrink.

Not abruptly, but gradually. And as it does, their role begins to shift. Not eliminated, but reoriented. From managing instability to supporting stability. This is how institutional resistance fades. Not because everyone agrees, but because the alternative becomes harder to justify.

Systems that require constant correction carry a cost where systems that hold reduce costs. That difference compounds and eventually, it becomes visible enough that resistance loses its foundation. Not through removal, through adaptation. Because the system does not make institutions obsolete, it makes them more effective within a simpler structure. This is a critical point. Resistance does not need to be defeated, it needs to become unnecessary. That is what this system does. It removes the conditions that sustain resistance. Uncertainty. Risk of disruption. Lack of visibility.

As those conditions decline, so does the need to resist. And what replaces it is not agreement, but acceptance. Not because everyone reaches the same conclusion at the same time, but because the system continues to work. And systems that consistently work do not require universal approval, they require continued use.

That is what carries this forward. Not consensus, not persuasion, but performance that makes resistance less and less relevant over time. Until eventually, the system is no longer something to resist. It is simply how things work. And at that point, the final shift becomes possible. Not adoption at the edges, but full integration across the system.

The shift from idea to reality

Systems do not require universal agreement to begin changing. They rarely receive it.

People will disagree on solutions. On pace. On design. On tradeoffs. That is normal.

Consensus is not the beginning of change. Recognition is. Large systems rarely begin because everyone agrees at once. More often, enough participants simply conclude the current explanation no longer solves the problem they are living inside. Agreement expands after visible success, not before it. That distinction matters because waiting for universal consensus often becomes a way of preserving systems long after better alternatives begin emerging.

The important threshold is not "Does everyone agree?" It is: "Do enough people recognize the current structure no longer resolves the problem?"

Once that threshold is crossed, the conversation changes.

The argument is no longer whether something should evolve.

The argument becomes how.

At some point, every system crosses a line. Not a visible one, not a declared one, but a real one. It is the point where something stops being discussed as an idea and starts being recognized as something that exists. Up to now, this system has been understood, explained, explored, tested in parts, seen in specific environments and adopted in limited ways.

But still, for many, it remains conceptual. Something that works. Something that makes sense. Something that could expand.

This is where that perception changes. Because once a system begins to operate in real conditions, produce consistent outcomes, expand through use, and align behavior across participants, it no longer depends on explanation to be taken seriously, it depends on performance. And Performance is what turns structure into reality.

Change begins quietly. Long before legislation. Long before institutions move. Long before headlines announce anything important. It begins when enough people stop treating instability as inevitable and start recognizing it as structural.

That recognition does not guarantee action. But it changes what becomes possible. Because once a system becomes visible, people begin asking different questions. Not: "How do I survive inside this?" but "What would actually work better?" And once that question becomes legitimate, something important changes.

Ideas that once sounded unrealistic suddenly deserve examination.

Structures that once seemed impossible begin feeling necessary.

That moment matters because recognition is only the beginning.

Eventually, every idea reaches a harder threshold.

It must stop sounding persuasive.

And start proving itself.

At first, that shift is subtle. Nothing dramatic changes. The system is still growing. Still expanding. Still integrating. But the conversation begins to sound different. People are no longer asking: "Would this work?" They are asking: "Where is this working?" That is the turning point. Because once that question becomes the focus, the system is no longer hypothetical, it is observable. And observable systems behave differently. They create reference points. Examples that can be studied, compared, replicated, begin to generate their own evidence. Not in controlled environments but in real ones.

That evidence compounds. Each successful application reinforces the next. Each environment that stabilizes adds to the pattern. Each participant that benefits strengthens the signal. And over time, the system becomes easier to understand, not because it is explained better, but because it is seen more often. This is how ideas become structures. Not through declaration, but through repetition.

At the same time, something else is happening. The existing system is still operating but it is no longer the only frame of reference. Participants now have something to compare it to. Not historically, not theoretically, currently. They can see where stability exists and where it does not. Where participation holds and where it breaks. Where planning works and where it fails.

This comparison changes expectations. What once felt normal begins to feel inefficient. What once felt unavoidable begins to feel solvable. And that shift in expectation is powerful. Because systems are not only shaped by how they function, but they are also shaped by what people are willing to accept.

As expectations rise, tolerance for instability declines. Not because people demand change, but because they have seen that better conditions are possible. This is where the system begins to move from alternative to standard. Not formally, not completely, but perceptually. And perception drives behavior. More participants choose stability where it is available. More activity flows into aligned structures. More decisions are made with the expectation that conditions will hold. This accelerates integration. Not by force, but by preference. And preference, once established at scale, becomes direction.

At this point, the system no longer needs to be introduced, it needs to be extended. Across more environments, across more sectors, and across more layers of the economy. Not because it is required, but because it is expected. This is the moment where the transition becomes irreversible. Not in the sense that nothing can change but in the sense that the direction is set.

The system has demonstrated that it can stabilize participation. That it can reduce volatility. That it can support growth without collapse. And once those conditions are proven, not once, but repeatedly, they become the standard by which all systems are judged. From that point forward, the question is no longer: "Should this exist?" it becomes: "Why doesn't this exist everywhere yet?" And that question does not require advocacy to spread. It spreads on its own. Because it is grounded in experience.

And that is where this leads. A system that does not need to be explained to be trusted. A system that does not need to be defended to be maintained. A system that does not need to be restarted when conditions change. A system that holds.

So, the final question is no longer about what is broken, it is about what comes next. Because once a system like this is understood, once it is seen not just as possible, but as functional, it stops being an abstract idea. It becomes a choice. Not a forced one, not an immediate one, but a real one. A choice between continuing to operate inside a system that requires constant correction or building one that holds.

That choice does not need to be made all at once, it is made gradually. Through participation. Through adoption. Through use.

And once enough of the system begins moving in that direction, reversal becomes increasingly difficult.

Because systems that consistently work do not fade, they replace. Not through argument, through reality. And once reality shifts, everything built inside it shifts with it. At some point, the shift becomes undeniable. Not because it is declared, but because it is experienced.

But adoption alone is not enough. Systems still have to hold under pressure. They must survive downturns, shocks, political cycles, technological disruption, and periods where confidence weakens. That is the next test. Not whether alignment can begin, but whether aligned systems can remain stable when stress arrives.

The question is no longer: "Does this work?" It becomes: "Why doesn't this exist everywhere yet?" And once that question takes hold, direction is no longer debated, it is followed.

Chapter 8 – The Moment After Understanding

There's a moment that happens after something becomes clear. Not when you first hear it, not when you first consider it, but when it settles. When it stops feeling like an idea and starts feeling like something real. That's where you are now. You've seen the problem. You've felt the disconnect. You've followed the structure. You've watched it move from concept to function to reality. And now there's a different kind of question forming. Not: "Does this make sense?" But: "What happens next?" That question matters. Because this is where most ideas lose momentum. They either ask too much, too quickly, become too technical, too fast, or stay too abstract to act on.

And when that happens, even the strongest ideas fade. Not because they were wrong, but because they never translated into something people could move toward. This is where we do something different. We don't rush. This is not a call to act immediately. It's not a demand to replace anything. Because people don't resist better systems. They resist losing stability before something better is proven.

That doesn't happen here. We don't overwhelm. And we don't pretend that understanding alone creates change, because it doesn't. Understanding creates something else, awareness. And awareness changes how you see the system. Understanding changes the questions people ask. At first, people ask "Could this be true?" But eventually the question changes.

Once a problem feels structural, curiosity becomes evaluation. "How would this begin?" "What could fail?" "What would build trust?" "How would people know whether it was actually working?" That shift matters. Because systems do not earn legitimacy through explanation. They earn legitimacy through observed performance. Recognition creates openness. Trust requires evidence.

And openness is not the same thing as agreement. People will reasonably disagree on pace, implementation, tradeoffs, and risk. Some will remain skeptical for long periods. Others will want evidence before participation. That is not failure, it is how serious systems are evaluated. Understanding does not eliminate caution. In many cases, it increases it. Because once an idea becomes real enough to matter, people begin asking harder questions. Not whether improvement sounds appealing, but whether improvement survives contact with reality.

Once you see misalignment, you can't unsee it. Once you recognize drift, you start to notice it everywhere. It shows up in places you weren't looking before. A raise that doesn't feel like progress. A business decision that makes sense on paper but not in reality. A system adjustment that fixes one problem and creates another. These aren't new experiences. What's new is that you can now see what connects them. Not bad decisions, not lack of effort, but disconnection.

Once you understand what an anchor does, you start to feel when it's missing. That shift is permanent. But it's not the same as action. And it doesn't need to be. Not yet. Because systems like this are not built in a single step. They are built in layers. That pace is not a limitation, it's a requirement. Because systems that move faster than people can understand them...create resistance. And systems that move slower than people can recognize their value, lose momentum.

Maya had spent most of her career solving problems that looked manageable on paper and far more complicated in reality.

Labor shortages, employee turnover, escalating healthcare costs, forecasting challenges and productivity expectations that rose faster than predictability.

She had seen ambitious ideas before. Most sounded compelling in presentations. Far fewer survived contact with execution.

That made her cautious. Not cynical. Cautious. Because systems are easy to imagine and difficult to operationalize.

When she first encountered the idea of alignment, her reaction was not enthusiasm.

It was skepticism. Not "Would this be nice?" But "Could this actually function without creating more instability than it solves?" Because recognition is not trust. Recognition only creates the conditions where trust becomes possible.

Maya had learned something over years of operations leadership: systems rarely fail because the intention was wrong. They fail because complexity shows up where no one expected it. Reporting breaks. Incentives drift. Administrative friction grows. Good ideas become difficult to execute at scale. That experience made her skeptical in a specific way. Not resistant to change, resistant to unintended consequences. If something this large was going to work, it had to survive operational reality—not just optimism.

This has to move in between those two. Fast enough to be seen, slow enough to be trusted. Trust rarely arrives through promises.

People trust what they can observe, what they can compare, and what survives scrutiny.

That means durable systems usually begin where outcomes can be measured clearly enough to evaluate and limited enough to adjust if something does not work as intended. In places where the risk is manageable, the scope is contained, and the results can be observed.

A system of this scale does not go live all at once. No serious institution would replace the operating rules of an economy without first testing them against reality. Before legal obligations change, the framework can operate in parallel, calculating outcomes, comparing results, validating assumptions, and exposing implementation errors under real-world conditions.

That process matters because confidence should be earned rather than assumed. Systems become trustworthy when they can demonstrate that their measurements are accurate, their mechanisms behave as expected, and their outcomes remain stable under scrutiny. The goal is not rapid deployment. The goal is responsible deployment.

That's why the next step is not about convincing anyone. It's about where this begins. And where it begins is not where most people expect. It doesn't start at the highest level. It doesn't require sweeping policy. And it doesn't depend on universal agreement. It starts where alignment can be created and observed.

At this point, something subtle begins to shift. You are no longer reading this as a theory. You're beginning to map it. You're thinking: "Where could this work?" "What would this look like in practice?" "How would this apply here?"

That shift is important. Because it means the system is no longer external. It's becoming contextual. And once something becomes contextual, it becomes actionable.

That's how systems begin to move. Not through universal adoption, but through initial application. Those first applications are not special. They are simply the places where clarity exists, conditions allow, and someone decides to try something different.

Because when an approach proves reliable, it rarely stays isolated. People notice. Others adapt it. Results become harder to ignore. Over time, what once felt experimental begins to feel practical.

And eventually, what feels practical becomes expected.

But that comes later.

Right now, nothing has changed yet. Not in the system around you. Not in the structures you interact with every day. But something has changed in how you see it. And that matters more than it seems. Because once you can see alignment you start to look for it. And once you start to look for it, you start to find where it can exist.

Where change actually begins

When people think about change at this scale, they tend to imagine it starting at the top – federal policy, national programs, sweeping reform – something large enough to match the size of the system itself. That assumption feels logical. If the system is large, the solution must be large. But that's not how systems actually change. They don't begin at scale, they begin where they can hold. Because trying to change everything at once does not create stability. It creates friction. It forces alignment before alignment has been proven. And when that happens, even strong ideas fail. Not because they don't work, but because they weren't allowed to demonstrate that they do.

That's where this system starts. In environments where three things can be clearly seen; what is being produced, who is participating, and what it costs to sustain. That's it. No full-system overhaul. No immediate replacement. No universal agreement required. Just enough clarity for alignment to exist.

These environments already exist. Inside companies managing complex labor structures. Inside regional supply chains trying to stabilize cost and output. Inside networks where coordination already matters more than scale. Not as theory, as pressure points where alignment already has value. They are not hypothetical. They show up in places where work is coordinated, output is measurable, participation is visible. You see them in organizations, networks, regional clusters, contained economic ecosystems, and places where activity is already connected, just not fully aligned.

That's where the system can begin to take shape. Not by forcing change but by refining what is already there. Because the goal at this stage is not transformation, it's demonstration. To show, in real conditions, that when output, participation, and cost are connected, the system behaves differently. More stable. More predictable. More coherent. That proof does not need to be large. It needs to be clear. Because clarity scales faster than complexity.

Once something is clearly working in one place it becomes easier to understand in another. That's how expansion begins. Not through mandate but through recognition. And recognition spreads in a specific way. First, internally, inside the environment where the system is applied.

Participants begin to notice decisions are easier to make. Outcomes are easier to understand. Planning holds longer. Not perfectly, but consistently enough to change behavior.

Then, externally, others begin to observe the difference. Not through explanation, but through comparison. "Why does that environment feel more stable?" "Why do decisions there seem to hold?" "What are they doing differently?"

Those questions are the beginning of replication. Because once something is visible, it becomes repeatable. And once it becomes repeatable, it becomes scalable.

But this stage is important for another reason, it keeps risk contained. Nothing at the system level is disrupted. No existing structure is removed. No participant is forced to change. The current system continues to operate uninterrupted. This is not replacement. It's parallel emergence. And that changes how people engage with it. Because instead of evaluating a new system against uncertainty, they evaluate it against experience. They can see both, side by side. And when people can compare directly, they don't need to be convinced, they decide. That decision is what drives adoption. Not policy, not pressure, preference. People move toward what works. Businesses adopt what stabilizes them. Networks expand what improves coordination.

This is how the system grows. From contained environments to connected ones. From connected ones to broader integration. Each step building on the last. Each expansion grounded in something that has already been proven. This is not a leap, it's a progression. And progression matters. Because it preserves something critical, trust.

That's when something changes. Not structurally at first, behaviorally. Participants begin to make decisions with the expectation that alignment will hold. They plan differently. They invest differently. They engage differently. Because the system they are operating in behaves differently. That behavioral shift is what carries the system forward. Not theory, not explanation, but use. And use is what turns a working model into a working system.

At this point, something important becomes clear, change is not something that is delivered. It's something that is built. In places where it can be seen. In ways that can be repeated. At a pace that can be trusted. That's where this begins, not at the highest level but at the most real one. And from there, it moves.

The parallel system phase

At this point, something important needs to be made clear, this system does not begin by replacing the current one. It begins by existing alongside it. That distinction is not a detail. It is the reason this works. Because the fastest way to create resistance is to force a choice before a comparison can be made.

Parallel should not be misunderstood to mean separate economies operating independently. The same businesses still operate. The same people still work. The same markets still function. What changes is that aligned structures begin operating inside existing systems where participation, output, and stability can be measured more clearly. In practice, this looks less like replacement and more like phased integration. Some environments adopt aligned mechanisms earlier. Others continue operating traditionally until outcomes become visible enough to justify broader expansion. The distinction matters because serious transitions rarely begin by replacing everything. They begin by proving enough to expand responsibly.

If people are asked to abandon what they know before they can see something better, the answer will almost always be no. Not because they reject improvement but because they reject uncertainty.

That's why this phase exists. The parallel system phase. Where nothing is taken away. Nothing is removed. Nothing is disrupted before something stronger is in place. The current system continues, fully. People still earn income the way they always have. Businesses still operate within existing structures. Markets still function the way they do today

At the same time, something new begins to operate within it. Not outside, not in opposition, but inside. In specific environments where alignment can be created and observed. This is not duplication, it's differentiation. Two systems operating at once, one requiring constant interpretation and one creating consistent relationships. And that difference becomes visible very quickly. That comparison is what drives everything that follows. Because when systems operate side by side, something becomes possible that has never been available before, direct evaluation. Not theoretical, not predictive, but observed. People can see which system stabilizes outcomes. Which system reduces uncertainty. Which system holds over time.

They don't have to interpret data, they experience the difference. And experience changes behavior faster than explanation ever can. This is where the system gains its first real advantage. Not through scale, but through clarity. Because once people can see how something works, they don't need to be convinced to try it. They choose to. That choice matters. Because voluntary adoption behaves differently than forced change. It spreads faster. It encounters less resistance. And it builds stronger trust.

This is why the parallel phase is not a temporary workaround, it is a structural requirement. Without it, the system would need to prove itself through argument. With it, the system proves itself through performance. That difference is everything.

At this stage, participation is optional. No one is required to engage with the new structure. No one is forced to change how they operate. But those who do participate begin to experience something different. Not dramatically at first, but noticeably. Decisions begin to hold longer. Outcomes become more predictable. Planning requires less adjustment. Not perfectly, but consistently enough to change how people engage. That consistency is what builds momentum. Because people don't adopt systems based on promises, they adopt systems based on results they can rely on.

And reliability is something that can only be demonstrated over time. That's what this phase provides, time to observe, time to compare, time to build trust without pressure. While this is happening, something else becomes visible, the limitations of the existing system. Not because it gets worse, but because there is now a point of comparison. Where before, instability felt normal, now it feels unnecessary. Where before, constant adjustment felt expected, now it feels inefficient. That shift is subtle but it's powerful. Because it changes the standard.

Once people see that alignment is possible, they begin to expect it. And expectation drives behavior. Businesses begin to explore where alignment can improve operations.

Networks begin to organize around more stable structures. Participants begin to move toward environments where outcomes hold.

This is how adoption begins to scale. Not all at once but through movement. From one environment to another. From one network to the next. Each step guided by something simple, what works.

This is also where one of the most common concerns begins to fade, the fear of disruption. Because nothing is being taken away. The existing system remains intact while the new system proves itself. That removes the risk that usually accompanies change. And when risk is reduced, participation increases. Not because people are told to engage, but because they feel safe enough to explore. This is how systems grow without forcing compliance. Through opportunity. not obligation.

Over time, something else begins to happen. The environments where the system is active begin to connect. What started as isolated applications becomes a network. And networks behave differently than individual systems. They reinforce each other. They share stability. They expand faster than single points of adoption. This is where the system begins to move beyond demonstration and into integration. Still not replacing the existing structure, but increasingly interacting with it. Influencing behavior across a wider range of participants.

At this point, the question is no longer: "Should this system exist?" It becomes: "Why would you not use it where it works?" And that question changes everything because it reframes adoption from risk to opportunity. That is what carries the system forward. Not pressure, not policy, but performance that can be seen, compared, and chosen.

That's the role of the parallel phase. To create a space where something new can exist without requiring something else to disappear. To allow comparison before commitment. To build trust before scale. Because once trust exists, expansion is no longer something that needs to be driven. It happens on its own. And that's what comes next.

What has to exist for this to work

Up to this point, we've been careful. We've focused on understanding, on behavior, on how the system feels when it works. But at some point, a different question becomes unavoidable. Not: "Does this make sense?" But: "What actually has to be in place for this to function?" Because if this is going to move beyond concept, if it's going to operate in real environments, then it has to stand on something. Not theory, structure. And that structure does not need to be complicated but it does need to be clear. Because systems don't fail when they are imperfect, they fail when they are undefined.

So, what does this system require? At its core, only three things. Not new ideas, not new behavior, just a consistent way to connect what already exists.

1. A way to measure output consistently

Every system produces something, whether it is goods, services, or some other value. That part isn't new. We already measure output. We track it. We report it. We build entire economic narratives around it. But the way we measure output today is disconnected from how people experience it. It exists at a distance. It's aggregated, abstracted, removed from participation

That's where the breakdown begins. Because if output cannot be meaningfully connected to the people inside the system, it becomes a number without context.

This system doesn't require new output. It requires output to be measured in a way that can be connected. Not just how much is produced, but what that production represents inside the system. That shift is subtle but it's critical. Because once output can be connected it can be used. What that means in real terms is simple: The system stops telling you how much is produced and starts telling you what that production means for you.

2. A way to track participation clearly

Every system depends on participation from labor, skill, time, and contribution. Again, nothing new. We already track participation in pieces. In employment. In hours worked. In productivity metrics.

But those measurements are fragmented. They don't resolve into a single understanding of: What does participation actually mean in the system? That's why people constantly ask: "Is this worth it?" "Am I being compensated fairly?" "Does this scale over time?"

Those questions exist because participation has no consistent reference point. This system creates one. Not by redefining work, but by linking participation directly to output. So that contribution is no longer interpreted, it is understood. And once participation is clear, alignment becomes possible. That removes the question people ask every day: "Is this actually worth it?" Because the answer is no longer guessed. It's built into the system.

3. A way to keep cost within the same structure

This is where most systems break. Not at output, not at participation, at cost. Because cost moves independently. Prices shift. Expenses change. Access fluctuates. And when cost is disconnected from both output and participation, stability disappears. That's what creates the constant need for correction whether in adjustments, policies or other intervention.

This system does not eliminate cost movement, it connects it. So that cost exists within the same structure as output and participation. Not controlled, aligned. That's the difference. Because when cost is part of the same system, it stops drifting. This is where stability becomes real. Not because prices stop moving, but because they stop moving independently of everything else.

These elements do not need to be perfect to function. They need to be consistent enough to maintain relationship. Every real system contains imperfect measurement, incomplete information, and changing conditions. Stability comes less from precision than from coherence. The purpose is not to calculate reality flawlessly. It is to prevent the key relationships underneath the system from drifting too far apart before correction becomes necessary.

What this means in practice

At this point, it might sound like something complex is being introduced. It's not. Nothing here requires inventing new behavior. People don't have to change how they work. Businesses don't have to change how they operate. Markets don't have to change how they move.

What changes is the structure underneath those actions. The connection between them. Instead of output existing in one place and participation being measured in another and cost moving independently.

They exist inside the same frame. That's it and that's enough. Because once those three elements are connected, everything else begins to stabilize. Not because it is controlled, but because it is aligned.

Why this is already possible

Another concern usually appears here, "If this is so simple, why doesn't it already exist?" The answer is not technical. We already have the capability to measure output to track participation, to observe cost, at a high level and increasingly, at a detailed one.

The barrier has never been capability, it has been connection. We built systems to observe. We did not build systems to align. That's the shift happening here. Not new data, new relationships. And those relationships can be established with tools that already exist gradually. In contained environments at a scale that can be tested and refined. This is not a future dependency, it's a present capability.

It's just as important to be clear about what this system does not need. It does not require centralized control or complete system replacement or even immediate universal adoption. It also does not require perfect measurement, perfect participation tracking, or perfect cost stability.

Because perfection is not what creates stability, consistency does. As long as the system holds its relationships, even imperfectly, it works. And as it is used, it improves. That's how durable systems evolve.

This structure does not sit above the system, it sits inside it. It operates where work happens. Where decisions are made. Where value is created. It becomes part of how organizations operate. How networks coordinate. How environments stabilize.

Not as an added layer, as a connecting one. That's why it doesn't feel disruptive. Because it doesn't replace what people are doing. It makes what they are doing make sense.

The Threshold

At some point, a threshold is crossed. Not when everything is perfect, but when the structure holds well enough to be relied on. That's when behavior changes. People stop questioning whether the system will hold and start planning as if it will.

That shift is what turns a working model into a working system. And that threshold is not theoretical, it is something that can be reached. In specific environments, with defined participation, and with measurable output

That's all it takes. Because once the structure holds in one place it can hold in another.

What comes next

Now the system has a place to begin. A way to operate alongside the current system. A structure that allows it to function.

They begin with those who have the clearest reason to act. Not the loudest voices not the largest institutions, but the ones closest to the problem and the ones who benefit most from solving it. That's where movement starts.

It doesn't start with policy

There's a natural instinct to assume that change begins at the policy level. That legislation drives adoption. That governments initiate transformation. But policy does not lead systems like this, it follows them. Because policy operates on validation. It requires evidence. It requires stability. It requires something that can be observed and trusted.

That statement deserves precision. Policy still matters enormously. Large systems require legal frameworks, institutional administration, standardized rules, and public accountability. The point is sequencing. Durable policy usually stabilizes systems that have demonstrated viability rather than creating legitimacy by declaration alone. Evidence creates trust. Trust creates participation. Policy helps scale what people already recognize as working.

This system builds that first. In real environments, with real outcomes. Only after that does policy begin to engage. Not to create the system, but to support what is already working. That's an important distinction. Because it removes a major barrier. This does not require political alignment to begin. It requires functional alignment. And that can happen anywhere.

The first movers are not who you expect

It's easy to assume that the largest organizations move first. That scale drives adoption. But scale often slows it. Large systems carry inertia. They are built around existing structures. They are optimized for current conditions. They are cautious by necessity.

The first movers tend to be different. They are close enough to the problem to feel it. Flexible enough to try something new. Motivated enough to seek stability.

Not reckless, not experimental for its own sake, but practical. They are looking for something that works. And when they find it, they use it.

Businesses seeking stability

Because instability has a cost. And that cost shows up long before it appears in numbers. It shows up in hesitation. In delayed decisions. In missed opportunities.

Systems that reduce that cost don't need to be explained. They get used. One of the first groups to move are businesses operating inside uncertainty. Not because they are failing, because they are adapting constantly. They deal with fluctuating costs, unpredictable labor alignment, and shifting demand. They are already adjusting every day.

So, when something reduces that need for constant adjustment, they notice. Because stability has value. Not just financially, operationally. Strategically. It allows planning to hold. It reduces friction in decision-making. It creates consistency across operations.

That's not theoretical value, it's immediate. And when something provides immediate value, it gets adopted. Not universally, but repeatedly.

Networks that need coordination

The next group is networks. Not individual organizations, connected ones. Supply chains. Industry ecosystems. Regional collaborations. Anywhere coordination matters.

Because networks amplify misalignment. When one part shifts, everything else adjusts. That creates complexity and complexity creates cost. Not just in money but also in time, in effort, in uncertainty.

So, when a structure appears that connects output, participation, and cost, networks benefit quickly. Because alignment at one point improves alignment across the system. That creates leverage and leverage accelerates adoption. Because the benefit is not isolated, it spreads through the network.

Environments that need predictability

There is another group that moves early environments where predictability matters more than optimization. Places where stability is more valuable than short-term gain. Where consistency matters more than volatility. Where planning matters more than reaction.

These environments don't need perfection, they need reliability. And when they find a system that provides that, they adopt it. Not because it is new, but because it works.

Individuals who recognize the difference

At the same time, individuals begin to move. Not all at once, not in coordination, but in response. People who experience alignment even in a limited way, begin to make different decisions. They choose environments where outcomes hold. They prefer systems where effort connects. They engage where participation makes sense.

Not because they were told to, but because they can see the difference. That individual movement matters. Because systems are built from participation. And participation follows understanding.

Why adoption feels natural

At this stage, something important becomes clear, adoption is not being driven, it is being pulled. By usefulness, by clarity, and by results that hold.

That's why it doesn't feel forced. There are no mandates, no requirements, no external pressure, just a simple dynamic: People move toward what works. And what works spreads.

The pattern of expansion

This creates a predictable pattern. It starts with contained environments, practical adopters, and clear use cases. Then it moves to connected systems, expanding networks, and shared benefits. Then further to broader environments, cross-system interaction, and wider recognition. Each step building on something that has already been proven. Each step reducing uncertainty. Each step increases trust.

This is how scale happens. Not through a single moment, through a sequence. At this point, the system is no longer waiting to be adopted, it is being used. In specific places. By specific participants. For specific reasons. That's enough. Because systems don't need universal adoption to grow, they need successful application. Once that exists, expansion follows.

Working scale does not mean perfect scale. It means contained enough to learn from. A region. An industry. A pilot environment. A voluntary structure where outcomes can be compared honestly rather than assumed. "What happens to retention?" "...to financial planning?" "...to business predictability?" "...to income stability?" or ...to investment behavior?" "What improves?" "What breaks?" "What requires adjustment?" Real trust comes from answering those questions publicly. Not assuming success before testing begins.

Some pilots would likely underperform. Some assumptions would prove incomplete. Some environments would expose friction theory could not predict. That should be expected. Real trust comes less from avoiding failure and more from responding visibly when failure occurs. Systems become credible when they improve under pressure rather than collapse because of it.

Maya had learned something important over years of operations work:

People rarely resist change because they hate improvement.

They resist change because they fear instability.

Especially when the current system, however frustrating, still mostly works.

That made one principle obvious.

No system like this earns trust by demanding belief.

It earns trust by reducing uncertainty.

Showing measurable improvement.

Creating enough predictability that people begin trusting what they experience more than what they fear.

That is where serious adoption begins.

The role of policy (later, not first)

Eventually, policy engages. Not to initiate, but to formalize. To support expansion. To standardize structure. To integrate systems more broadly. But by that point, the system is already functioning. Already trusted. Already understood in practice. That changes how policy interacts with it. Because it is no longer speculative, it is established.

There is a moment when something shifts. Not visibly, but meaningfully. When the question changes from: "Who would try this?" To: "Who isn't using this yet?" That's the point where adoption accelerates. Because at that point, the system is no longer competing as an idea, it is competing as a structure. And structures that reduce correction tend to outperform those that depend on it. Not over time, immediately. Because at that stage, not participating begins to carry its own cost. In missed stability, missed efficiency, and missed alignment. And when non-participation has a cost, participation increases.

What comes next

Now we have a system that can begin. A way for it to operate safely. A structure that supports it. And a clear path for early adoption.

The final step is not about mechanics. It's about direction. Because once something is working, and once it is being adopted, the only question left is: Where does this lead? Not eventually, but practically.

At this point, the system is no longer a question. It has moved through every stage that matters. It has been understood. It has been tested in concept. It has been structured. It has begun to operate. It has started to be adopted.

So, the final question is not about whether it works, it's about where it leads. Because every system, once it begins to move, creates direction. Not all at once, but inevitably. And that direction matters more than any single step along the way.

This does not end in a program

Programs often exist to compensate for instability after it occurs. Infrastructure exists to reduce instability before it compounds. That difference matters. One continually reacts. The other supports function. Roads, electrical systems, and digital networks are not constantly debated because they became part of what allows everything else to work. The long-term role of alignment is closer to that logic than to temporary intervention.

It's important to be clear about this. This does not lead to a program. It's not something temporary, or optional or something layered on top of everything else. Programs require maintenance, they require adjustment, they require constant intervention to remain effective. That's because they operate outside the system, trying to correct it.

That's not what this is. This leads to infrastructure. Something the system depends on. Something that supports everything inside it. Something that does not need to be constantly adjusted to function. Infrastructure doesn't tell people what to do, it allows what they do to work. That's where this goes.

A system that holds

If you step back, the shift is simple. Right now, the system moves, but it doesn't hold. Growth happens. Effort increases. Output expands. But the connection between those things is inconsistent. That's why everything feels unstable.

Holding does not mean permanence. Markets will still change. Technology will continue reshaping labor. External shocks will still arrive. Tradeoffs will remain. The difference is not the elimination of uncertainty. It is the ability of the system to absorb uncertainty without repeatedly pushing ordinary participants into instability.

This changes that. Not by slowing movement, but by allowing it to hold so that growth translates into stability. So that effort translates into progress. So that participation translates into meaning. Not occasionally, consistently. That consistency is what changes everything. Because once the system holds, people begin to rely on it. And once people rely on it, they begin to build on it.

This is where the impact becomes visible. Not in theory, but in behavior. When people trust that the system will hold, they plan further ahead. They take measured risks. They invest with more confidence. Not because conditions are perfect, but because they are predictable. That predictability is what drives real growth. Not short-term expansion, but sustained progress.

Businesses operate differently. They are no longer managing constant instability. They are building within a structure that supports them. That reduces friction. It reduces the need for continuous adjustment. It allows focus to shift from correction to creation.

Networks behave differently. Coordination improves because alignment in one part of the system strengthens the places it connects. That's what allows stability to spread faster than traditional change. Not through mandate, but through connection.

And individuals experience something that has been missing, clarity. Not just about what they earn, but what it means. Not just about what things cost, but how it fits into the system. That clarity reduces hesitation. And when hesitation decreases, participation increases.

The reduction of complexity

Something else happens as this system expands. Complexity begins to decline. Not because the system becomes simpler in structure but because it becomes simpler to operate within, but because fewer corrections are needed.

That's how systems simplify, not by design, but by function. Today, complexity comes from correction. Policies layered on top of policies. Adjustments reacting to adjustments. Systems built to manage instability.

All of that exists because the system does not hold on its own. When alignment is built into the structure, the need for correction decreases. Fewer interventions are required. Fewer reactive measures are needed. Fewer systems are built to manage problems that no longer exist. That reduces administrative burden, regulatory complexity, and operational friction. Not by removing oversight, but by reducing the need for it. That's a different kind of efficiency. And it compounds over time.

What happens at scale

As this system expands, something shifts. Not just in behavior, in expectation. What was once seen as an improvement becomes the standard. People no longer ask: "Does this work?" They assume it does. They begin to expect that effort will translate. That growth will hold. That participation will make sense.

That expectation reshapes the system. Because systems ultimately reflect what people expect from them. And once alignment becomes the expectation, misalignment becomes unacceptable. Not ideologically, practically.

At this stage, the system is no longer being introduced, it is being extended. Across more environments. Across more networks. Across more layers of the economy. Not because it is required, but because it is relied on. That's when direction becomes clear. Not as a plan but as a pattern. A pattern of adoption. A pattern of stability. A pattern of outcomes that hold. And patterns, once established, do not need to be forced, they repeat.

The role of the reader

This is where the book comes back to you. Not with a demand, not with a directive, but with clarity. You now understand what the system is missing. What connects it. How it begins. And how it grows.

That understanding does not require immediate action but it changes how you see the system. And how you evaluate what happens within it. You begin to recognize where alignment exists and where it doesn't. but more importantly, where it could.

That awareness is where participation starts. Not in a single decision, but in a series of them. Where you choose what systems to engage with. What environments to trust. What structures make sense. That's how change actually happens. Not through one moment, through many.

The final shift

At the beginning of this book, the system felt unclear, disconnected, unstable. Difficult to explain. Now, it has shape. Not just as a problem, as a solution. And more importantly, as something that can exist in the real world. That's the shift, from: "Something is wrong" to: "There is a way to fix it" And from there to: "This can be built"

Understanding matters. Recognition matters. But eventually every serious idea reaches a harder threshold. The moment where explanation stops being enough. Where structure must survive questions. Assumptions must survive testing. And confidence must survive scrutiny. That threshold matters. Because trust cannot be requested. It must be earned. Not through optimism. Not through ideology. Through performance. Through measurable outcomes. Through proof. And that is where the conversation becomes more difficult. Because once a system deserves serious consideration, the next question becomes unavoidable: "Can it actually withstand the hardest questions we can ask?"

And there's another question forming underneath that.

Not just about the system, but about you. "Where would this show up in your world?" "What would this change in your decisions?" "What would it take for you to trust it?" Because that's where understanding stops being theoretical. And starts becoming something real.

Because serious ideas eventually earn a different kind of responsibility. Not applause. Examination. The moment something begins sounding possible is the moment skepticism becomes useful. Questions sharpen structure. Criticism exposes weak points. Adversarial thinking improves durability. If this deserves to be real, then it deserves to be pressure-tested honestly

Chapter 9 – The Moment the System Must Be Proven

Up to this point, we've built something that makes sense. You've seen the problem clearly. You've felt the misalignment. You've followed the logic of a system that reconnects what has been drifting apart. And if you're being honest with yourself. It probably feels right.

But feeling right is not enough. Not here. Because this is where most ideas fail. They sound good. They look clean on paper. They even work under perfect conditions. But the real world is not built on perfect conditions. It's built on pressure. And if a system cannot hold under pressure, it doesn't matter how elegant it is. It will break.

Elena had learned something difficult about good ideas. Most sound better before payroll. Before slow quarters. Before rising costs. Before customers suddenly pull back.

As a small business owner, she had seen policies announced by people who never had to make payroll on a Friday while hoping receivables arrived by Monday.

That made her skeptical. Not resistant, just skeptical.

Because survival changes how people evaluate risk.

Elena had learned something else over years of running a business: systems often look strongest before constraints appear. Before labor shortages. Before delayed payments. Before healthcare costs rise faster than expected. Before one bad quarter forces impossible tradeoffs. That experience made her cautious in a very practical way. She did not need elegant theory. She needed confidence that the system would still make sense on difficult days.

Because businesses rarely fail under ideal conditions. They fail when pressure compounds faster than predictability.

When she first encountered the idea of alignment, her reaction was simple: "Okay, but what breaks when reality hits?" That question matters because systems are not proven when conditions are ideal. They are proven when pressure arrives and the system still holds.

This is where everything changes. Up to now, we've been answering a question: *"Does this make sense?"* From this point forward, the question becomes: *"Does this actually hold?"* Those are not the same question. Because a system can make sense and still fail the moment it's tested. And the system we're talking about doesn't get tested lightly. It gets tested constantly. Every day. Every decision. Every shift in the economy.

We're not looking for theory. We're not looking for isolated examples. We're not looking for a system that works when everything is calm. We are looking for something much harder. A system that holds when things are not stable. When pressure shows up. When the environment changes faster than expected. When behavior shifts in ways no model predicted. Because that's not the exception. That's the system we actually live in.

Most systems are designed for stability. But they don't operate in stable environments. That's the disconnect. We build models that assume predictable growth, controlled inflation, rational behavior, and balanced inputs. Then we apply them to a system that is constantly shifting, emotionally driven, uneven in participation, and unpredictable in outcome.

And when those systems fail, we don't question the structure. We adjust the inputs. We tweak policy. We shift incentives. We intervene. But we don't ask the harder question: *"Was this system ever designed to hold under pressure?"* You've already seen the answer. Not in theory. In real life. When pressure hits the system today, it doesn't absorb it. It fragments. Different parts of the system react in different ways. Costs move faster than income. Wages lag behind productivity. Growth expands without stabilizing anything. And suddenly, what used to feel connected starts pulling apart. Not because anything stopped working. Because nothing is holding it together.

Every time the system is tested, we see the same thing: Something improves. Something else destabilizes. We raise wages and costs follow. We slow inflation and growth weakens. We stimulate growth and stability doesn't reach people. Each move helps. But no move holds. And over time, that creates something deeper than inefficiency. It creates fatigue.

You don't just see it in numbers. You feel it in decisions. You hesitate more. You calculate more. You second-guess more. Not because you've changed. Because the system has. When outcomes are inconsistent, behavior becomes defensive. People don't stop participating. They just participate differently. More cautiously. More selectively. More protectively. And when that happens across millions of people the system itself begins to slow. Not because it ran out of energy. Because it lost confidence.

Because everything we've built so far, every idea, every connection, every explanation, depends on one thing: That it doesn't just work when things are calm, that it works when things are not. Because if it only works under ideal conditions, it's not a solution. It's a scenario. And scenarios don't change systems. structures do.

We don't ask: *"Does this improve outcomes?"* We ask: *"Does this prevent disconnection?"* That's the standard. Because disconnection is the root problem. Not wages, not prices, not growth. Those are symptoms. The real failure is that they don't move together. So, the test becomes simple: When pressure enters the system do those relationships hold? Or do they break apart?

Every system we've used so far is built to react. Something changes → we respond. But reaction happens after the break. After the disconnect. After the instability is already felt. That's why it always feels like we're catching up. Because we are.

No serious system survives untouched by failure. Not economic systems. Not businesses. Not institutions.

The question is never: "Will problems emerge?" The question is: "Can the system recognize problems early enough to adapt before instability compounds?"

Because resilient systems are not systems that avoid pressure. They are systems built to absorb pressure, learn from mistakes, and improve without breaking.

Any serious implementation would require adjustment. Unexpected behavior would surface. Some incentives would work differently than intended. Early assumptions would need revision. That is not evidence of failure. That is how durable systems mature.

Structure works differently. It doesn't wait for things to break. It keeps them connected as they move. So, when pressure shows up the system doesn't need to recover. It holds. Not improvement, not optimization, not temporary balance, we are looking for something that holds under pressure. That maintains connection and scales with change. Something that reflects real participation. Anything less than that and we're right back where we started. Because this is where they are exposed. This is where assumptions break. Where models fail. And where trade-offs reappear.

And what once felt complete starts to unravel. That's not failure. That's reality. We need to answer the question that actually matters, not whether this system sounds right. Not whether it feels intuitive. But whether it can survive the same conditions that have broken every system before it. Because if it can't, nothing we've built so far matters. And if it can, then everything changes. Not gradually. Not theoretically. Structurally. Because for the first time we would have something the system has never had, a way to move without coming apart.

We're not going to assume it works. We're not going to protect the idea. We're going to test it. Directly. Under the same conditions that have broken everything else. Recession. Inflation. Rapid growth. System shock. Not to prove that it performs. But to see if it holds. Because that is the only proof that matters. Not in theory, not in isolation, but where systems fail. Under pressure. That's where we go next.

And serious testing does not mean assuming success. Some assumptions may fail. Some incentives may behave differently than expected. Certain environments may expose weaknesses theory alone cannot anticipate. That should be expected. Systems become durable not because pressure never exposes flaws, but because flaws can be identified early enough to strengthen the structure before instability compounds. The objective is not perfection under pressure. It is continuity under pressure.

Why these failures are structural (not policy)

At this point, a reasonable question starts to form. If every system we've built breaks under pressure Why? Is it bad policy? Poor timing? Imperfect execution? Or something deeper?

Because if the problem is policy, then the solution is adjustment. But if the problem is structural, no amount of adjustment will ever be enough.

We keep making the assumption that the system works. We've been taught to believe that. Not perfectly, not consistently, but fundamentally. So, when something goes wrong, the instinct is clear: Fix the policy. Adjust the rate. Increase the wage. Stimulate demand. Tighten supply. And in isolation, those actions make sense. They target visible problems. They produce measurable changes. But they all rest on the same assumption, that the system itself is sound.

What if that assumption is wrong? Because if the structure itself allows disconnection, then every policy is operating inside a flawed framework. Which means even when policy works it works temporarily. Even when outcomes improve, they don't hold. Even when we correct one problem another emerges. Not because policy failed. Because it was never addressing the root.

Let's look at what policy actually does

Policy is designed to influence behavior. It can encourage participation, restrict excess, redirect resources, and stabilize short-term conditions. But policy does not define relationships. It does not determine how output connects to participation or how participation connects to income or how income connects to cost.

It assumes those relationships already exist. And that's the flaw. You can think of it like this policy is how you adjust the system. Structure is what the system is built on. If the structure is sound, adjustments refine it. If the structure is weak, adjustments compensate for it. And compensation never ends. It just shifts. From one problem to the next.

When relationships are missing, policy becomes reactive because without a structure holding the system together, every policy must respond to symptoms. You see it clearly. Inflation rises so policy tightens. Growth slows so policy stimulates. Wages lag so policy intervenes.

Each response targets a specific issue. But none of them reconnect the system. So, the cycle continues. This creates a loop where a problem appears → policy responds, the response creates pressure somewhere else, a new problem appears → policy responds again. Each step feels necessary. Each step is logical. But the system never stabilizes. Because the loop never addresses the connection between the parts. It only manages the distance between them.

Why can't policy solve a structural problem? Because policy operates on the surface. Structure operates underneath. Policy can move things. Structure determines how they stay connected. And if the structure allows disconnection, then policy is constantly compensating for something it cannot fix. This is why trade-offs keep appearing. You've heard them before:

- Stability vs growth
- Wages vs inflation
- Efficiency vs fairness

As if choosing one requires sacrificing another. But what if those trade-offs aren't real? What if they are not constraints but symptoms? Because in a connected system growth does not destabilize. Wages do not chase cost. Efficiency does not come at the expense of stability. Those trade-offs only appear when the system is disconnected. So, we didn't inherit them. We created them. By building a system that cannot hold its own relationships. So, we keep managing the trade-offs instead of eliminating them. We say: "We can't have both" or "That's just how the system works" or "Every gain comes with a cost"

And over time, that becomes accepted. Not because it's true. Because we've never seen a system where it isn't. But look closely at the pattern. Every time we push for higher wages, cost pressure follows. When we drive lower inflation, growth pressure follows. When we see increased growth, stability pressure follows. Each outcome creates a counterforce. Not randomly but predictably. Because the system is not holding those elements together. That's not a policy failure, that's a structural reality. Policy didn't create the disconnection. It's reacting to it. And no amount of refinement changes that. It looks like progress. It feels like improvement. But over time, it fades. Because nothing is maintaining the relationship underneath.

So, let's be clear about what this means. This is not an argument against policy. Policy still matters. It always will. But policy cannot do the job of structure. And right now, we are asking it to. That's why nothing fully resolves, because we are solving at the wrong level. Trying to manage outcomes instead of defining relationships. Trying to correct behavior instead of connecting the system.

To be precise, tradeoffs do not disappear entirely. Every serious system still faces competing priorities, resource constraints, and difficult choices. The argument here is narrower and more important: many of the tradeoffs we have normalized may be less fundamental than they appear. Some are symptoms of relationships that fail to remain connected under pressure. When systems drift apart, progress in one area often creates instability somewhere else. Alignment reduces those unnecessary tensions. It does not eliminate difficult decisions entirely.

Policy remains essential. Legal frameworks still matter. Institutions still matter. Oversight still matters. Large systems require administration, rules, accountability, and public legitimacy. The distinction is not whether policy matters. It is what policy is being asked to do. Policy works best when it supports relationships already capable of holding rather than continuously compensating for relationships that remain disconnected.

Serious systems must also survive institutional scrutiny. Questions of constitutional authority, due process, implementation boundaries, and public accountability matter because systems this large cannot rely on good intentions alone. They must be structured clearly enough to survive challenge, revision, and interpretation over time. That reality strengthens serious design rather than weakening it.

Once you see that, something shifts. You stop asking: “What’s the right policy?” And you start asking: “What’s the right structure?” Because the structure determines whether anything holds. And that leads to the real question which now becomes unavoidable. If policy cannot create connection and adjustment cannot restore it what happens when the structure itself changes? Not improved, but rebuilt. Because if the system has always been reacting, we are about to test something different. A system that doesn't react to pressure. A system that holds under it.

What happens when you introduce structure? Not adjustments, not improvements, but structure. Because if the problem is connection, then the solution must be something that holds it.

The first true stress test

If a system only works when things are stable it doesn't work. That's not a criticism. It's a standard. Because stability is not the environment we live in. Pressure is. So, now we test it where systems actually fail. Not in controlled conditions. Not in ideal scenarios. But in the environments that have broken every system before it:

- Inflation
- Recession
- Rapid growth

Not to see if the system performs. But to see if it holds. Because performance can be managed. Holding cannot be faked.

We're not asking "Does output increase?" or "Do wages improve?" or "Do prices stabilize?" Those are outcomes. We're asking something more fundamental: When pressure enters the system do the relationships stay connected? Because that is what has always broken.

Stress test one, inflation

Let's start where most people feel it first. Prices begin to rise. In the current system, this creates immediate separation. Costs move quickly. Income lags behind. Value becomes uncertain.

So, behavior changes. Households pull back. Businesses adjust defensively. Policy reacts after the fact. The system doesn't absorb the pressure. It fragments.

Now run that same condition through structure. Prices still rise. Pressure still exists. Nothing about reality disappears. But something critical changes: The relationship between output, participation and, cost remains connected. Because cost is no longer drifting independently. It is tied to the same reference structure as participation and output.

Inflation would still create pressure. Scarcity would still exist. Supply disruptions, energy shocks, and external constraints would still influence cost. The claim is not that inflation disappears. The claim is that inflation becomes less destabilizing because the underlying relationships remain connected rather than separating under stress.

Stress test two, recession

Now take the opposite condition. Demand slows. Opportunity contracts. Participation becomes uneven. In the current system, effort disconnects from opportunity. Businesses pull back. Hiring slows. Risk disappears.

Again, not because people stopped trying, but because the system no longer connects participation to outcome.

Run that through structure

Demand still slows. That part is real. But participation does not disconnect from output. Because the system defines that relationship continuously. So instead of contraction leading to disconnection which leads to hesitation, you get contraction leading to adjustment which maintains alignment. The system responds, but it does not break.

No serious system survives untouched by failure.

Not businesses. Not institutions. Not economies.

The question is never whether problems emerge.

The question is whether the system can recognize problems early enough to adapt before instability compounds.

Because resilient systems are not systems that avoid pressure.

They are systems designed to absorb pressure, learn, and improve without breaking.

Stress test three, rapid growth

Now take the condition that should be easiest. Growth accelerates. Output increases. Innovation expands. In the current system, this creates a different kind of break. Growth does not translate evenly. Stability separates from expansion. Some move forward quickly. Others feel no change. So even in growth you hear uncertainty.

Run that through structure

Growth still accelerates. But now participation scales with output. Cost remains tied to the same system. Value maintains meaning.

So instead of "growth creates separation which creates uneven stability, you get "growth creates expansion which maintains connection. The system doesn't just grow. It holds while growing.

What does this system eliminate? Not volatility. Not change. Not pressure. Those are part of any real system. What it eliminates is: Disconnection. Because once disconnection is removed the system no longer works against itself. And that changes behavior immediately. Because behavior is not driven by numbers. It's driven by trust. When people can see how effort connects, how change is absorbed, or how outcomes remain consistent.

They stop reacting. And they start participating. This is the first time the system can hold under pressure. Not because it resists change but because it stays connected through it. That's the difference.

So, what have we proven? Not that the system performs better, but that it does something no other system has done: It holds its internal relationships under the exact conditions that have always broken them. And that changes the entire standard. We are no longer comparing: growth rates, policy effectiveness, or short-term outcomes.

Proof would not arrive as a headline. It would arrive gradually. Quietly. In measurable ways. "Would households begin planning further ahead?" "Would emergency expenses create fewer crises?" "Would businesses hire with more confidence?" "Would turnover slow?" "Would investment become easier to justify?" "Would periods of economic pressure create less instability than before?" Those are the signals that matter. Because serious systems are judged by behavior. Not theory. Not promises. Outcomes.

We are comparing: Which system holds and which system comes apart. Now that we've seen this system hold under pressure the question shifts again. Not: "Does it work?" But: "What does this change in how people actually behave?" Because if the system holds behavior changes. And when behavior changes everything else follows. This changes real life behavior. Not theory, not structure, but decisions. Because that's where systems become real.

That change would not occur evenly. Some people would remain cautious longer. Some organizations would adapt faster than others. Trust would expand unevenly. Certain environments would respond immediately while others would resist until outcomes became impossible to ignore. That unevenness is normal. Systems rarely shift all at once.

Serious systems are not proven through flawless execution. They are proven through disciplined learning. A pilot that reveals weaknesses is not failure. A contained test that identifies unintended consequences is not failure. That is responsible design.

What matters is whether the structure becomes stronger after pressure, not weaker. Because systems that cannot tolerate learning rarely survive long enough to matter.

What this changes in real life behavior

If this only works at the system level, it's not enough. Because people don't live inside systems. They live inside decisions. Small ones, constant ones, every day. And those decisions are shaped by one thing above all, whether the system makes sense. Right now, most decisions are defensive. Not because people are cautious by nature, but because the system has trained them to be. You've felt it. Before you make a decision, there's a pause: "Will this hold?" "Is this the right time?" "What happens if something shifts?"

That pause isn't hesitation. It's adaptation. The system teaches behavior. When outcomes are inconsistent people don't stop participating, they adjust how they participate.

They take fewer risks. They delay commitments. They protect more than they pursue. Not because they lack ambition. Because the system no longer feels reliable. And that changes everything because participation is not just activity. It's confidence. It's willingness. It's forward motion. And when that changes the entire system behaves differently.

Maya and Elena approached the question differently.

Maya wanted to know: "Can this survive execution?"

Elena wanted to know: "Can this survive reality?"

Neither question came from ideology.

They came from responsibility.

Because systems sound very different when people depend on them.

Different questions. Same standard. Neither cared whether the idea sounded elegant. They cared whether it held. "Could workers plan further ahead?" "Could businesses absorb shocks more predictably?" "Could pressure stop compounding into fragility?" That is the threshold serious systems eventually face. Not admiration. Performance.

Now shift the structure. Nothing about the individual changes. Same skills. Same effort. Same ambition. But the system underneath them is different. It holds. It connects. It makes sense. The first change is invisible. It doesn't show up in numbers immediately. It shows up in how decisions feel. That pause? It starts to disappear. Not all at once. But consistently. Because the question: "Will this hold?" no longer dominates every decision.

Start with the individual, right now, most people are managing uncertainty. Even when things look stable, they're constantly translating: "What does this income actually mean?" "Will this cost stay where it is?" "Is this progress real?"

That translation layer never goes away. Because nothing is holding those relationships in place. With structure, that translation disappears because the system already defines the relationships. So instead of asking: "Is this enough?" You understand what this represents. That's a subtle shift. But it changes everything.

Decisions become clearer. Not easier, just clearer. You can accept a raise without recalculating its real value. You can plan expenses without assuming they will drift. You can make commitments without building in uncertainty. All because the system itself is consistent.

Now, look at behavior over time. When decisions become clearer, they become faster. More confident less defensive and that changes participation. People stop playing defense. Right now, many decisions are about protection. Avoiding loss. Managing risk. Preserving stability.

With structure, decisions shift toward building, expanding, and moving forward. Not because risk disappears. Because it becomes understandable.

Now look at the skilled worker, someone who invests in their ability. Who improves over time. Who expects that improvement to translate into a better life. Right now, that expectation is uncertain. Because costs may outpace income. Value may not translate. Growth may not reach them. So even progress feels conditional.

With structure, that expectation holds because participation is tied to output. So, when skill increases, contribution increases. The system reflects that. Not eventually, not unevenly, structurally. That changes motivation. Not artificially, naturally. Because when effort consistently connects to outcome people don't need incentives to participate, they want to.

Now look at the entry-level worker

This is where the system often feels most disconnected. Early participation feels uncertain. Growth feels distant. Stability feels out of reach. So, the question becomes: "Does this path actually lead anywhere?"

With structure, the path becomes visible, even at the beginning. Because the system defines: what participation represents. How it connects to output. How it scales over time. So instead of hoping, people understand.

Now shift to the business

Right now, businesses operate inside instability. They deal with unpredictable cost structures. Fluctuating labor alignment. Demand that shifts without warning.

So, behavior becomes defensive. They start pricing cautiously. They start hiring more carefully. They start investing more selectively. Not because they lack opportunity but because they lack clarity. With structure, relationships become coherent. Labor, output, and cost are aligned.

So, businesses are not guessing. They understand what labor represents. How pricing connects. How growth translates.

That doesn't remove competition. It removes confusion. And that changes how businesses operate. They move from reaction, adjustment, and protection to planning, investment, and expansion. Because the system supports forward movement.

Now look at the household.

This is where everything converges. Because households don't think in systems, they think in life. "Can we afford this?" "Can we plan ahead?" "Will this hold?"

Right now, those answers are uncertain. Even when income rises. With structure, those answers stabilize because income reflects participation. Participation reflects output. Cost remains aligned.

So, planning becomes possible again. Not perfectly, but reliably. And that changes behavior immediately. Households commit more confidently, plan further ahead, and participate more fully.

Because they are no longer guessing. This is the shift that matters most. Not numbers, behavior. Because behavior drives spending, investment, innovation, and growth.

And behavior is driven by whether the system makes sense. Right now, it doesn't fully make sense. That's why participation is uneven. That's why decisions feel heavy. That's why progress feels inconsistent.

With structure, it does, and when it does, people don't need to be pushed. They move. Because forward motion feels safe again. This is the feedback loop reversed. Right now: instability leads to hesitation. Hesitation leads to reduced participation. Reduced participation leads to weaker system.

With structure: Stability leads to confidence. Confidence leads to participation. Participation leads to stronger system. This is not behavioral engineering. Nothing is forced, nothing is artificial. The system simply reflects reality. And when it does, behavior aligns naturally.

So, what have we actually changed? Not effort, not ambition, not capability, we've changed the environment those things exist in. And that changes everything. Because when the environment holds, people don't hold back.

Now we've seen that the system holds under pressure and that behavior changes when it does. So, the question becomes even sharper: Is there anything else that can do this? Because if there isn't, then the choice is no longer between options, it's between continuing with a system that fragments or moving to one that holds. This changes something that nothing else has. Not better, not improved, fundamentally different.

What this solves that nothing else can

By now, you've seen three things clearly. The system we have does not hold under pressure. The failure is structural, not policy-driven. And when structure is introduced, both stability and behavior change.

So, the question becomes unavoidable: Is there anything else that can do this? Not partially, not temporarily, but completely. Because that's the standard now. We are no longer asking: "What improves outcomes?" "What reduces pressure?" or "What manages instability?"

We are asking something more precise: What keeps the system connected as it moves? Because that is the only thing that holds. Let's be honest about what we've tried.

We haven't lacked ideas. We've built entire systems around wage policy, monetary control, fiscal stimulus, and regulatory frameworks.

Each one designed to improve part of the system. And each one has done something useful while none of them have done what we actually need. They improve pieces, not the system. Wage policy can raise income. Monetary policy can influence cost. Fiscal policy can stimulate activity. Regulation can shape behavior.

But none of them define how those things relate to each other. So, even when they work, they work in isolation. And isolation is the problem. Because the system is not made of independent parts, it is made of relationships. Between output and participation. Between participation and income. Between income and cost. If those relationships are not defined, everything else becomes unstable.

So, every solution becomes partial and partial solutions create predictable outcomes. Improvement in one area creates pressure in another. Adjustment to compensate start to repeat the same outcomes.

This is not failure, it's limitation. Existing systems cannot close this gap because they were not designed to. They were designed to measure, influence, and respond. Not to connect. And that is more important than anything else. You cannot combine disconnected tools into a connected system.

This is where intuition often misleads. It feels like: "If we just use the right mix of policies, we can balance the system." But balance is not connection. Balance is temporary. Connection is structural. That's why the system always drifts back. Even after improvement, even after correction, even after progress. Because nothing is holding the relationships in place. Let's look at the alternatives clearly, not to dismiss them, but to understand what they actually do.

Alternative One – better policy

The idea: Refine what we already have. Be more precise, more targeted, and more responsive. And this has value. Better policy does improve outcomes, but it cannot solve disconnection. Because it operates after movement occurs, not within it.

Alternative Two – more control

The idea: If the system is unstable, control it more tightly. Set boundaries. Limit movement. Constrain outcomes. But control does not create alignment, it restricts behavior. And over time, that creates new distortions. Because the underlying relationships are still not defined.

Alternative Three – market correction alone

The idea: Let the system self-correct. Allow forces of supply and demand to rebalance everything. And in some areas, they do. But markets reflect relationships, they don't define them. So, if the underlying structure is disconnected, market corrections will always be uneven.

All three approaches share the same limitation. They operate on outcomes, not structure. They influence behavior, not relationships. They respond to movement, they don't hold it. So, they cannot do what this system does because this system is not a policy or a control mechanism or a reactive tool. It is a defined relationships between what the system produces and how people participate, and what things cost.

That relationship exists continuously. Not after the fact, not in response, always. This is the difference that matters. Everything else tries to improve alignment, approximate balance, and reduce instability.

This defines alignment from the start. And that removes the trade-offs we've accepted. Because trade-offs only exist when parts are disconnected. When you improve one area and it creates pressure in another. But when the system is connected, growth does not destabilize. Wages do not chase cost. Efficiency does not reduce stability. They move together. This is not an optimization, it's not making the current system better. It's changing what the system is doing. From managing disconnected parts to maintaining connected relationships. That's why there is no direct comparison, because you can't compare policy vs structure or control vs alignment or reaction vs connection, because they are solving different problems.

So, the question changes again. Not: "Is this better than what we have?" But: "Is there anything else that can maintain connection under pressure?" And the answer becomes clear. We've seen what breaks, why it breaks, what holds, how it changes behavior. And no existing system defines the relationship. maintains it continuously, scales with change, and holds under pressure.

All at the same time. So, this is the first time this has been solved. This is the first time the problem is being addressed at the structural level rather than the reactive level. And that has a consequence. Because once a problem is solved at the structural level, it doesn't compete with alternatives, it replaces them. Not by force, by function.

That statement deserves humility. Many systems have solved pieces of this problem. Others improved stability for specific periods or environments. The claim being made here is narrower: no widely adopted framework has consistently defined and maintained the relationship between output, participation, and cost as a continuously connected structure. That distinction matters because solving part of instability is different from addressing the condition producing it.

This book is not asking the reader to accept technical claims on trust. Its purpose is to make the structure visible—to explain why the system behaves the way it does and why an alternative architecture may be worth examining. But understanding a structure and proving a structure are not the same thing.

That is why the work exists in layers. The manuscript explains the principles. The technical appendices test those principles against mathematics, implementation requirements, administrative realities, and operational constraints. The legislative framework examines what legal authority, constitutional safeguards, and institutional mechanisms would be required to put those ideas into practice.

Each serves a different purpose. The goal is not belief without scrutiny. The goal is a framework that can be understood, tested, challenged, refined, and ultimately evaluated on its merits rather than its promises.

This is the moment alternatives fall away. Not because they are wrong, but because they are incomplete. They still have a role, but not this role.

So, what are we left with? Not a range of competing systems. Not a set of options to choose from. But a single distinction – a system that reacts, adjusts, and fragments under pressure. Or a system that connects, holds, and maintains alignment. That's no longer a preference, it's a difference in capability.

And that leads to the final question, "if this is the only system that holds under pressure, maintains connection, changes behavior, and eliminates structural trade-offs, then what happens if we don't build it?" Not collapse, not failure, something more subtle. And more permanent.

What happens if we don't build it

At this point, it would be easy to assume the stakes are dramatic: that if we don't build this, something breaks. But that's not what happens. Not immediately, not visibly. The system doesn't collapse. It continues. It grows. It adjusts. It responds.

On the surface, it keeps functioning, just as it has. That's what makes this difficult to see. Because nothing forces a decision. But something subtle keeps expanding. Not failure, distance. The distance between effort and outcome, growth and stability, and income and meaning.

That distance doesn't show up all at once, it widens gradually, quietly. You've already seen this happen. Not as a single moment, but as a pattern. Where progress feels smaller than it should. Where stability feels harder to maintain. Where decisions feel heavier than they used to. Not because things stopped working, but because they stopped connecting. And over time, that becomes normal.

That's the real shift. Not collapse, normalization. Where constant adjustment feels expected. Uncertainty feels built in. Stability feels temporary.

And people adapt. Adaptation isn't always progress. We tend to assume that when people adapt, the system is working. But adaptation can also mean people are compensating for something the system no longer provides.

So, behavior changes quietly. Not in obvious ways, in consistent ones. People take fewer risks. They delay longer commitments. They prioritize short-term certainty. Not because they lack confidence in themselves, but because they lack confidence in the system. And that has a compounding effect because participation is not just activity, it's willingness. And when willingness declines, the system begins to change from the inside.

Growth starts to feel different. Not because it stops, but because it doesn't translate. You can have strong output, expanding markets, and increasing productivity, and still feel disconnected, because growth alone does not create stability.

So, we start managing around the gap instead of closing it. We add more adjustments. We increase intervention. We build more layers. All trying to stabilize outcomes without fixing the connection underneath them. That creates complexity, not clarity. More rules. More responses. More systems within systems.

And over time that complexity becomes its own barrier. Because complexity doesn't build trust, it replaces it. When a system becomes harder to understand, people rely less on it and more on their own protection. So, the system becomes less participatory. Not because access disappears, but because confidence does. And participation without confidence is limited.

This is how systems slow without failing. Nothing breaks, but everything becomes heavier. Decisions take longer. Movement becomes cautious. Opportunity feels less certain. Not because the system stopped moving, but because it stopped carrying people forward with it. And that becomes the new baseline. Not temporary, expected. Where stability is something you manage. Progress is something you question. Participation is something you limit

Not consciously, naturally. This is the cost of not building structure. Not collapse, drift. And drift has a unique characteristic; it doesn't force urgency, it reduces clarity. Which makes change less likely. Drift often feels manageable precisely because its cost arrives gradually. One delayed decision. One postponed investment. One family choosing caution over opportunity. One business avoiding expansion because uncertainty feels too expensive. No single moment looks dramatic. But accumulated hesitation changes systems over time just as powerfully as sudden disruption.

Because when something is clearly broken, people act. But when something slowly disconnects, people adapt. And adaptation can mask the problem because life continues, work continues, and growth continues. But underneath, the system is becoming less effective at connecting those things together. So, the question isn't "will it break?" It's: "What does it become if nothing changes?" It becomes a system that requires constant effort to navigate. Not to succeed, to stay stable. Where every gain must be defended. Every decision must be calculated. Every step forward carries uncertainty.

Not because of external shocks, but because the system itself does not hold alignment. And over time, that shapes expectations. People stop expecting stability, consistency, or clear progress, and start expecting adjustment, volatility, and uncertainty.

Once that happens, something important changes. Not in the system, but in how people relate to it. They stop trusting it to carry them forward and start managing their position within it. That is a fundamental shift, from participation to navigation.

So, now the choice becomes clear. Not between good and bad, but between a system that continues to drift or one that holds its structure. Because both will continue. Both will function and both will move, but only one will maintain connection. And that brings us to the final step. We've seen what breaks and why it breaks. We've seen what holds and what it changes. We've also seen what happens if we don't act.

So now the question is no longer analytical. It's simple. "What do we choose?" Not as a theory, not as a concept, but as a direction. The point where the decision becomes obvious. Because at some point understanding becomes choice. And that's where we are now.

The point where the decision becomes obvious

By now, nothing here should feel abstract. You've seen how the system behaves, why it breaks, what holds, what changes when structure is introduced, and what happens if we choose not to build it.

At the beginning of this book, the problem felt familiar but unclear. Something was off. Things weren't translating. Movement was happening, but it wasn't holding

Now the shape of that problem is clear. And more importantly, so is the shape of the solution. This is the point where ambiguity starts to disappear. Not because every question has been answered, but because the most important one has.

This system is not failing because people are not working hard enough. It is not failing because growth stopped. It is not failing because we ran out of intelligence, effort, productivity, or tools. It is failing because the parts are not connected. And once that becomes clear, a lot of other arguments begin to fall away. Because disconnected systems always produce the same kind of experience. Effort that doesn't fully translate. Progress that doesn't fully hold. Growth that doesn't fully reach. Stability that doesn't fully last.

Different decade, different policy, different pressure, same pattern. That is not bad luck, that is structure. And structure changes the nature of the question. For most of this conversation, publicly, politically, economically, we've been asking the wrong thing. We've asked: "How do we raise wages?" "How do we lower costs?" "How do we improve growth?" "How do we reduce instability?"

Those are not useless questions but they are downstream questions. They assume the structure is basically sound and the outcomes just need better management. What this chapter has shown is something harder and more important. The structure itself is incomplete. So, the real question is not: "How do we manage the system better?" It is: "How do we connect the system so it can finally hold?" That is a different question. And it produces a different answer.

This is where the decision stops being theoretical. Because once you can see the problem structurally, you can no longer solve it cosmetically. Once you know the issue is disconnection, adjustment starts to look different. Not wrong, just insufficient. That is a hard shift for people to make, because adjustment feels safer. It feels familiar. It feels responsible. You don't have to rethink the whole system, you just improve what is already there. But that only works when the system underneath is sound. And if it isn't, improvement becomes maintenance. Correction becomes routine. Instability becomes managed instead of removed.

That is where we have been living. And once you see that clearly, the decision starts to simplify. Because the choice is no longer between two good options. That is the illusion, that we are comparing two equally viable paths. We are not. We are comparing a system that reacts after separation and a system that maintains connection before separation occurs. A system that constantly adjusts and a system that structurally holds. A system that teaches people to defend themselves from instability and a system that allows them to participate with confidence.

That is not a small distinction, that is the whole distinction. And once the distinction is clear, the direction changes. At first, people ask whether a new system is necessary. That is a natural question. But eventually, if the argument has held, if the proof is there, if the structure truly does what nothing else can do, the question changes. It becomes:

Why are we still protecting a system that keeps coming apart when we can now see what would hold it together? That is the moment the decision becomes obvious. Not because everyone agrees, not because debate disappears, not because complexity goes away, but because the central issue is no longer hidden. And once something central is visible, it reorganizes everything around it. This is how large shifts actually begin. Not with consensus, with recognition.

People do not all change their minds at once. That is not how systems move. What happens instead is quieter and stronger. Enough people begin to see the same thing. Enough leaders begin to recognize the same limit. Enough workers, businesses, thinkers, builders, policymakers, and participants begin to feel that the old explanations no longer account for what they're living through. That is when the center of gravity moves. Not through force, through clarity. And clarity has a different kind of power. It does not need to shout, it just needs to remain true under pressure. That is what this system has now done.

None of this removes uncertainty completely. Serious systems still require refinement, oversight, disagreement, and adaptation over time. But once a structural problem becomes visible, continuing to ignore it becomes its own decision. The question shifts from whether adjustment feels safer to whether repeated instability is actually safer than responsible change.

At the beginning of the book, the reader may have been skeptical. That is appropriate, they should be. Any argument this large should earn belief. But skepticism changes when each objection is met not with rhetoric but with structure. If the problem is real, show it. If the pattern repeats, explain why. If the solution is different, define how. If it holds under pressure, prove it. If it changes behavior, make that visible. If nothing else can do it, say so clearly. If the cost of not building it is real, state it calmly.

Chapter 10 – What Alignment Feels Like

By this point, we have spent a great deal of time discussing systems. Wages. Productivity. Purchasing power. Misaligned incentives. Structural drift. Taxes. Participation. Economic behavior. All of those things matter. But economics often struggles with an important question: *What does any of this actually feel like in real life?*

We have spent much of this book diagnosing the problem. Why wages feel disconnected from productivity. Why stability feels increasingly fragile. Why effort no longer seems to create the same sense of progress it once did.

Before asking how alignment changes institutions, markets, and incentives, it is worth pausing to ask a simpler question: *What would alignment actually feel like in ordinary life?*

Policy conversations tend to become abstract. Charts. Percentages. Growth rates. Deficits. Tax structures. Economic indicators. Yet ordinary people do not experience the economy through spreadsheets. They experience it in moments. At the grocery store. When a raise arrives and somehow still feels too small. When a car repair suddenly changes the entire month. When saving money feels impossible. When planning for the future begins to feel unrealistic. Or when hard work slowly starts to feel disconnected from progress.

This chapter is not about economic theory. It is about lived experience. What changes when people no longer feel like they are constantly losing ground? What changes when effort begins to feel connected to stability again? What changes when planning begins to feel rational? When opportunity feels survivable? When communities feel less fragile? The purpose of this chapter is not to promise perfection.

No economic system eliminates struggle. No system guarantees equal outcomes. No framework removes hardship, uncertainty, competition, or risk. Life will still happen. People will still struggle. Businesses will still fail. Hard decisions will still exist. But healthy systems should do something important, they should make effort matter. They should make stability feel possible. And they should allow ordinary people to believe that if they contribute, work hard, and participate, life can slowly become more secure rather than more fragile.

The Feeling of Stability

Most people are not asking for luxury. They are not asking for yachts, private jets, or homes with ocean views. They are not asking to stop working, stop trying, or stop striving for more.

Most people are asking for something much simpler. They want to know that if they work hard, show up, and do what they are supposed to do, life will eventually feel stable. Not perfect. Stable.

Stability should not be confused with comfort or ease. Many people would still struggle financially at times. Different households would still experience different outcomes. Emergencies would still happen. Jobs would still change. Some seasons of life would remain difficult. Stability simply means the distance between effort and recovery becomes shorter. It means setbacks feel survivable more often than catastrophic. The goal is not to eliminate hardship. It is to make hardship less likely to permanently disconnect people from progress.

Today, stability feels increasingly out of reach. For millions of people, life has become a constant exercise in financial calculation. A trip to the grocery store becomes math. A prescription refill becomes math. A car repair becomes math. A child's school expense becomes math. Families do not plan around opportunity nearly as much as they plan around avoiding disaster.

The problem is not simply that things cost more. The deeper problem is uncertainty.

A person can survive hardship when hardship feels temporary. What breaks people down is the feeling that even when they are doing everything right, the ground keeps moving beneath them. A raise disappears into rent increases. Overtime disappears into insurance premiums. A second job creates exhaustion but still does not create breathing room. The future becomes something to survive until rather than something to build toward.

That feeling changes inside an aligned system. Not because everyone suddenly becomes wealthy. Not because struggle disappears. And not because bad luck stops happening. Life still happens. Cars still break down. Medical emergencies still occur. Businesses still fail. Recessions still happen. Families still face difficult seasons.

Alignment is not a promise that life becomes easy. It is a framework designed to make effort matter again.

Remember Marcus?

If you remember, Marcus works in a distribution warehouse. He works hard, picks up overtime when it is available, and tries to save where he can. He is careful with money, but for years life has felt like the same story playing on repeat. Rent climbs faster than his paycheck. Groceries take a bigger bite out of the budget. Health insurance gets more expensive. His savings account slowly grows for a few months, only to disappear the moment something unexpected happens.

Marcus is not irresponsible. He is not lazy. He is doing exactly what society has long told people to do: work hard, show up, stay disciplined, and build a life. Yet despite doing all of those things, progress still feels fragile.

Now imagine Marcus inside an aligned economy. His paycheck still matters. His work still matters. He still earns raises based on skill, performance, and contribution. His employer still competes, still grows, and still rewards good people. But something important feels different.

That difference would not appear overnight. Marcus would still have stressful months. Unexpected expenses would still interrupt plans. Some years would feel stronger than others. But slowly, the pattern underneath life begins changing. Progress stops feeling temporary. Recovery takes less time. A setback no longer erases every gain quite so easily. The shift is subtle at first. Then cumulative. And over time, what once felt fragile begins feeling manageable.

When the economy grows, the benefits of that growth no longer feel disconnected from ordinary life. His purchasing power stops quietly moving backward every year. The cost of building a stable life stops accelerating faster than the life he is trying to build.

Marcus is not suddenly wealthy. That is not the point. But for the first time in years, he no longer feels like he is falling behind while doing everything right.

That difference matters more than many policy conversations acknowledge.

Because for most people, the dream was never excess. The dream was stability. Enough breathing room to handle an emergency. Enough confidence to plan six months ahead. Enough predictability to think about buying a home, starting a business, helping a child through school, or simply taking a vacation without feeling guilty about it for six months afterward.

That emotional shift changes behavior. People make better decisions when they are not operating from constant financial stress. They take more calculated risks. They invest in themselves. They pursue training. They leave jobs that are abusive instead of staying trapped because one missed paycheck could collapse everything.

Families begin thinking about the future again. Communities become more stable because desperation stops driving every decision. This matters because instability changes people. When individuals feel trapped for long enough, trust erodes.

Trust in employers. Trust in institutions. Trust in government. Trust that effort still matters. Trust that tomorrow can be better than today. Eventually, people stop planning. They stop believing. And when enough people stop believing, economies weaken in ways statistics often fail to capture.

An aligned economy does not promise equal outcomes. It does not guarantee success. It does not eliminate competition. What it attempts to restore is something far more basic:

The belief that if people contribute, participate, and work hard, the system will stop quietly moving farther away every year.

That may sound like a small thing. It is not. The difference between surviving and building a life is often smaller than policy debates make it seem. Sometimes, it is simply the difference between waking up every morning wondering what will go wrong and believing that if something does go wrong, life will still hold together.

That feeling matters because stability is not the reward at the end of a healthy economy. Stability is the foundation that allows people to build one.

What Work Feels Like

For many people, work no longer feels connected to progress. That may sound strange in a country built around the idea that hard work creates opportunity, but for millions of workers, the disconnect feels real.

People are working. In many cases, they are working harder than ever. Longer hours. More responsibility. More education. More certifications. More hustle.

Yet despite all of it, something feels off. For many workers, effort no longer feels proportional to progress. The reward for hard work still exists, but increasingly, it feels smaller, more fragile, and harder to hold onto than it once did.

Eventually, something dangerous begins to happen. People stop believing effort changes outcomes. That erosion matters more than many economic discussions acknowledge. Because economies are not only built on labor. They are built on belief. The belief that showing up matters. The belief that learning a skill matters. The belief that taking on more responsibility matters. The belief that tomorrow can look different than today.

When people stop believing effort changes outcomes, behavior changes. Some people stop trying. Some stop investing in themselves. Some stop chasing promotions. Some stop believing ownership, savings, or advancement are realistic goals. Others burn themselves out chasing progress that always feels one step further away.

None of this happens overnight. It happens quietly. Year after year. One small disappointment at a time.

An aligned economy attempts to restore something that should never have weakened in the first place, the relationship between effort and progress. Not perfectly. Not equally. And not without competition.

That relationship will never be perfect. Hard work does not guarantee success in every circumstance. Talent, timing, opportunity, luck, health, and external conditions will still matter. Some people will advance faster than others. Some efforts will fail despite discipline and sacrifice. Alignment cannot eliminate uncertainty. The purpose is narrower, but important: to make the connection between contribution and the possibility of progress stronger and more visible than it feels today.

People will still earn different outcomes. Some people will work harder. Some people will take bigger risks. Some people will create businesses, invent products, or build organizations that create enormous value. Success still exists. Ambition still exists. Competition still exists. But the connection between contribution and stability becomes easier to see.

Think again about Marcus. Marcus still works hard. He still picks up overtime. He still wants promotions and better opportunities. Nothing about his work ethic changes. What changes is how his effort feels. Instead of overtime helping him barely keep pace with rising costs, extra effort begins creating actual progress. A raise no longer feels temporary. Additional training feels worthwhile.

Saving money begins to feel meaningful because inflation and instability are no longer quietly consuming every gain before he has the chance to use it. That emotional shift matters. Because work is not just economic. Work is psychological. People want to feel useful. They want to feel respected. They want to believe that effort has meaning beyond survival.

Most people do not expect life to be easy. They understand that success requires sacrifice. What becomes demoralizing is sacrifice without movement. Working hard and still feeling stuck. Trying harder and still feeling fragile. Watching every gain disappear before life feels different.

An aligned economy cannot guarantee success. No system can. But it can make a different promise - that work once again feels connected to the possibility of building something. A better future. A safer household. A stronger retirement. A business. A home. A life that slowly becomes more stable instead of more uncertain.

That change affects more than paychecks. It changes behavior. When people believe work matters again, they train more. They invest more. They stay engaged. They take smarter risks. They begin trying again because effort finally feels worth something again. And perhaps most importantly, people begin thinking about the future differently.

Not as something constantly slipping away, but as something they can still build toward.

What Planning Feels Like

One of the quietest consequences of instability is that people stop planning. Not because they stop caring. Because planning begins to feel unrealistic. When every unexpected expense threatens to erase progress, the future becomes difficult to trust. People still think about buying homes. They still think about retirement. They still think about education, travel, starting businesses, or finally replacing the car that has been breaking down for three years. But thinking about something and believing it is possible are very different things.

For many households, financial planning slowly shifts into financial survival. The goal becomes get through this month, then get through the next one, then, hopefully nothing breaks. That constant uncertainty changes behavior in ways that are easy to overlook. People postpone dental care. They delay medical appointments. They avoid pursuing certifications or additional education because the cost feels too risky. They stop saving because emergencies repeatedly consume what little progress they make.

Even ordinary decisions begin carrying emotional weight. A weekend trip feels irresponsible. Replacing worn furniture feels indulgent. Taking time off feels dangerous. A family dinner out becomes something to debate instead of enjoy. Tires that should be replaced wait another month. A broken appliance becomes a source of anxiety instead of inconvenience.

The future stops feeling like something people build toward. It becomes something they hope does not get worse. That emotional shift matters. Because stable economies depend on future-oriented behavior.

People buy homes when they believe tomorrow will be manageable. They invest in training when they believe opportunity still exists. They start businesses when risk feels survivable. They have children, move communities, and make long-term commitments when the future feels stable enough to support those decisions.

An aligned economy does not eliminate uncertainty. Life will always carry uncertainty. But it changes the relationship people have with it.

Imagine Marcus again. For years, planning felt fragile. Saving money felt frustrating because every gain seemed temporary. One car repair, medical bill, or rent increase could erase months of discipline. Retirement felt distant. Homeownership felt unlikely. The future often felt like something happening to him instead of something he was shaping.

Now imagine a different feeling. Marcus still budgets. He still works hard. He still worries about unexpected expenses because life does not suddenly stop being expensive. But for the first time in years, planning begins to feel rational again. A savings account slowly grows and stays intact longer. A raise creates breathing room instead of disappearing overnight. Training for a better role feels worthwhile because advancement feels connected to something real.

Instead of constantly asking: *What goes wrong next?* he begins asking: *What could come next?* That is a profound psychological shift. Because planning changes behavior. People who believe stability is possible tend to make better long-term decisions. They save more. They prepare more. They invest in themselves. They think beyond immediate survival. And importantly, they become more resilient when hardship arrives. Because hardship always arrives.

An aligned economy is not built on the assumption that people will never struggle. It is built on the belief that struggle should not permanently erase the possibility of progress.

Most people are remarkably resilient when they believe effort still matters. What wears people down is repeated instability without recovery. Working hard. Trying to plan. Trying to improve. Only to feel like the future keeps moving farther away.

An aligned economy attempts to restore something many people quietly miss, the ability to imagine a future and reasonably believe they might actually reach it. That matters more than many economic models account for. Because people build different lives when tomorrow feels possible.

What Opportunity Feels Like

For many people, opportunity does not disappear all at once. It slowly starts to feel too risky. A better job may exist, but changing employers feels dangerous when missing even one paycheck could create a crisis. A promotion may require additional training, but the cost feels impossible to justify when money already feels stretched.

Starting a business sounds exciting in theory, but terrifying in practice when failure could threaten housing, healthcare, or financial survival. Over time, uncertainty quietly reshapes ambition. People stop asking: *What could I build? a*nd begin asking: *What can I afford to risk* *losing?* That shift matters. Because healthy economies depend on people believing they still have room to grow. People learning new skills. Changing careers. Taking calculated risks. Starting businesses. Investing in ideas. Trying, failing, and trying again.

When people feel trapped, economies become less dynamic. Talent gets stuck. Potential goes unused. Innovation slows, not because people stop caring, but because survival leaves little room for experimentation.

This is one of the quiet contradictions in the current economy. We often celebrate entrepreneurship, ambition, and innovation while building conditions that make risk feel increasingly dangerous for ordinary people. It is easier to take risks when failure is survivable.

An aligned economy attempts to restore that balance. Not by removing consequences. Consequences still matter. Bad ideas still fail. Businesses still close. Poor decisions still carry costs. Competition still exists. But the penalty for trying no longer threatens to permanently destabilize a person's life.

Think about someone who has spent years working a steady job while quietly imagining something more. Maybe it is opening a small landscaping company. Starting an online business. Launching a local service company. Going back to school for a trade. Taking the risk of moving into management. Today, many people avoid those decisions because the margin for failure feels too thin. One setback feels catastrophic. A single wrong decision can take years to recover from.

Inside an aligned economy, the emotional equation changes. Risk still feels uncomfortable. But it becomes more survivable. The floor beneath people feels stronger. That matters because people are more willing to invest in themselves when they believe failure will not permanently ruin them. More people pursue training. More people experiment with small businesses. More people move toward better opportunities instead of remaining trapped in situations that no longer serve them. And importantly, success still belongs to those who create value.

Not everyone would suddenly become entrepreneurial or ambitious in the same way. Some people prefer stability over risk. Others value consistency more than expansion. That is normal. The point is not to pressure people toward bigger goals. The point is that opportunity feels available again for those who want to pursue it. Risk becomes a choice rather than something reserved only for people who can afford failure.

An aligned economy does not remove ambition. It protects it. Because ambition works best when people believe the game is still worth playing. That includes workers. Small business owners. Tradespeople. Professionals. Entrepreneurs. Young people deciding whether effort still matters. And older workers deciding whether reinvention is still possible.

Opportunity feels different when progress feels realistic. People begin saying yes to things they once assumed were impossible. A new certification. A business loan. A career change. A second chance. Not because fear disappears, but because hope finally feels rational again. That feeling matters. Because societies become stronger when people believe they still have a future worth building.

What Communities Feel Like

Economies do not exist in spreadsheets. They exist in communities. In neighborhoods. In schools. In small businesses. In local restaurants. In churches. In little league fields. In factories, offices, warehouses, hospitals, and construction sites where ordinary people spend most of their lives. And when economic instability grows, communities feel it long before economists measure it.

You can often see it before you can quantify it. A downtown storefront stays empty a little longer. A family delays moving into a better home. A small business closes and never reopens. Volunteer organizations struggle to find support. Schools quietly stretch thinner. People stop spending time together because everyone is working more hours just to stay afloat. Stress slowly becomes normal. Not dramatic. Just constant.

That constant pressure changes communities in ways that are easy to overlook. People become more isolated. More cautious. Less trusting. They pull inward. They spend less locally. They participate less. Not because they stop caring. Because survival quietly narrows their focus.

When enough households feel unstable at the same time, the effects compound. Local businesses lose customers. Hiring slows. Communities become more economically fragile. And eventually, people begin leaving when opportunity elsewhere feels like the only option.

Many towns across America know this story well. A factory closes. An industry shifts. A local employer shrinks. And over time, what disappears is not only jobs. What disappears is confidence. The belief that the community still has a future.

An aligned economy cannot solve every local challenge. Communities will still rise and fall. Industries will still change. Technology will still reshape work. Some regions will still struggle more than others. But stability at the household level creates something powerful, resilience.

When more families feel financially stable, communities behave differently. People shop locally more often. Small businesses survive longer. Families become more involved in schools and local organizations. People invest more time where they live because they no longer feel like they are barely keeping up.

Communities become stronger not because people suddenly have unlimited money, but because they finally have enough breathing room to participate again. That matters more than it may seem. Because healthy societies depend on more than economic output. They depend on social trust. People believing they belong somewhere. Believing their work matters. Believing their children may have a better future. Believing that effort still has meaning. Those things are difficult to measure. But they are impossible to ignore once they begin disappearing.

That does not mean every struggling town suddenly recovers or every community begins thriving again. Local leadership still matters. Industry still shifts. Geography still matters. Some regions will continue struggling longer than others. But stronger household stability changes the conditions communities operate inside. It gives people more capacity to participate, invest locally, and believe staying is worthwhile. Recovery becomes more possible, even if never guaranteed.

An aligned economy attempts to strengthen something many conversations about economics overlook the everyday stability that allows communities to function. Not perfectly. Not equally. And not without struggle. But with a stronger foundation beneath ordinary people trying to build ordinary lives. Because most people do not measure success in economic theory.

They measure it in simpler ways. Can I afford to stay in the town where I grew up? Can my kids build a future here? Can I retire without fear? Can I support local businesses? Can I build something that lasts?

These are not abstract questions. They are the questions communities quietly ask every day. And the answers shape far more than local economies. They shape trust. Hope. Belonging. And ultimately whether people believe the future is something worth investing in together.

The Difference Between Surviving and Building a Life

Most people are not asking for extraordinary lives. They are asking for ordinary lives that feel possible. A stable paycheck. A reliable home. A chance to save. The ability to recover when something goes wrong. The confidence to believe hard work still leads somewhere.

That matters because there is an important difference between surviving and building a life. Survival is reactive. Building is intentional. Survival asks: *How do we make it through this month?* Building asks: *What could life look like five years from now?* Survival focuses on avoiding disaster. Building focuses on creating possibility.

Many people today are surviving. Working hard. Doing their best. Trying to make responsible decisions. Trying to save. Trying to move forward. Yet still feeling like stability remains just out of reach. That feeling slowly changes how people see themselves. Ambition shrinks. Patience wears thin. Trust erodes. People stop dreaming smaller before they stop dreaming entirely.

The first thing many people abandon is not hope. It is expectation. The expectation that effort will eventually matter. The expectation that discipline will eventually pay off. The expectation that life will become more stable instead of more fragile.

That emotional shift affects far more than household budgets. It changes families. Communities. Trust in institutions. Trust in work. Trust in one another. Because people who feel trapped eventually begin to believe the future belongs to someone else.

An aligned economy attempts to restore something simple, the ability to believe that ordinary effort can still create an ordinary good life. Not luxury. Not guarantees. Not perfection.

Life will still be difficult sometimes. People will still struggle. Businesses will still fail. Hard decisions will still exist. But struggle begins to feel temporary again instead of permanent. That difference matters. Because people can endure hard seasons when they believe recovery is possible.

What wears people down is instability without recovery. Trying harder and still feeling fragile. Sacrificing more and still losing ground. Watching the future feel smaller every year.

The purpose of alignment is not to eliminate hardship. It is to reconnect effort to progress strongly enough that stability becomes realistic again for ordinary people. And when stability feels realistic, behavior changes.

People invest in themselves. Families plan again. Workers pursue better opportunities.

Businesses hire with greater confidence. Communities strengthen. The future begins to feel like something people can participate in instead of something happening to them.

That may sound like a modest goal. It is not. Healthy economies are not built only on growth. They are built on belief. The belief that participation matters. The belief that contribution matters. The belief that tomorrow can still be better than today.

But belief is not built through slogans or promises alone. People trust systems after repeated experience teaches them trust is reasonable. Stability must become visible. Recovery must become credible. Participation must feel worthwhile often enough that confidence slowly rebuilds through lived experience rather than rhetoric.

For generations, that belief formed the quiet foundation of the American promise. Not that life would be easy. Not that outcomes would be equal. But that effort had meaning. That if people worked hard, contributed, and stayed disciplined, life would gradually become more stable.

For many people, that promise feels increasingly fragile. Alignment is an attempt to rebuild it. Not through slogans. Not through blame. And not through resentment. But through a system intentionally designed to reconnect effort, participation, and stability. Because most people are not asking for special treatment. They are asking for something much simpler, a fair chance to stop surviving, and finally begin building a life. For many people, that possibility alone would feel like progress.

It is important to understand what alignment does not promise.

Alignment does not make life easy. It does not make outcomes equal. It does not eliminate risk, hardship, disappointment, or uncertainty. People will still face setbacks. Businesses will still succeed and fail. Industries will still rise and decline. Economic systems cannot guarantee outcomes, nor should they attempt to.

What alignment changes is the relationship between effort and stability. When participation, productivity, compensation, and economic obligations remain connected to the same underlying reality, the path between contribution and security becomes more reliable. The objective is not a guarantee of success. The objective is a system where stability is less dependent upon luck, timing, or structural misalignment and more closely connected to meaningful participation in the economy itself.

Fair chance should not be confused with guaranteed outcomes. Life will remain uneven. Some people will succeed more than others. Some decisions will still fail. Hardship will still arrive unexpectedly. The difference is not equality of result. It is whether ordinary participation once again feels capable of producing ordinary stability.

Chapter 11 – How Daily Economics Changes Behavior

In the previous chapter, we explored what alignment might feel like in ordinary life. What stability feels like. What work feels like. What planning feels like. What opportunity feels like. What stronger communities feel like. But feeling matters only if the system supporting it actually works.

That raises an important question: *What changes inside the economy to make those experiences possible?* This is where many conversations about reform begin to lose people. The discussion becomes technical. Abstract. Dense. A debate between economists, politicians, and policy experts using language that often feels disconnected from everyday life. But beneath all of that complexity sits a much simpler question:

What happens when an economy becomes more aligned with the people participating in it?

How do wages behave differently?

How do businesses make decisions?

How does hiring change?

How do incentives shift?

What happens to investment, risk, productivity, and competition?

And perhaps just as importantly: *What does not change?* Because an aligned economy is not built on the idea that markets stop functioning. Competition still exists.

Businesses still compete. Innovation still matters. Risk still matters. Success still matters. People still make better and worse decisions.

Good companies still outperform bad ones. Strong leadership still matters. The difference is not that economic life becomes easier. The difference is that incentives begin pulling in the same direction more often than they work against one another.

Workers benefit when productivity improves. Businesses compete for talent without constantly fighting against household instability. Growth becomes more connected to participation. Success becomes easier to sustain because more people have the stability needed to participate in it.

This chapter is not about theory. It is about practical behavior. What changes in the decisions businesses make. What changes in the choices workers make. What changes in risk-taking, investment, mobility, and growth. Because healthy economies are not only built through policy. They are built through millions of ordinary decisions people make every day. And when incentives change, behavior changes with them.

That change would not happen evenly. Some businesses would adapt quickly. Some households would remain cautious for years. Certain industries would respond faster than others. Some leaders would recognize opportunity early while others would hesitate until results became harder to ignore. Human behavior rarely changes all at once. But incentives matter because repeated experience slowly reshapes what people believe is rational. Over time, behavior that once felt risky begins feeling normal again.

What Businesses Feel Like

Businesses do not experience the economy the same way workers do. But they feel instability too. Just differently. For workers, instability feels personal. For businesses, instability feels operational. Hiring becomes harder. Turnover becomes more expensive. Training investments disappear when employees leave after six months. Planning becomes reactive. Margins become fragile. Customers become less predictable. The business environment slowly becomes harder to trust.

Many conversations about economics treat workers and businesses as if they exist in opposition to one another. As if one side's gain must always come at the other's expense. But in reality, most healthy businesses depend on healthy workers. And healthy workers depend on healthy businesses. The relationship is more connected than political conversations often acknowledge.

Think about a company struggling with constant turnover. The problem is not always wages alone. Sometimes workers leave because schedules are unstable. Sometimes they leave because a small raise somewhere else feels necessary just to stay afloat. Sometimes they leave because financial instability turns every decision into short-term survival. Managers hire. They train. They watch people leave. Then they start over. Again and again. That cycle is expensive. Not only financially. Operationally. Culturally. Emotionally. It wears organizations down. Especially for small businesses and operators already working inside narrow margins.

Imagine a manufacturing supervisor trying to maintain productivity while half the team is constantly rotating.

Or a restaurant owner retraining staff every few months. Or a logistics company struggling to maintain reliability because labor instability keeps disrupting consistency. Most leaders do not want instability. They adapt to it.

An aligned economy changes part of that equation. Not because businesses suddenly become more generous. And not because competition disappears. Competition still exists. Margins still matter. Poor leadership still fails. Bad businesses still struggle. Strong businesses still outperform weaker ones. But something important changes, the operating environment becomes more stable. Workers with greater household stability tend to stay longer. Training investments last longer. Productivity becomes more consistent. Planning becomes easier. Hiring becomes less desperate and more strategic. Absenteeism often falls. Burnout becomes easier to manage. Customers become more predictable because household spending becomes less fragile.

That does not mean retention problems disappear. Difficult jobs remain difficult. Some industries will still experience high turnover. Leadership quality will still matter enormously. Poor management will still push people away. Labor shortages may still emerge. But even modest improvements in workforce stability often compound over time. Small gains in retention can produce disproportionately large improvements in training, reliability, morale, and operational continuity.

That matters because businesses do not only operate on profit. They operate on predictability. A company can survive difficult conditions. What makes planning difficult is volatility. Constant turnover. Constant retraining. Constant uncertainty around labor, pricing, demand, and workforce reliability. This becomes especially important for smaller employers.

Large corporations often absorb instability better. They have scale. Cash reserves. Dedicated departments. Sophisticated forecasting. Small businesses often do not.

For a local contractor, restaurant owner, machine shop, landscaping business, or family retailer, losing one good employee can materially change operations. One hiring mistake matters. One difficult quarter matters. One unexpected disruption matters.

Inside an aligned economy, businesses still compete. But they compete inside a more stable environment. And stability changes behavior. Companies invest more confidently in training because workers are more likely to stay. Managers spend less time replacing talent and more time developing it. Leaders become more willing to think long term because constant disruption no longer consumes every decision.

Importantly, this is not about removing accountability. Businesses still have to create value. Poor leadership still creates failure. Bad strategies still fail. Inefficient companies still struggle.

Alignment does not protect businesses from competition. It attempts to reduce unnecessary friction that prevents healthy businesses from functioning well in the first place. Because most operators are not asking for perfection. They are asking for predictability. Reliable workers. Reliable customers. Reliable demand. Enough stability to make good decisions without constantly reacting to the next disruption.

In many ways, businesses want the same thing households want, the ability to plan. And when businesses can plan, they build. They hire. They invest. And they create opportunities that strengthen the broader economy around them.

What Hiring and Retention Feel Like

One of the least discussed costs in modern business is instability. Not market instability. Not supply chain instability. People instability. Hiring. Turnover. Burnout. Constant retraining.

The quiet exhaustion that comes from trying to build reliable teams in an environment where many workers feel financially trapped, emotionally drained, or constantly searching for the next opportunity simply to stay ahead of rising costs.

For many employers, especially frontline managers and operators, labor instability has become normal. A position opens. Applications come in. Someone is hired. Training begins. The employee learns the job. Then six months later, they leave. Sometimes for a slightly better wage. Sometimes for a schedule that works better. Sometimes because another employer offered marginally more stability. The process starts over again. Recruit. Interview. Train. Adapt. Hope they stay. Repeat.

Most people think of turnover as a labor problem. In reality, it is often an economic symptom. When households feel unstable, workers become more reactive. A small wage increase somewhere else matters more. A shorter commute matters more. A slightly better schedule matters more. The margin for error becomes smaller because financial fragility turns ordinary decisions into survival decisions.

That reality creates friction for everyone. Workers feel stuck. Managers feel frustrated. Businesses struggle to maintain consistency. Customers experience declining service, delays, or errors. And productivity quietly weakens. Not because people stopped caring. Because instability changes behavior.

Imagine a supervisor responsible for maintaining performance in a warehouse, factory, hospital unit, restaurant, or logistics operation. The challenge is not simply finding workers. The challenge is keeping good workers long enough for experience to matter.

A stable team operates differently than a revolving door. People know the systems. They trust one another. Communication improves. Training costs fall. Errors decline. Institutional knowledge stays inside the business. Good employees often help train future good employees. That kind of stability compounds over time. But instability compounds too. High turnover forces managers into constant reaction mode. Experienced workers burn out covering gaps. Training becomes rushed. Standards slowly decline. Morale weakens. Eventually, leaders stop building teams and begin simply trying to survive staffing shortages.

An aligned economy does not eliminate turnover. People will still leave jobs. Some businesses will still struggle to retain talent. Poor leadership will still drive people away. That should not change. But something important shifts. Workers operating from greater financial stability tend to make longer-term decisions. Instead of constantly reacting to immediate pressure, people become more willing to invest in roles that offer growth. Training feels more worthwhile. Career development feels more realistic.

Loyalty becomes easier when survival no longer dominates every decision. That benefits employers too. Retention improves. Hiring becomes less desperate. Managers spend less time replacing talent and more time developing it. Businesses gain confidence to invest in people because those investments are more likely to last. Importantly, higher stability does not eliminate competition for talent.

Easier should not be confused with automatic. Workers will still pursue better opportunities. Some organizations will continue struggling with retention. Ambitious employees may still leave for advancement. Labor mobility remains healthy in functioning markets. The difference is that decisions become less reactive and more intentional. Workers increasingly leave because opportunities genuinely fit better—not simply because financial instability forces constant movement.

Higher stability does not eliminate competition for talent. It improves it. Businesses still compete for great workers. Strong leadership still matters. Healthy cultures still matter. Good compensation still matters. But competition becomes more productive. Instead of constantly fighting instability, employers compete by creating environments people genuinely want to stay in.

This matters because healthy labor markets are not built on people feeling trapped. They are built on people feeling capable of choosing. Workers choosing better opportunities. Employers choosing stronger investments in people. Managers building teams that grow stronger instead of restarting every few months. Most operators understand this intuitively. Stable teams outperform unstable ones. The challenge has always been creating the conditions where stability is realistic.

Alignment attempts to strengthen those conditions. Not by forcing loyalty. Not by protecting poor performance. But by making stability easier to sustain for the people and businesses trying to build something worthwhile.

What Productivity Feels Like

Productivity is one of those words economists use often and ordinary people rarely think about. Most workers do not wake up wondering whether productivity increased this quarter. Most business owners do not describe success using abstract economic terminology. But almost everyone experiences productivity. They feel it when work runs smoothly. When teams function well. When training pays off. When problems get solved faster. When customers are happier. When effort produces results instead of frustration.

At its core, productivity is not complicated. It is simply the ability to create more value with the same effort—or the same value with less waste. Healthy economies depend on it. Businesses depend on it. Workers depend on it.

The challenge is that productivity becomes difficult to sustain when instability becomes normal. A worker worried about eviction performs differently than a worker with breathing room. A burned-out employee performs differently than someone who feels invested in the future. A constantly rotating workforce performs differently than an experienced team that trusts one another. A business constantly reacting to labor shortages operates differently than one able to plan ahead.

None of this should be controversial. People generally perform better when stability exists. The problem is that modern conversations about productivity often focus only on outputs while ignoring conditions. We celebrate efficiency. Technology. Performance. Growth. But we often overlook the environment required to sustain them.

Imagine two companies operating similar facilities.

The first experiences constant turnover. Workers leave frequently. Managers retrain endlessly. Experienced employees burn out covering staffing gaps. Mistakes happen more often. Morale weakens. Leaders spend more time reacting than improving.

The second company experiences greater workforce stability. Training lasts. Institutional knowledge stays. Teams trust one another. Managers spend less time replacing people and more time improving operations. Small problems get solved before becoming expensive ones.

The difference between those companies is not simply labor cost. It is operating stability. And stability compounds. That matters because productivity is not only about effort. It is about alignment.

When workers feel invested, they tend to care more.

When businesses feel stable, they tend to invest more.

When households feel secure, distraction declines.

People train more. Learn more. Stay longer. Build stronger teams. Over time, small improvements begin stacking on top of one another.

The result is not dramatic overnight transformation. It is something more realistic, an economy that wastes less human potential.

People still work hard. Competition still exists. Some companies still outperform others.

Innovation still matters. But productivity begins feeling less like extraction and more like participation.

This matters because people are generally willing to work hard when they believe hard work creates something meaningful. For themselves. For their families. For their employers. For the future they are trying to build.

An aligned economy does not create productivity by demanding more from people. It creates better conditions for people to succeed. And when conditions improve, performance often follows.

Of course, conditions alone never guarantee performance. Leadership still matters. Training still matters. Execution still matters. Poor systems can still underperform even in stable environments. Strong competitors will still outperform weaker ones. The argument is not that better conditions guarantee stronger outcomes. It is that healthier conditions make stronger outcomes easier to sustain more consistently.

What Consumer Demand Feels Like

Businesses do not only depend on workers. They depend on customers. And customers behave differently when instability becomes normal.

When households feel financially fragile, spending becomes reactive. People delay purchases. Put off repairs. Avoid risk. Wait longer to replace appliances, vehicles, clothing, or household items. Discretionary spending becomes harder to justify because uncertainty quietly changes decision-making.

The question becomes less: *What do we want to buy?* and more: *What can we safely afford to risk right now?* That shift matters. Because economies do not slow all at once. They often slow quietly.

A family skips eating out.

A contractor postpones replacing equipment.

A homeowner delays repairs another season.

A small business owner cancels expansion plans.

One decision may seem small. Millions of decisions begin changing the direction of an economy. Businesses feel this quickly. Demand becomes harder to predict. Sales become more volatile. Customers become more price sensitive. Planning becomes harder because consumer behavior becomes less stable.

This creates a difficult cycle. Households pull back because uncertainty grows. Businesses respond cautiously because demand weakens. Hiring slows. Investment slows. Consumers grow more cautious still.

Nobody necessarily caused the cycle. But everyone feels it.

An aligned economy attempts to strengthen something markets quietly depend on, confidence. Not irrational confidence. Not endless spending. And not debt-fueled consumption disconnected from reality. Stable confidence. The belief that tomorrow is manageable enough to make reasonable decisions today.

Imagine Marcus again. His refrigerator is failing.

In a fragile economy, replacing it feels stressful. Even if he technically has the money, uncertainty changes behavior. What if rent increases again? What if hours get cut? What if the car breaks down next month?

So, Marcus waits. Repairs what he can. Stretches the problem longer. Not because he wants to, but because uncertainty tells him to.

Now imagine Marcus operating from greater stability.

Life is still expensive. Unexpected problems still happen. But because planning feels more realistic, replacing the refrigerator becomes an inconvenience instead of a crisis.

This makes a big difference because stable households tend to make healthier economic decisions. They spend more predictably. Repair things sooner. Invest in education more confidently. Support local businesses more consistently. Take calculated risks. Plan further ahead. That does not mean unlimited consumption. Or endless growth.

Healthier decisions do not necessarily mean more spending. In many cases, they mean steadier spending. More savings. Better maintenance. Smarter borrowing. Longer planning horizons. Less financial whiplash. Healthy economies depend not only on consumption, but on households making decisions from stability instead of fear.

Healthy economies are not built on reckless spending. They are built on participation. People participating in ways that feel sustainable.

Businesses benefit from that too. Predictable customers create better planning. Better planning supports hiring. Hiring strengthens communities. Communities create stronger local economies. The cycle begins reinforcing itself instead of fighting itself.

Importantly, this does not eliminate downturns. Markets still fluctuate. Businesses still struggle. Consumer confidence still changes. Economic cycles still exist. But an aligned economy attempts to reduce unnecessary fragility. Because economies perform better when ordinary people are not forced to make every decision through the lens of financial fear. And when enough households feel stable enough to participate, businesses notice.

What Long-Term Investment Feels Like

Healthy economies are not built only through spending. They are built through investment. Businesses investing in equipment. Workers investing in skills. Families investing in homes. Entrepreneurs investing in ideas. Communities investing in local growth. And perhaps most importantly, people investing in the belief that the future is worth preparing for.

Investment is ultimately an expression of confidence. People rarely invest when survival feels uncertain. Businesses rarely expand when demand feels unpredictable. Families rarely make long-term commitments when stability feels fragile. The future has to feel believable before people begin building toward it. That challenge affects more than households. Businesses experience it too.

Imagine a company deciding whether to purchase new equipment. Expand a facility. Hire additional workers. Open a second location. Invest in training programs. Launch a new product line. None of those decisions happen in a vacuum. Leaders ask questions: *Will demand still be there? Will we be able to keep good employees? Can we reasonably predict labor costs? Will customers remain stable enough to support growth?*

When uncertainty dominates, businesses often delay. Not because leaders lack ambition. Because instability changes behavior. Expansion feels riskier. Long-term thinking becomes harder.

Protecting the present often takes priority over building the future. That reaction is understandable. But when enough businesses become cautious at the same time, economies begin slowing in ways that are difficult to see in the moment. Hiring slows. Expansion slows. Training slows. Innovation slows. Not because opportunities disappeared, but because confidence weakened.

An aligned economy attempts to strengthen something often overlooked, the conditions that make long-term thinking feel reasonable again. Businesses still face risk. Bad investments still fail. Poor strategy still carries consequences.

Competition still matters. But when workers become more stable, customers become more predictable, and labor becomes more reliable, long-term decisions become easier to justify. A company becomes more willing to train workers because retention improves. A manufacturer becomes more willing to invest in equipment because demand feels steadier. A small business owner becomes more willing to expand because household spending feels less fragile. Communities become more attractive to invest in because local participation feels stronger. That stability compounds. Not overnight. And not perfectly. But over time.

Think about someone considering opening a second landscaping crew. Buying another delivery truck. Expanding a family-owned machine shop. Hiring a manager for the first time. These are not abstract economic decisions. They are ordinary risks taken by ordinary people trying to build something. And those decisions matter. Because healthy economies are often built through thousands of small acts of confidence rather than a handful of massive decisions.

A new hire.

A new storefront.

A certification program.

A new piece of equipment.

A first-time homeowner fixing up a property.

A local business renovating instead of closing.

Small decisions accumulate. And over time, they shape the direction of communities, industries, and economies.

Importantly, an aligned economy does not remove failure. Some investments will still fail. Some businesses will still struggle. Some risks will still not work out. Because risk is part of growth. But healthier systems make recovery more realistic. Failure becomes something people can learn from rather than something that permanently destabilizes their future. This matters because people are more willing to invest in businesses, in communities, in themselves, and in one another when tomorrow feels stable enough to believe in.

What Small Business Feels Like

Small businesses experience the economy differently than large corporations. A difficult quarter feels different when there is no massive cash reserve. Hiring feels different when losing one employee changes the entire operation. Unexpected costs feel different when margins are already thin.

For many small business owners, the economy is not something they watch on television. It is something they feel every morning when they unlock the door. A contractor checking whether enough jobs are booked for next month. A restaurant owner wondering whether rising food costs will erase already narrow margins. A machine shop deciding whether replacing equipment is possible this year, or too risky. A landscaping company debating whether there is enough stability to add another crew. A family retailer wondering whether customers will still be spending six months from now.

These are not abstract economic questions. They are practical ones. Questions about survival. Questions about timing. Questions about whether the future feels stable enough to take the next step. That matters because small businesses are often operating closer to the edge than people realize. One bad quarter matters. One hiring mistake matters. One major customer leaving matters. One piece of broken equipment matters. And one talented employee leaving can change an entire operation.

Many small business owners become reluctant economists without ever intending to. They watch fuel prices. Interest rates. Insurance costs. Customer demand. Hiring markets. Supplier pricing. Not because they enjoy uncertainty, but because instability affects nearly every decision they make.

Imagine a local contractor considering whether to hire another crew. The work exists. Demand looks promising. But uncertainty changes behavior.

Will customers still move forward with projects if costs rise? Will skilled workers stay? Will material prices jump again? Will financing tighten?

Instead of expanding, the safer decision often becomes: *Wait and see.* That hesitation matters. Because small businesses create enormous amounts of local opportunity. Hiring. Training. Apprenticeships. Career mobility. Local investment. Community resilience. When small businesses hesitate, communities often feel it quickly. Growth slows. Hiring slows. Opportunity narrows.

An aligned economy attempts to strengthen something small business owners rarely say directly but almost always want predictability. Not guarantees. Not protection from competition. And certainly not freedom from risk. Risk is part of business. Competition should still matter.

Good operators should outperform poor operators. Strong service should still win. Healthy businesses should still grow. But healthier conditions change behavior. Workers with greater stability tend to stay longer. Customers spend more predictably. Planning windows become longer. Training investments last. Expansion feels more realistic.

Owners begin making decisions based less on survival and more on growth. That matters because most small business owners are not trying to build billion-dollar companies. Many simply want something dependable. A stable operation. Reliable employees. Customers they can count on. Enough consistency to build something lasting. Enough confidence to believe the next investment might actually pay off.

That shift would not happen uniformly. Some industries remain volatile by nature. Seasonal businesses still experience uncertainty. Local economic conditions still matter. Access to financing still matters. Strong operators will still outperform weaker ones. But when survival pressures ease even modestly, owners often gain the breathing room needed to think further ahead than the next payroll cycle or difficult quarter.

In many ways, small business owners want the same thing workers want, the ability to plan. The ability to grow. And the feeling that hard work is building something instead of constantly fighting against instability. When enough small businesses begin feeling that way, communities often grow stronger too.

What Leadership Feels Like

Leadership feels different when instability becomes normal. Most people imagine leadership as power. Control. Big decisions. Corner offices. Strategy meetings. But leadership, especially operational leadership, often feels far less glamorous than people imagine. It feels like pressure. Pressure to hit numbers. Pressure to retain people. Pressure to protect margins. Pressure to solve problems with incomplete information. Pressure to make difficult decisions while knowing those decisions affect real people.

For many leaders, the economy is not theoretical. It shows up in staffing meetings. Production delays. Missed shipments. Unexpected turnover. Rising insurance costs. Customer slowdowns. Budget reductions. Capital requests that suddenly no longer make sense.

Leadership often becomes an exercise in managing instability. A plant manager trying to maintain output while struggling to fill shifts. A hospital administrator balancing staffing shortages against burnout. A regional operations leader trying to maintain service while turnover quietly erodes consistency. An executive team debating whether long-term investments remain possible when every quarter feels increasingly reactive.

Good leaders adapt. They always have. But adaptation comes at a cost. The more instability enters the system, the shorter planning horizons become. Instead of asking: *What should this organization look like three years from now?* leaders begin asking: *How do we get through the next six months?*

That shift matters because leadership changes when survival becomes the priority. Training becomes harder to justify. Long-term investments get delayed. Hiring freezes become easier to rationalize. Risk tolerance shrinks. Improvement projects slow. Innovation becomes secondary to immediate performance. None of this necessarily reflects poor leadership. Often, it reflects the environment leaders are operating inside.

Most executives, operators, and managers are not trying to create instability. They are responding to it. And when enough instability exists, leadership becomes reactive instead of strategic.

An aligned economy attempts to change part of that equation. Not by eliminating pressure. Leadership should still be difficult. Competition should still matter. Results should still matter. Organizations should still be accountable. Poor leaders should still struggle. Strong leaders should still outperform weaker ones. That should not change. But healthier operating conditions change leadership behavior. Stable workers improve retention. Stable households strengthen demand. More predictable planning environments reduce constant reaction. Managers spend less time filling holes and more time developing people. Executives spend less time triaging disruption and more time building systems that improve performance. Planning horizons grow. Training becomes easier to justify. Long-term thinking becomes more realistic. This matters because leadership works best when people have enough stability to lead forward instead of constantly defending against disruption.

Better conditions do not eliminate difficult decisions. Leaders will still face downturns, staffing problems, difficult markets, strategic mistakes, and hard tradeoffs. Strong organizations will still outperform weaker ones. The difference is that leadership becomes less consumed by avoidable instability and more capable of focusing on capability, systems, and long-term performance.

Think about the difference between managing crisis and building capability. One survives. The other improves. One reacts. The other plans. One protects against loss. The other creates opportunity. Healthy organizations need both. But no company becomes exceptional by remaining permanently trapped in reaction mode. And no economy becomes stronger when leadership increasingly shifts from building the future to simply managing instability.

At its best, alignment attempts to create better conditions for leadership to function the way strong leaders prefer to lead: building teams. Developing talent. Improving systems. Investing in people. Solving problems. And creating organizations capable of growing stronger over time. Because leadership feels different when the future feels buildable again.

And when leaders begin building again, the effects rarely stop at the top. They spread throughout entire organizations.

What Business to Business Economics Feels Like

Most people think about the economy through the lens of consumers. Buying groceries. Paying rent. Replacing appliances. Managing household expenses.

But much of the economy happens long before products ever reach customers. Businesses depend on other businesses. Manufacturers depend on suppliers. Contractors depend on distributors. Hospitals depend on equipment providers. Restaurants depend on food suppliers. Retailers depend on logistics networks. Machine shops depend on raw materials. Construction firms depend on subcontractors. Technology companies depend on infrastructure providers.

Modern economies are built through relationships between businesses. And when instability grows, those relationships feel it too. A supplier suddenly raises prices. Shipping becomes unpredictable. A contractor delays payment because cash flow tightened. A customer reduces orders unexpectedly. Inventory costs increase. Lead times stretch. Planning becomes harder. What often looks like inflation or disruption to consumers frequently begins much deeper in the chain. For businesses, predictability inside those relationships matters as much as price.

Imagine a regional manufacturer supplying components to larger industrial customers. Orders arrive inconsistently. Customer forecasts shift frequently. Hiring becomes difficult because staffing needs constantly change. Investments in equipment become harder to justify because predictability weakens. Eventually, leadership begins operating defensively. Not because growth no longer matters, but because survival feels more urgent.

Now imagine greater stability throughout the broader economy. Customers order more consistently. Labor markets stabilize. Demand becomes easier to forecast. Planning windows grow longer. Supplier relationships strengthen because both sides feel less reactive. That matters because healthy business relationships are built on predictability. Trust. Reliability.

The confidence that commitments made today will still make sense six months from now. Greater predictability strengthens contracts, planning, supplier relationships, and long-term cooperation between companies.

Importantly, this does not eliminate negotiation. Or competition. Or difficult market conditions. Businesses will still compete aggressively. Prices will still fluctuate. Supply disruptions will still happen. Industries will still cycle. Healthy economies still require discipline. Efficiency. Innovation. Strong execution. But healthier systems reduce unnecessary friction.

And friction matters. Because when enough businesses stop operating defensively, the economy begins behaving differently. Companies invest more confidently. Suppliers hire more steadily. Partnerships strengthen. Planning horizons grow. Growth becomes easier to sustain because businesses spend less time reacting to instability and more time building capability.

Most successful businesses already understand this. Stable partners tend to outperform unstable ones. Reliable customers matter. Reliable suppliers matter. Reliable demand matters.

In many ways, business-to-business economics comes down to a simple idea, healthy companies build stronger relationships when the environment around them feels stable enough to plan. And when enough businesses begin planning again, entire economies often become stronger with them.

What Business to Government Feels Like

For many businesses, government feels less like a partner and more like weather. Unpredictable. Expensive. Difficult to plan around. Sometimes helpful. Sometimes disruptive. Often unavoidable.

That feeling matters because businesses do not operate in isolation. They operate inside systems. Permits. Regulations. Infrastructure. Contracts. Tax structures. Labor rules. Compliance requirements. Public investment.

Whether a company is building homes, manufacturing equipment, transporting freight, running a hospital, or opening a second restaurant location, government quietly shapes much of the environment businesses operate inside.

The challenge is not usually that rules exist. Healthy economies need rules. Contracts matter. Standards matter. Safety matters. Fair competition matters.

Most serious operators understand this. The frustration often comes from unpredictability, rules shifting, timelines changing, incentives feeling temporary, or planning becoming difficult because the operating environment no longer feels stable enough to trust.

Imagine a manufacturer considering expansion. The capital exists. Demand appears strong. Leadership believes growth makes sense. But uncertainty changes behavior. Will permitting timelines delay the project? Will workforce incentives still exist in two years? Will infrastructure investments happen? Will future policy suddenly alter the economics of expansion?

Instead of investing, many organizations slow down. Wait. Delay. Reduce scope. This becomes especially important for businesses working directly with government. Construction firms. Defense contractors. Healthcare providers. Engineering companies. Infrastructure suppliers. Technology vendors. Public transportation providers.

Thousands of businesses depend not only on customers, but on governments functioning predictably. A delayed payment matters. An unclear requirement matters. A procurement process stretching months longer than expected matters.

Policy instability changes behavior the same way market instability does. It shortens planning windows.

Healthy business-to-government relationships are rarely about agreement on every issue. They are about trust. Clear expectations. Stable rules. Reasonable oversight. The belief that businesses can plan because the environment surrounding them feels consistent enough to navigate.

An aligned economy attempts to strengthen part of that relationship. Not by removing accountability. Government should still regulate where necessary. Fraud should still face consequences. Unsafe practices should still face scrutiny. Public money should still require oversight.

But healthier systems reduce unnecessary friction. Businesses benefit when rules are understandable. When incentives are durable. When planning feels possible. When infrastructure investments become more reliable. When permitting becomes more predictable. When public and private systems work toward shared stability instead of constantly reacting to uncertainty. That matters because governments and businesses ultimately depend on one another more than many conversations acknowledge.

Healthy businesses and healthy public institutions ultimately depend on one another more than many conversations acknowledge. One creates jobs, investment, and local resilience, the other provides the infrastructure, legal stability, and operating conditions businesses depend on to function well. Neither functions particularly well when trust weakens. And neither benefits when uncertainty becomes the norm.

Most operators are not asking government to disappear. They are asking for consistency, fairness, and predictability. The ability to make long-term decisions without feeling like the rules constantly shift beneath them.

In many ways, business-to-government relationships work best when they resemble healthy partnerships: clear expectations. Mutual accountability. And enough stability to build something that lasts.

What Risk Feels Like

Risk is one of the most misunderstood parts of the economy. People often talk about risk as though it belongs only to investors. Executives. Entrepreneurs. Large corporations. Financial markets. But risk exists everywhere.

A worker deciding whether to change jobs.

A parent deciding whether to go back to school.

A small business owner considering expansion.

A company investing in new equipment.

A manager deciding whether to hire.

A manufacturer opening another production line.

A family buying a first home.

Much of economic life is ultimately a series of decisions about risk. The question is rarely: *Should risk exist?* Healthy economies require risk. Innovation requires risk. Investment requires risk. Growth requires risk. The real question is different: *What kind of risk are people being asked to take?*

There is productive risk. And there is fragile risk. Productive risk creates opportunity. Fragile risk creates fear. Those distinctions matter.

Imagine a worker considering a better opportunity.

In a healthier system, the decision feels difficult, but manageable. There may still be uncertainty. A learning curve. The possibility things may not work out. But failure feels survivable. If the new role does not work, recovery still feels possible.

Now imagine that same decision inside greater instability. Missing one paycheck threatens rent. Healthcare uncertainty grows. Savings barely exist. One wrong decision could create years of financial consequences.

The opportunity may still exist but the risk feels very different. People become more cautious. Not because they lack ambition. Because fragility changes behavior.

Businesses experience this too. A manufacturer considering automation. A contractor expanding into a new region. A hospital system investing in technology. A local restaurant opening a second location. A logistics company purchasing additional trucks. When conditions feel stable, leaders take calculated risks. They evaluate. Model outcomes. Prepare contingencies. Move forward when confidence exists. But instability changes decision-making. Leaders become defensive. Expansion slows. Hiring pauses. Capital investments get delayed. Risk tolerance shrinks. Not because leaders suddenly become timid, but because uncertainty changes incentives.

The objective is not to slow automation, discourage innovation, or preserve inefficient work for its own sake. Productivity growth remains one of the most important drivers of human progress. Better tools, better systems, and better technology should continue to be adopted wherever they create genuine value.

The challenge arises when productivity gains and economic participation begin moving in different directions. If automation increases output while simultaneously reducing participation opportunities, the benefits of that productivity can become increasingly disconnected from the people and communities that helped create the conditions for growth in the first place.

The framework therefore does not prohibit automation. It allows innovation to proceed while attaching participation continuity responsibilities to significant displacement events. The goal is simple: productivity gains should strengthen the system that produced them rather than sever participation from the value being created.

This matters because economies become weaker when too much productive risk turns into fragile risk. Fewer people start businesses. Fewer workers pursue advancement. Fewer companies invest. Fewer communities grow. The economy slowly becomes more defensive. More cautious. More reactive.

An aligned economy attempts to strengthen something risk depends on recovery. Not success, recovery. Because healthy systems do not eliminate failure. Some businesses should fail. Some ideas will not work. Some investments will disappoint. Some careers will change direction.

Risk matters because it helps economies adapt. But healthy systems create conditions where failure does not permanently remove people from participation. A failed business becomes a lesson instead of financial ruin. A career change becomes disruption instead of catastrophe. An investment setback becomes manageable instead of devastating.

This matters because people are surprisingly willing to take risk when they believe recovery is realistic. Entrepreneurs try again. Workers retrain. Businesses reinvest. Communities rebuild. The future remains believable.

At its best, an aligned economy does not remove risk. It improves the relationship people have with it. Risk begins feeling constructive again instead of punishing. Calculated instead of desperate. Productive instead of fragile. And when enough people begin taking healthier risks, economies often become more dynamic, more innovative, and more resilient in return.

What competition Feels Like

Whenever people hear ideas about economic reform, one concern tends to appear quickly: *What happens to competition?* It is a fair question. Because healthy economies need competition. Competition drives innovation. Efficiency. Better products. Better services. Better ideas. It pushes companies to improve. It rewards strong execution. It creates incentives for people to build something better. Without competition, systems often stagnate. Complacency grows. Innovation slows. Consumers lose. That should concern everyone.

An aligned economy is not built on the idea that competition disappears. In many ways, it depends on competition remaining strong. What changes is not whether competition exists. What changes is what businesses are competing against—and what they are competing for.

Today, many businesses spend enormous energy competing against instability. Competing against labor shortages. Against burnout. Against unpredictable turnover. Against fragile consumer demand. Against planning environments that feel increasingly difficult to trust. Against short-term pressures that make long-term decisions harder to justify.

Much of modern competition becomes reactive. Who can survive disruption best? Who can absorb volatility longest? Who can tolerate instability better than everyone else? Large organizations often hold advantages there. Scale helps. Cash reserves help. Market leverage helps. Smaller businesses frequently struggle more. Not because they lack capability, but because instability hits them harder.

An aligned economy attempts to shift more competition back toward value creation. Who builds the best product? Who provides the best service? Who develops people best? Who creates stronger customer relationships? Who innovates better? Who executes better? Who solves problems better? This matters because healthy competition should reward performance more than fragility tolerance.

Imagine two manufacturers.

One constantly loses workers, struggles with planning, and operates reactively and the other develops talent, invests in systems, and builds long-term capability. In a healthier environment, the stronger operator should win. Not because the market protects them, but because execution matters.

Or imagine two restaurants.

One invests in culture, quality, and consistency.

The other cuts corners and burns through staff.

Competition should reward the better operation. Strong businesses should still outperform weaker ones. Better ideas should still win. Poor leadership should still struggle. Consumers should still have choices. Markets should still discipline bad decisions.

Alignment is not an argument against competition. It is an argument for healthier competition. Competition built more around value creation and less around who can best survive instability.

Importantly, this does not eliminate difficult outcomes. Companies will still fail. Industries will still shift. New competitors will still disrupt old ones. Some workers will still lose jobs. Some businesses will still struggle to adapt. Creative destruction is part of healthy markets. But there is a difference between healthy pressure and unnecessary fragility. Healthy pressure improves systems. Fragility exhausts them. Healthy competition encourages innovation. Fragility encourages short-term survival.

This matters because people generally support competition when it feels fair. When effort matters. When rules feel consistent. When success feels earned. And when failure reflects poor execution more than unstable conditions no one can reasonably control.

At its best, an aligned economy attempts to create stronger conditions for competition to work the way people often imagine it should. By rewarding innovation, rewarding discipline, rewarding strong leadership, rewarding better ideas, and creating an environment where more people and businesses feel like they genuinely have a chance to compete.

Reaction vs. Participation

Much of modern economic life feels reactive. People react to rising costs. React to layoffs. React to unexpected bills. React to inflation. React to changing schedules. React to labor shortages. React to shifting regulations. React to uncertainty they did not create and often cannot control.

Over time, that reaction changes behavior. Quietly. Gradually. In ways people often feel before they can explain.

A worker postpones training because money feels too tight.

A family delays replacing a car because uncertainty feels too high.

A business postpones hiring because demand feels too unpredictable.

A manufacturer delays investment because customer forecasts feel unstable.

A local contractor avoids expansion because labor feels unreliable.

None of those decisions are irrational. They are rational reactions to instability. This matters because economies are not only shaped by policy. They are shaped by behavior. And behavior changes depending on whether people feel stable enough to participate, or fragile enough to react.

Reaction and participation often look similar from the outside. People still work. Still spend. Still make decisions. But the mindset underneath changes everything. Reaction asks: *How do I avoid losing ground?* Participation asks: *How do I move forward?* Reaction shortens planning windows. Participation extends them. Reaction protects against loss. Participation creates opportunity. Reaction makes people cautious. Participation makes calculated risk feel worthwhile. Reaction tends to shrink behavior. Participation tends to expand it.

Imagine Marcus again.

In a fragile environment, Marcus reacts. He delays replacing appliances. Avoids pursuing training. Stays in jobs longer than he wants because change feels too risky. Keeps savings liquid because uncertainty feels constant. The goal becomes: *Do not fall behind*.

Now imagine greater stability. Marcus still budgets. Still worries about money sometimes. Still makes careful decisions. But something changes. He begins participating again. Training feels worthwhile. Changing jobs feels survivable. Planning for a home feels rational. Saving begins feeling meaningful instead of temporary.

The question slowly changes from: *What goes wrong next?* to: *What becomes possible now?* That shift matters. Because reaction compounds. But participation compounds too.

That compounding would rarely appear dramatically. Some periods would still weaken confidence. Recessions would still interrupt momentum. External shocks would still create hesitation. Participation grows unevenly because trust rebuilds unevenly. But when systems repeatedly reinforce the relationship between effort and stability, confidence becomes easier to rebuild after disruption.

When households begin participating more fully, businesses respond. Hiring grows. Investment becomes easier to justify. Training increases. Planning horizons expand. Communities strengthen. Confidence slowly becomes more durable. And confidence matters more than many economic conversations acknowledge. Because confidence is not optimism. It is trust. Trust that effort matters. Trust that planning makes sense. Trust that participation has value. Trust that setbacks are survivable. Healthy economies require that trust. Not blind trust. Earned trust. The kind that develops when people repeatedly experience a connection between effort and progress.

An aligned economy attempts to strengthen that relationship. Not by removing hardship.

Not by eliminating competition. And not by promising certainty. Uncertainty will always exist. Life will always change.

The goal is different. It is to create conditions where more people, businesses, and communities spend less time reacting, and more time participating. Because economies grow strongest when people stop asking: *How do I survive this?* and begin asking: *What can I build next?*

Extraction vs. Participation

Throughout this book, we have returned to a recurring idea that participation strengthens economies. And extraction weakens them. But what does that actually mean? Because "extraction" can sound abstract. Political. Even accusatory. That is not how it is being used here. Extraction is not the act of creating value, building businesses, investing capital, or taking risk. Those activities remain essential. Extraction occurs when economic participation becomes increasingly disconnected from productive circulation, allowing value to accumulate in ways that no longer remain connected to productive circulation within the broader system that produced it. Extraction is not success. It is not wealth. It is not entrepreneurship. And it is certainly not an argument against people benefiting from hard work, innovation, or smart decisions.

Success, profit, scale, and wealth creation remain essential to healthy economies. Businesses should absolutely benefit from innovation, discipline, strong leadership, and risk-taking. The distinction being made here concerns feedback loops. Does success strengthen broader participation over time—or increasingly disconnect from it? That question matters because healthy systems work best when value creation reinforces stability rather than quietly weakening the conditions participation depends on.

Healthy economies should absolutely reward success. The question is different: *Does success strengthen participation—or disconnect from it?* Participation happens when value creation strengthens the broader system. A business succeeds and hires more people. Workers gain stability and spend locally. Communities strengthen. Suppliers grow. Training expands. Investment compounds. Growth spreads. The cycle reinforces itself.

Extraction feels different. It occurs when value increasingly leaves the broader system without strengthening participation around it. Sometimes that looks dramatic. A company stripping assets without reinvesting in workers, capability, or long-term health. A financial structure rewarding short-term gains while weakening long-term resilience. A community losing jobs while value quietly concentrates somewhere else.

But often extraction feels quieter than that. Harder to see. People work harder but feel less stable. Communities generate value but struggle to keep opportunity. Businesses become increasingly focused on short-term reactions instead of long-term capability. Households spend more time surviving than building. The challenge is that economies can still grow while participation weakens. Markets can rise. Profits can increase. Technology can advance. And yet many people still quietly feel disconnected from the benefits of growth happening around them.

Over time, extraction changes incentives. Businesses become more short-term. Communities struggle to retain opportunity. Workers increasingly feel disconnected from growth happening around them. The economy may still expand, but participation weakens—and when participation weakens, long-term resilience becomes harder to sustain.

An aligned economy attempts to strengthen the opposite pattern. Not by punishing success. Not by limiting ambition. And not by pretending everyone contributes equally. Some people will still create extraordinary value. Some businesses will still outperform competitors. Some leaders will still make better decisions. That's OK but the goal is different. It is to create stronger feedback loops between success and participation.

When businesses succeed, workers benefit more consistently. When workers stabilize, businesses gain stronger customers and more reliable talent. When communities strengthen, opportunity becomes easier to sustain. Growth becomes more connected, more durable, and more participatory. That matters because healthy economies work best when success feels connected instead of isolated. Not perfectly. No system achieves that perfectly. But direction matters. And direction shapes incentives.

Imagine two different futures.

In one, growth increasingly disconnects from ordinary participation. The economy still functions. But more people feel left behind. Planning shrinks. Trust weakens. Communities grow more fragile. People increasingly react instead of build.

In the other, success strengthens participation. People feel effort matters again. Businesses invest more confidently. Workers participate more fully. Communities become more resilient. The future begins feeling more buildable.

Neither future appears all at once. Both emerge gradually from the incentives societies choose to strengthen. At its core, alignment is an argument for participation.

For systems that reward success while strengthening the broader conditions that allow more people to contribute meaningfully to the future being built around them. Because healthy economies are strongest when growth feels connected, not extracted.

What Daily Economics Makes Possible

By now one thing should be clear, daily economics matters. Not only in theory. In practice. In kitchens. In factories. In offices. In hospitals. In warehouses. In classrooms. In restaurants. In small businesses. In family budgets. In hiring meetings. In investment decisions. And in the quiet choices people make every day about whether the future feels worth building toward. Because economies are not shaped only through large events. Not only recessions. Not only elections. Not only major policy shifts.

Economies are shaped through repetition. Repeated decisions. Repeated incentives. Repeated experiences. A worker deciding whether additional training feels worth the effort. A family deciding whether planning ahead feels realistic. A small business owner deciding whether to hire. An executive approving long-term investment instead of delaying it another quarter. A contractor taking the risk of expanding. A supplier investing in better capability. A community choosing to build instead of retreat.

One decision alone rarely changes much. But millions of decisions begin changing everything.

That matters because many of the challenges discussed throughout this book did not emerge overnight. Drift rarely announces itself. It compounds. Quietly. A little more instability each decade. A little less purchasing power. A little more fragility. A little less confidence that effort still creates progress. Eventually, people adapt. Not because they stop caring. Because reaction slowly replaces participation.

Short-term thinking becomes normal. Planning shrinks. Risk tolerance weakens. Trust erodes. Businesses become more defensive. Workers become more cautious. Communities become more fragile. Nobody necessarily intends the outcome. But incentives shape behavior. And behavior compounds.

Healthier systems compound too. Stable workers tend to strengthen businesses. Stable businesses tend to invest more confidently. Predictable demand strengthens planning. Planning strengthens hiring. Hiring strengthens communities. Communities strengthen participation. Participation strengthens resilience. The cycle begins reinforcing itself instead of working against itself. Not perfectly. No economy works perfectly. And not immediately.

Healthy systems rarely feel dramatic. They feel steadier, more durable, more resilient. The future feels less fragile. This matters because daily economics ultimately determines what people believe is possible.

Whether effort feels worthwhile.

Whether opportunity feels realistic.

Whether planning feels rational.

Whether communities feel buildable.

Whether businesses feel confident enough to invest.

Whether ordinary people believe they still have a meaningful place in shaping the future around them. That possibility matters. Because healthy economies are not built only on growth. They are built on belief. The belief that participation matters. The belief that contribution matters. The belief that tomorrow can still be better than today.

And when enough people begin believing that again, behavior changes. People plan. Build. Hire. Learn. Risk. Invest. Participate. Not because someone tells them to, but because the system finally begins giving them reasons to believe it is worth doing.

That is what daily economics makes possible. Not perfection. Not guarantees. Not a world without struggle. But something more practical: a healthier relationship between effort, stability, opportunity, and participation. And over time, those small shifts can begin changing far more than people expect.

None of this implies a world without friction. Serious economies still face tradeoffs, mistakes, changing industries, technological disruption, political disagreement, and periods of instability. The claim is narrower, but meaningful: healthier incentives tend to create healthier patterns of behavior over time. And healthier patterns matter because behavior compounds.

Before We Move Forward

At this point, one thing should feel increasingly clear: economies are not experienced only through numbers. They are experienced through behavior. Through hiring decisions. Through business investments. Through family planning. Through leadership choices. Through risk. Competition. Trust. Participation. And through the countless small decisions people make every day about whether the future feels stable enough to build toward.

That matters because economic systems rarely succeed or fail all at once. They evolve. Slowly. Quietly. Through incentives, behavior, and repeated decisions.

When instability grows, behavior changes. Workers become more cautious. Businesses shorten planning windows. Leaders become reactive. Families postpone decisions. Communities grow more fragile.

People adapt. Not because they stop caring, but because the environment surrounding them quietly changes what feels rational. Healthier systems change behavior too. Workers invest in themselves. Businesses hire more confidently. Small business owners expand. Leaders plan further ahead. Communities stabilize. None of this forces better decisions. It changes the conditions under which decisions are made.

Risk begins feeling productive instead of dangerous. Competition begins rewarding stronger execution instead of mere survival. Participation becomes easier to sustain. None of this happens perfectly. And none of it happens overnight.

Healthy systems are not built through slogans. Or optimism. Or wishful thinking. They are built through incentives strong enough to consistently reinforce healthier behavior over time. That is ultimately what alignment attempts to strengthen, a system where participation feels worthwhile again. Where effort feels connected to progress. Where businesses feel stable enough to invest. Where workers feel secure enough to plan. Where communities feel resilient enough to grow. And where success becomes more connected to the broader health of the system instead of increasingly detached from it.

If Chapter 10 explored what alignment feels like and Chapter 11 explored how healthier daily economics changes behavior, then the next question becomes unavoidable: can a system like this survive reality?

But by now, another question should naturally begin emerging: *If these ideas sound reasonable in theory, what happens when they encounter reality?* What about bad actors? What about manipulation? What about unintended consequences? What about political resistance? What about businesses trying to game the system? What about people who choose not to participate? What about failure?

Those questions matter. They deserve serious attention. No system survives scrutiny by avoiding difficult conversations. And alignment should not ask people to suspend skepticism. It should invite it. Because the real test of any idea is not whether it sounds good in theory, but whether it remains durable when challenged.

And that is where we turn next.

Chapter 12 – The Hard Questions

By now, skepticism is not only reasonable. It is necessary. Because ideas that sound compelling in theory often become more complicated when they encounter reality. Incentives behave differently than expected. Systems produce unintended consequences. Good intentions collide with imperfect human behavior. Political resistance emerges, markets react, and institutions adapt. And sometimes, problems appear in places no one initially anticipated.

Large systems also face another reality: legal boundaries matter. Constitutional authority matters. Administrative clarity matters. Due process matters. Public legitimacy matters. Serious frameworks cannot depend only on good intentions or strong outcomes. They must survive institutional scrutiny, legal challenge, democratic disagreement, and revision over time. That reality strengthens serious design rather than weakening it.

Economic systems are no exception. Every serious economic framework eventually faces difficult questions. What happens during recession? What happens when people try to game the system? What about businesses acting in bad faith? What about manipulation? What about capital flight? What about inflation? What about people who choose not to participate? What about unintended consequences? What happens when political systems distort good ideas? Those questions matter. They should matter. Because healthy skepticism is not cynicism. It is discipline.

No serious system survives scrutiny by avoiding difficult conversations. Strong ideas should withstand pressure.

They should survive disagreement. They should remain durable even when examined from uncomfortable angles.

Alignment should be no different.

Up to this point, this book has focused on something practical, what misalignment feels like. What healthier participation might feel like. How daily economics changes behavior for workers, businesses, families, and communities. But understanding possibility is only part of the conversation. The harder question is whether those possibilities remain realistic when they encounter friction. Because friction always exists. People are imperfect. Businesses are imperfect. Governments are imperfect. Markets are imperfect. No system removes self-interest.

No structure eliminates bad actors. No framework escapes tradeoffs. And any serious proposal that assumes otherwise deserves skepticism. That is not an argument against trying to improve systems. It is an argument for designing systems strong enough to survive reality. Which means the next step in this conversation is not advocacy. It is stress testing. Not: *Could this work in theory?* But: *Does it still work when things go wrong?*

That is where we turn next. It is also worth stating something plainly before continuing: some criticism would likely be right. Certain assumptions may prove incomplete. Some incentives may behave differently than expected. Some ideas may require revision. Serious systems improve through pressure, not protection. The purpose of skepticism is not merely to defend existing assumptions. It is to reveal weak ones early enough to improve them.

The Question Behind Every Question

Most skepticism surrounding economic reform eventually arrives at the same place. Not immediately. People often begin with different concerns. Inflation. Taxes. Government overreach. Corporate behavior. Labor incentives. Political feasibility. Market reactions. Unintended consequences. But beneath nearly all of those questions sits a deeper one: *Can people actually be trusted to behave responsibly inside a system like this?*

It is a fair question. Because every economic system ultimately depends on human behavior. Workers make choices. Businesses make choices. Investors make choices. Governments make choices. Consumers make choices. And people are imperfect. Always have been. Always will be.

That reality matters because many large ideas fail for the same reason. They assume ideal behavior, perfect compliance, perfect incentives, perfect leadership, perfect participation, or perfect information. No serious system should rely on any of those things.

Healthy systems are not built around ideal people. They are built around real people. Ambitious people. Short-sighted people. Ethical people. Self-interested people. Responsible people. Irresponsible people. Creative people. Greedy people. Disciplined people. And occasionally, people actively trying to exploit weaknesses. That should not surprise anyone.

Every successful system already accounts for imperfect behavior. Businesses do. Strong companies do not assume every employee will always make perfect decisions. They build incentives. Processes. Oversight. Accountability. Training. Risk controls. Checks and balances. Not because leadership distrusts people, but because leadership understands people. Financial institutions do the same. Markets do the same. Legal systems do the same. Even households do the same. Families save for uncertainty because uncertainty exists.

Good systems plan for imperfection. They do not pretend imperfection disappears. This matters because skepticism about alignment often sounds like this: *"This sounds good if everyone behaves responsibly."* But that standard is impossible.

No economic system works because everyone behaves responsibly. The current system certainly does not. Fraud exists now. Manipulation exists now. Short-term thinking exists now. Bad incentives exist now. Poor leadership exists now. Regulatory capture exists now. Rent-seeking exists now. People already game systems.

The real question is different: *Which incentives become easier to exploit—and which behaviors become easier to reinforce?* That is the more useful question. Because systems shape behavior. Not perfectly. But meaningfully. People respond to incentives. Businesses respond to incentives. Governments respond to incentives. Markets respond to incentives. The issue is rarely whether bad behavior exists. It always will. The issue is whether systems reward it too easily. Or make healthier behavior easier to sustain.

No incentive structure perfectly predicts behavior. Some people will still exploit systems. Some organizations will still prioritize short-term advantage. Some unintended consequences will emerge. The objective is not flawless alignment. It is improving the probability that healthier participation becomes easier to sustain than unhealthy extraction over time.

Imagine two workplaces.

In one, poor performance carries little consequence while strong performance goes largely unrewarded. Eventually, behavior changes. Motivation weakens. Standards slip. Frustration grows.

Now imagine another. Clear expectations. Fair accountability. Meaningful opportunity. Reasonable stability. Poor behavior still exists. But healthier behavior becomes easier to reinforce. Over time, culture changes.

Economic systems function similarly. No structure eliminates greed. Or manipulation. Or selfishness. Or poor decision-making. Healthy systems reduce unnecessary fragility while strengthening incentives for productive participation.

This matters because critics are often asking the wrong first question. Not: *Could someone exploit this system?* Every system can be exploited. The better question is: *Does this system reward healthier participation more consistently than the alternative?* That is the standard serious systems should be measured against. Not perfection. Improvement. Not ideal outcomes. Better incentives. Not the elimination of bad behavior, but stronger conditions for good behavior to become easier, more sustainable, and ultimately more normal.

Because before debating inflation, bad actors, political resistance, or implementation, there is one foundational reality worth accepting. That no system succeeds by assuming perfect people. The real test is whether imperfect people can still produce healthier outcomes inside it.

And that is where the harder questions begin.

What Happens in a Recession?

Every economic system eventually faces the same test: What happens when conditions worsen? Not during expansion. Not during optimism. Not during strong markets. During contraction. When confidence weakens. Demand slows. Businesses become cautious. Consumers pull back. Investment declines. Because recessions are not unusual events. They are recurring realities. Healthy economies experience them. Fragile economies experience them. No serious framework should assume they disappear.

That matters because one of the first reasonable questions people ask about alignment is simple: *What happens during recession?* It is a fair concern. Especially because many economic systems reveal their strengths, and weaknesses, under pressure.

Some systems perform reasonably well during expansion but become highly unstable during contraction. Fragility compounds. Layoffs accelerate. Consumers retreat. Business investment freezes. Communities weaken. Recovery becomes harder. And once confidence breaks, fear often spreads faster than growth ever did.

That pattern matters because recessions are not only financial events. They are behavioral events. People respond. Families delay spending. Businesses pause hiring. Investors become defensive. Managers reduce risk. Communities contract inward. Again, none of that behavior is irrational.

In uncertain conditions, caution often feels responsible. The problem emerges when caution compounds faster than resilience. One business cuts hiring. Another delays investment. Consumers spend less. Demand weakens further. Layoffs begin. Confidence declines. The cycle reinforces itself. Economists sometimes describe this as a feedback loop.

Ordinary people usually describe it differently: *Everything suddenly feels harder at once.* That feeling matters. Because much of economic pain comes not only from the initial disruption, but from how deeply disruption spreads.

An aligned economy does not prevent recession. That should be stated clearly. No system removes economic cycles. Markets still fluctuate. Industries still change. Technology still disrupts. Poor decisions still happen. Global events still matter. Pandemics. Wars. Supply chain failures. Energy shocks. Financial crises. No framework eliminates uncertainty.

The question is becomes: *How resilient is the system when disruption arrives?* That matters because resilience changes outcomes.

Imagine two households.

Both experience unexpected hardship. A layoff. Medical issue. Business slowdown.

In one environment, even a temporary disruption creates immediate instability. Savings disappear quickly. Housing insecurity grows. Recovery feels fragile. Planning collapses.

In another, hardship still hurts. But recovery feels more survivable. There is more stability beneath the disruption.

More time to adapt. More ability to recover. The hardship remains real, but collapse becomes less likely.

Businesses experience recessions similarly. In fragile environments, short-term survival dominates. Layoffs happen quickly. Hiring freezes. Training disappears. Investment collapses. Planning windows shrink. Leaders become purely reactive.

In healthier environments, businesses still adjust. Cost discipline still matters. Difficult decisions still happen. But resilience allows stronger operators to preserve capability instead of dismantling it entirely. Recovery becomes faster because the underlying system stayed stronger. That matters because recessions are often worsened by fragility. Not simply the original shock. Fragility spreads disruption. Resilience absorbs more of it.

An aligned economy attempts to strengthen some of that resilience. Not by eliminating risk. Not by preventing downturns. And not by shielding everyone from consequences. Poor decisions still carry costs. Weak businesses may still fail. Industries may still restructure. That should not change. But stronger participation creates stronger foundations. More stable workers. More resilient households. Businesses better able to plan. Communities better able to absorb disruption.

The result is not recession avoidance. It is recession durability. It matters because the question serious people should ask is not: *Can this system stop hard times?* No serious system can. The better question is: *When hard times arrive, does the system help people recover—or push instability deeper?* That is the standard resilience should ultimately be measured against. Because economies are rarely judged by how they perform during easy years.

Durability should not be mistaken for immunity. Severe downturns would still create hardship. Businesses would still close. Families would still experience stress. Some industries would still contract sharply. The distinction is not whether pain exists. It is whether systems become strong enough that disruption spreads less destructively and recovery becomes more achievable afterward.

The real test comes when conditions become difficult. And whether the system bends, or breaks.

What About Bad Actors?

Eventually, every serious conversation about systems arrives at the same concern: *What happens when people try to exploit it?* It is a reasonable question. Because bad actors exist. Always have. Always will. Some people cut corners. Some businesses manipulate incentives. Some institutions protect themselves at the expense of broader outcomes. Some individuals seek benefits without contribution. Some organizations prioritize short-term extraction over long-term participation.

Human behavior does not suddenly improve because a system intends good outcomes. That reality matters. Because one of the easiest ways to dismiss any proposal is simple: *"People will just game it."* But that criticism deserves a more serious response. Not because it is wrong. Because it is incomplete.

Every system gets gamed. The current system certainly does. Fraud exists. Tax avoidance exists. Regulatory capture exists. Market manipulation exists. Corporate rent-seeking exists. Financial engineering exists. Abuse of public programs exists. Exploitative labor practices exist. Predatory pricing exists. Monopolistic behavior exists.

None of those things appeared because the current system failed entirely. They appeared because incentives created opportunities for exploitation.

Most attempts to game a system rely on the same assumption: that changing labels, paperwork, ownership structures, or legal forms changes the underlying reality being measured. Sometimes that works because the rules focus more on classification than substance.

The Alignment Economy takes a different approach. The framework looks first at what materially changed, not simply what paperwork changed. If the underlying economic reality remains substantially the same, changing the form alone does not necessarily change how the system evaluates participation, responsibility, or economic position.

That principle is important because healthy systems should respond to real economic behavior rather than becoming trapped in endless debates about technical labels. The goal is not to eliminate flexibility or legitimate business structures. The goal is to ensure that measurement remains connected to substance rather than appearance.

This matters because the real question is not: *Can bad actors exist?* They will. The better question is: *How expensive does the system make bad behavior and how rewarding does it make productive participation?* Healthy systems understand something important: Prevention matters. But incentives matter even more.

Imagine a workplace where poor performance faces no accountability while manipulation consistently outperforms contribution. Over time, behavior changes.

The strongest contributors disengage. Short-term thinking grows. Trust weakens. The culture deteriorates.

Now imagine another workplace. Strong expectations. Clear accountability. Meaningful rewards for contribution. Consequences for harmful behavior. Bad actors still exist. But exploiting the system becomes harder to sustain. Over time, healthier behavior becomes more normal.

Economic systems function similarly. An aligned economy should not assume perfect participation. Nor should it assume everyone acts in good faith. Some businesses will still exploit workers if incentives allow it. Some individuals will still seek benefits without contributing. Some organizations will still attempt regulatory arbitrage. Some investors will still chase short-term extraction. That should be expected.

Healthy systems plan for reality. Not idealism. That means stronger oversight where incentives create vulnerability. Better alignment between contribution and reward. Clear accountability. Transparent enforcement. And importantly, consequences meaningful enough to discourage exploitation without punishing productive participation.

That reality can take many forms. Misreporting participation. Manipulating classifications. Exploiting regulatory ambiguity. Structuring organizations to avoid responsibility. Short-term extraction disguised as efficiency. Benefit abuse. Fraudulent reporting. Regulatory arbitrage. These behaviors already exist in many forms today. Serious systems should assume similar pressures emerge under any structure and design accountability accordingly.

That balance matters. Because systems become unstable at both extremes. Too little accountability encourages abuse. Too much rigidity discourages innovation, entrepreneurship, and legitimate risk-taking. Healthy systems avoid both. They protect participation without suffocating initiative. That distinction becomes especially important because many conversations about economic reform unintentionally drift into two unhelpful positions. One assumes people are naturally selfish and systems cannot improve. The other assumes people will behave responsibly if given the chance. Neither position reflects reality.

Most people are neither saints nor villains. Most respond to incentives. Most adapt to expectations. Most behave somewhere between self-interest and contribution. Which means system design matters more than moral assumptions. A healthy system does not depend on extraordinary virtue. It makes healthier participation easier, stronger, and more sustainable than exploitation. Not perfectly. No system achieves that perfectly. But direction matters. Because over time, incentives shape norms. And norms shape behavior.

The goal of alignment is not to eliminate bad actors. That is impossible. The goal is to reduce how much damage bad actors can create while strengthening the incentives for productive participation to remain the better long-term choice. Because serious systems are not judged by whether bad behavior exists. They are judged by what behavior they consistently reward, and what behavior they make increasingly difficult to sustain.

What Happens if Money Leaves?

Few concerns appear faster in economic conversations than this one: *What happens when money leaves?* Or stated more bluntly: *What stops businesses, investors, or wealthy individuals from simply moving somewhere else?* It is an important question. And a fair one. Because capital is mobile. Businesses can relocate. Investors can move money. Supply chains can shift. Manufacturing can move. Tax structures influence behavior. That reality should not be ignored. Nor should it be treated emotionally.

Healthy systems require realism. Especially when discussing incentives. The concern itself is not new. Every country, state, and region already competes for investment. Lower taxes. Better infrastructure. Skilled labor. Regulatory predictability. Energy costs. Logistics networks. Market access. Political stability. All of those things influence where capital goes. That should surprise no one.

The mistake many conversations make, however, is assuming capital moves for a singular reason, taxes. Reality tends to be more complicated. Businesses rarely make major decisions based on a single variable. Strong operators think in systems. Can we find reliable labor? Can we forecast costs? Can we trust the infrastructure? Can we recruit talent? Can we move products efficiently? Will customers remain stable? Can we plan five or ten years ahead with confidence?

Predictability matters. Demand matters. Workforce capability matters. Institutional stability matters. Customer strength matters. In many industries, those variables matter as much, or more, than marginal tax differences.

Imagine two operating environments.

One offers lower taxes but greater instability. Weak infrastructure. High turnover. Volatile labor conditions. Unpredictable planning. Fragile demand.

The other offers slightly higher costs but stronger workforce participation. More predictable demand. Better planning stability. Stronger infrastructure. More durable consumer participation.

Many serious operators choose predictability because uncertainty becomes expensive. That matters because discussions around capital flight sometimes assume businesses behave like spreadsheets. In reality, businesses behave more like ecosystems. They optimize for survivability. For capability, talent, operational continuity, customer access, or long-term profitability.

That does not mean capital flight is imaginary. It is real. Some firms relocate. Some investors arbitrage systems. Some industries move aggressively toward lower-cost environments. That should be acknowledged honestly.

Some organizations would likely leave. Some investors would shift behavior. Certain industries may prove more sensitive than others. Competitive pressures would remain real. Healthy systems should plan for those reactions rather than assume participation happens automatically. The relevant question is not whether every participant stays. It is whether the broader environment becomes strong enough that productive participation remains attractive for enough participants to sustain growth.

Healthy systems should never pretend incentives do not matter. They absolutely do. The question is not: *Can capital move?* Of course it can. The better question is:

What makes productive participation more valuable than exit?

This matters because strong economies become difficult to leave when participation remains attractive. Reliable customers matter. Stable workers matter. Strong infrastructure matters. Skilled talent matters. Legal predictability matters. Healthy demand matters. Long-term planning matters. Those are competitive advantages too.

An aligned economy attempts to strengthen more of those advantages. Not through coercion. Not through punishment. And not through assuming businesses owe participation regardless of incentives.

Businesses should respond to incentives. That is rational. The objective is different. It is to create conditions where productive participation becomes the more attractive long-term choice. That means rewarding investment. Strengthening workforce stability. Improving planning confidence. Reducing fragility. Making demand healthier and more durable. Because businesses generally invest where they believe success is sustainable. Not simply where costs are lowest in a single moment.

Importantly, this conversation should avoid false extremes. One extreme says: *Businesses will leave no matter what*. The other says: *Businesses should simply stay out of obligation*. Neither position reflects reality. Most businesses stay where participation works. Where customers exist. Where capability exists. Where planning feels rational. Where long-term success feels achievable. That is not ideology. It is operational behavior. And healthy systems should be designed with operational behavior in mind. Because the real test is not whether capital can move. It always can. The real question is whether the system becomes strong enough that productive participation remains worth staying for.

What About Inflation?

Few economic concerns feel more immediate than inflation. People can debate markets. Taxes. Policy. Growth. Even unemployment. But inflation feels personal. Groceries cost more. Housing costs more. Insurance costs more. Utilities cost more. Savings lose purchasing power. Paychecks stretch less than they used to.

People feel inflation before they understand it. And because they feel it so directly, inflation becomes one of the first serious questions any economic proposal must answer: *Would this create more inflation?* It is a fair concern. Especially because inflation is not only an economic problem. It is a trust problem.

When purchasing power weakens, confidence weakens. Planning becomes harder. Savings feel less meaningful. Households become more reactive. Businesses shorten planning horizons. The future feels less stable. That concern deserves a serious response. Not dismissal. And certainly not simplistic promises. Because inflation is complicated.

Contrary to popular conversation, inflation rarely comes from one source. Sometimes it emerges from excessive money supply. Sometimes supply chains break. Sometimes labor shortages push wages upward faster than productivity. Sometimes energy costs rise. Sometimes housing shortages constrain supply. Sometimes corporate pricing power expands. Sometimes global disruptions ripple through local economies. Usually, inflation is not one thing. It's several things happening at once.

This matters because critics of stronger participation-based systems often worry about one specific risk: *If more people have stronger purchasing power, won't prices simply rise to absorb it?* In other words: *Does helping people participate more just create inflation somewhere else?* It is a serious question. And one worth examining honestly. The short answer is: *It depends on what drives the participation.*

And humility matters here. Inflation is notoriously difficult to model with precision because multiple forces often interact at once. Even well-designed systems can underestimate pressure. Supply constraints may emerge unexpectedly. Behavioral responses may differ from projections. External shocks may overwhelm assumptions. Serious systems should treat inflation as a continuing management challenge rather than a permanently solved problem.

If stronger participation comes only from more money chasing the same supply, inflation risk rises. That should be acknowledged plainly. Healthy systems should never pretend tradeoffs disappear. But participation and inflation are not automatically the same thing. The difference matters.

Imagine two scenarios.

In one, demand rises while supply remains constrained. Too few homes. Too little energy. Too few workers. Too little productive capacity. Prices often rise. That is basic economics.

In another, stronger participation also strengthens productive capacity. Workers participate more consistently. Training improves. Businesses invest more confidently. Planning horizons expand. Productivity strengthens. Supply becomes healthier. Participation becomes more sustainable. The economy grows more capable, not simply more expensive.

This matters enormously because inflation becomes most dangerous when systems experience imbalance. Too much demand. Too little supply. Too much fragility. Too little productive resilience.

Healthy systems attempt to improve both sides of the equation. Participation matters. But production matters too. Capability matters. Infrastructure matters. Housing supply matters. Energy matters. Workforce development matters. Long-term investment matters. This is one reason alignment places so much emphasis on participation rather than simple distribution. Participation strengthens productive systems. Workers contribute. Businesses expand. Communities stabilize. Capacity improves.

The objective is not merely stronger spending. It is stronger resilience beneath spending. That does not mean inflation disappears. It will not. Healthy economies still experience inflation. Some inflation is normal. Even useful. Growing systems often experience price pressure. Industries change. Demand shifts. Global events still matter. No serious framework eliminates those realities.

The question is different: *Does the system become more inflation-prone or more inflation-resilient over time?* This matters because fragile systems often create inflation from weakness. Supply shortages. Labor instability. Housing underinvestment. Poor planning. Short-term incentives. Weak productive capacity.

Healthy systems absorb pressure more effectively. Not perfectly. But more durably. Importantly, inflation concerns should not be dismissed as fear. They are rational. Especially for workers, retirees, households on fixed incomes, and people already feeling financially stretched.

Inflation disproportionately harms people with the least margin for error. That reality deserves respect. Which means any serious proposal should welcome scrutiny here. Not avoid it. Because the question should never be: *Could inflation happen?* Of course it could. The better question is: *Does the system strengthen enough productive resilience to make inflation easier to manage—and less destructive when it appears?* That is the more serious conversation. Because healthy economies are not judged by whether pressure exists. They are judged by whether they become strong enough to withstand it without quietly eroding the stability people depend on every day.

What About Businesses That Fail?

One concern often sits quietly beneath conversations about economic reform: *What happens to failure?* Because healthy economies require success. But they also require failure. That reality can feel uncomfortable. Especially when discussing ideas centered around participation, stability, and resilience.

People reasonably wonder: *Does a healthier system protect businesses from consequences? Does failure stop mattering? Does competition weaken?* Those concerns deserve a direct answer: No.

Failure still matters. And in many ways, it should. Healthy economies depend on experimentation. Risk-taking. Innovation. Competition. New ideas replacing weaker ones. Better execution outperforming poor execution. Some businesses succeed. Some businesses fail. That should not disappear.

Creative destruction, the process by which weaker ideas give way to stronger ones, remains an important part of functioning markets. Poor leadership still carries consequences. Weak execution still matters. Unsustainable business models still struggle. Changing markets still disrupt incumbents. Technology still reshapes industries. Consumer preferences still evolve. No serious economic system eliminates those realities. Nor should it.

The question is different: *What kind of failure are we talking about?* Because not all failure is the same. There is productive failure. And there is fragile failure. Productive failure teaches. Fragile failure destabilizes.

Imagine two businesses.

The first takes reasonable risk. Leadership makes thoughtful decisions. The market shifts unexpectedly. Demand weakens. The business struggles. Eventually, it closes.

Painful? Absolutely. But people recover. Workers find opportunities elsewhere. Owners apply lessons learned. Skills remain valuable. Communities absorb the disruption. The system bends.

Now imagine another environment. One disruption triggers collapse. Workers immediately lose stability. Communities lose key employers. Small suppliers fail alongside the larger business. Recovery feels distant.

Confidence weakens. Risk-taking shrinks. The system breaks more than it bends.

That matters because healthy systems should not eliminate failure. They should reduce unnecessary fragility surrounding failure. Businesses should still carry responsibility. Poor choices should still matter. Weak operators should not be artificially sustained forever. That creates stagnation. Misallocated resources. Reduced innovation. Poor incentives.

Healthy systems still require discipline. But healthier systems also create stronger recovery conditions. Workers retrain more easily. Entrepreneurs try again. Communities recover faster. Businesses take calculated risks because failure does not automatically become catastrophe. That relationship matters more than many conversations acknowledge. Because economies weaken when fear of failure becomes stronger than willingness to participate. Entrepreneurs stop starting businesses. Managers stop taking smart risks. Companies avoid investment. Workers stop changing jobs. Innovation slows. People become defensive. Not because ambition disappears but because fragility changes behavior.

An aligned economy attempts to improve that relationship. Not by removing accountability. And not by guaranteeing success. But by making recovery more realistic. Participation more sustainable. Risk more constructive. Failure remains possible. Necessary, even. But collapse becomes less contagious. The distinction may sound subtle. It is not.

Healthy systems are not measured by whether hardship exists. Hardship always exists. They are measured by whether people and businesses remain capable of rebuilding after hardship arrives. Because in healthy economies, failure is not supposed to permanently remove people from participation. It is supposed to teach, adapt, redirect, and ultimately allow stronger participation to emerge on the other side. That is not weakness. It is resilience.

What About People Who Opt Out?

Eventually, most conversations about economic systems arrive at a difficult question: *What about people who choose not to contribute?* It is an important concern. And one often discussed with frustration. Sometimes quietly. Sometimes directly. Because most people understand something instinctively, that healthy systems depend on participation. People working. Learning. Building. Taking responsibility. Contributing where they are able.

That expectation matters. Especially in systems built around reciprocity. People reasonably ask: *If participation matters so much, what happens when someone simply opts out? Does the system still reward people who choose not to contribute? Is responsibility still expected?* Those are fair questions. Because healthy societies rely on a balance that many people feel strongly about – that compassion matters. But accountability matters too.

That difference deserves careful attention. Especially because this conversation can become emotionally charged very quickly. Often for understandable reasons. Most people know someone who works hard, contributes consistently, and still struggles. Many also know situations where responsibility appears disconnected from outcomes. That frustration is real. And dismissing it helps no one.

But clarity matters here. Not everyone who struggles is refusing to participate. This is a critically important point. People lose jobs. Industries change. Health problems emerge. Families face disruption. Caregiving responsibilities arise. Economic shocks happen. Setbacks happen. Temporary instability happens. Healthy systems should create pathways back into participation when hardship interrupts it. That is resilience. Not dependency.

The harder question concerns something else, people who are capable of participation, but choose not to engage. That deserves an honest response. Because healthy systems should encourage contribution. Not weaken it.

An aligned economy should not reward disengagement more consistently than participation. That creates bad incentives. And bad incentives eventually weaken trust. Trust matters. Especially among people carrying responsibility every day. Workers. Parents. Business owners. Managers. Entrepreneurs. Communities. When people feel contribution no longer matters, participation weakens. That should concern everyone.

At the same time, healthy systems must avoid another mistake, assuming punishment alone creates stronger participation. Often, disengagement reflects something deeper. Broken incentives. Lost trust. Skills mismatch. Institutional failure. Economic instability. A feeling that effort no longer changes outcomes. Again, not always.

Personal responsibility still matters. But serious systems ask serious questions before assuming every outcome reflects individual failure. That distinction matters because healthy participation depends on both responsibility AND opportunity.

That statement also deserves humility. Human situations are rarely simple. Capability changes over time. Health changes. Caregiving responsibilities emerge. Economic conditions shift. Temporary disengagement should not automatically be confused with permanent unwillingness. Healthy systems distinguish between hardship, transition, and chronic avoidance thoughtfully rather than reactively.

People should be expected to contribute where they are able. That expectation should remain. Work matters. Effort matters. Contribution matters. Responsibility matters. Healthy societies function best when participation remains the cultural norm. But systems also function best when participation feels realistic. When training exists. When pathways upward exist. When work feels connected to stability. When contribution feels meaningful. When setbacks do not permanently remove people from opportunity. That balance matters. Too little accountability weakens trust. Too little opportunity weakens participation. Healthy systems require both.

An aligned economy attempts to strengthen that relationship. Not by removing responsibility. Not by guaranteeing outcomes. And not by pretending everyone contributes equally. People contribute differently. At different stages of life. Under different circumstances. That is reality.

The objective is simpler; create stronger conditions where participation becomes both expected and worth pursuing. Because the goal of a healthy economy is not merely to ask: *Are people participating?* The better question is: *Are we building a system where participation remains the strongest, most realistic, and most rewarding long-term choice?* That is the harder question. And the more useful one.

Why Change Feels So Hard?

Even if an idea appears reasonable on paper, another question quickly emerges: *Could something like this ever actually happen?* It is a fair question. Because economic systems are not changed in laboratories. They are changed through institutions. Politics. Public trust. Competing priorities. Conflicting interests. Human disagreement. And those realities are rarely simple.

By now, one thing should already feel clear - alignment is not a small adjustment. It asks difficult questions. About incentives. About participation. About long-term resilience. About what kinds of behavior healthy systems should reward more consistently.

Large questions create large resistance. That should surprise no one. Because systems, economic or otherwise, rarely change easily. Especially when many people benefit from the current arrangement. That statement should not be interpreted cynically. It is simply operational reality. Organizations resist change. Businesses resist change. Institutions resist change. Governments resist change. People resist change. Even when the existing system contains visible weaknesses. Why? Because uncertainty feels risky. Known problems often feel safer than unknown outcomes. That instinct exists everywhere. In families. In workplaces. In corporations. In governments. And in economies. The devil you know is always better than the devil you don't know...

This matters because conversations about economic reform often drift toward two extremes. One says: *The system is fine. Nothing substantial should change.* The other says: *The system is broken. Tear everything down.* Neither position tends to produce durable progress. Healthy systems evolve. They adjust. Adapt. Correct. Not because everything failed, but because maintenance matters.

No serious business ignores drift for decades simply because operations still technically function. Leaders evaluate. Refine. Adapt. Not emotionally. Operationally. Healthy economies deserve similar seriousness. This matters because alignment should not be understood as revolution. It is not an argument against markets. Not an argument against business. Not an argument against competition. And not an argument for centralized control.

Healthy markets still matter. Entrepreneurship still matters. Innovation still matters. Investment still matters. Success still matters. What changes is the attempt to strengthen participation beneath those things. That nuance matters politically. Because much of modern discourse struggles with complexity.

People often assume proposals must belong entirely to one side or the other. Pro-business or pro-worker. Growth or fairness. Competition or stability. Public or private. But reality rarely works in absolutes. Healthy systems usually require tension. Balance. Tradeoffs. That makes political conversation harder. But also, more necessary. Resistance will exist. Some concerns will be legitimate. Some criticisms will improve the idea. Some interests will resist change because uncertainty feels threatening. Some people will disagree honestly. That should be expected. Healthy skepticism strengthens serious ideas.

Some resistance would be principled. Some ideological. Some operational. Some economic. Some rooted in legitimate implementation concerns. Some rooted in institutional self-interest. That complexity matters because disagreement should not automatically be dismissed as obstruction. Serious systems improve when criticism separates meaningful weaknesses from reflexive resistance.

Weak criticism often fades under scrutiny. Strong criticism improves design. This matters because alignment should not require agreement from everyone. No serious framework ever achieves that. The real question is different: *Can enough people recognize the difference between change that feels disruptive and drift that becomes increasingly expensive to ignore?* That may ultimately be the harder political question. Because systems rarely change when frustration first appears. They change when enough people begin recognizing that maintenance is less costly than continued drift.

That is not ideology. It is how most institutions eventually evolve. Slowly, unevenly, and sometimes reluctantly. But often necessarily. And if healthier participation, stronger resilience, and more durable opportunity are worth pursuing, then political difficulty alone should not automatically end the conversation. It should simply make the conversation more serious.

What Could Go Wrong?

At this point, another question deserves direct attention: *What if parts of this are wrong?* It is not a cynical question. It is a serious one. Because every meaningful system carries risk. Every framework produces tradeoffs. Every policy creates unintended consequences somewhere. And every generation eventually discovers that even well-designed ideas behave differently once they encounter reality. That should create humility. Not paralysis.

Humility matters because economic history is full of examples where confidence exceeded caution. Systems overpromised. Incentives behaved unexpectedly. Good intentions collided with human behavior. Political realities distorted implementation. Short-term pressures weakened long-term outcomes. Ideas that looked coherent on paper struggled under real-world complexity. No serious proposal should pretend immunity from those risks.

Alignment should not. That matters because one of the fastest ways to lose credibility is to imply certainty where uncertainty clearly exists. There are things this framework could underestimate. Behavioral responses. Political resistance. Institutional complexity. Implementation challenges. Market adaptation. Global competitive pressures. Technological disruption. Human creativity, both productive and exploitative. Those risks deserve acknowledgment. Openly. Not defensively. Because healthy skepticism improves systems. Weak ideas fear scrutiny. Strong ideas evolve through it. Unfortunately, some unintended consequences may not appear immediately.

Imagine a policy intended to strengthen participation accidentally creating distortions somewhere else. A labor incentive functioning differently than expected. Capital responding more aggressively than modeled. Industries adapting unevenly. Regional disparities widening instead of narrowing. Administrative systems becoming too complicated. Or incentives unintentionally rewarding behavior that weakens long-term participation instead of strengthening it.

Those possibilities deserve serious attention. Not dismissal. Good systems improve through pressure testing. The real danger is not asking hard questions early enough. That applies to both change and stagnation. Because continuing current trajectories also carries risk. Drift has consequences. Weakening purchasing power has consequences. Shrinking participation has consequences. Rising fragility has consequences. Growing distrust has consequences. In other words, doing nothing is not neutral.

Often, public conversations unintentionally frame decisions as: *Change equals risk. Staying the same equals safety*. Reality rarely works that way. Stability can contain risk. Change can contain risk. The question is usually: *Which risks appear more manageable over time?* That is the more honest conversation. Because no serious person should ask: *Could something go wrong?* Of course something could. Something always does. The better question is: *Does the framework improve the probability of healthier long-term outcomes while remaining adaptable enough to correct mistakes when they emerge?*

That standard matters because successful systems are rarely flawless. They are responsive. They adjust, adapt, correct, and improve. No successful business survives decades without changing. No healthy institution avoids revision forever. Healthy systems evolve because reality changes. Economies should not be different.

That does not guarantee success. Nothing does. But uncertainty alone is not an argument against improvement. Especially when current trajectories carry uncertainty too. The real test is whether society remains willing to ask difficult questions honestly, including ideas it hopes succeed. Because healthy skepticism is not opposition. It is stewardship. And stewardship matters when the stakes involve how millions of people experience work, stability, participation, and opportunity over time.

Why Doing Nothing Is Still a Choice

After enough difficult questions, a temptation quietly emerges. A reasonable one. People begin thinking: *Maybe change simply creates too much risk. Maybe imperfect systems are safer than uncertain ones. Maybe it is better to leave things alone.* That instinct deserves respect. Because caution matters. Especially when discussing systems affecting millions of people.

Healthy skepticism is responsible. Thoughtful restraint is responsible. And history provides plenty of examples where confidence outran wisdom. But there is an important distinction worth remembering, caution and complacency are not the same thing. Because after discussing bad actors, inflation, political resistance, recession, unintended consequences, participation, capital movement, and failure, another question naturally emerges: *Compared to what?* Compared to what future? Compared to what trajectory? Compared to what risks? Because every serious decision carries tradeoffs. Including the decision to do nothing.

That question should not imply existing systems have failed entirely or that current structures contain no strengths worth preserving. Most systems contain both strengths and weaknesses. The question is not whether everything changes. It is whether important relationships have drifted far enough that thoughtful maintenance becomes necessary.

That reality deserves attention. Especially because economic drift rarely feels dramatic in the moment. It feels manageable. Incremental. Easy to rationalize. A little more instability. A little less purchasing power. A little more fragility. A little less confidence. A little more reaction. A little less participation. Quietly, gradually, often slowly enough that adaptation feels easier than correction. Until eventually, people begin mistaking adaptation for normalcy. Because humans are remarkably adaptable.

People adjust expectations. Families delay goals. Businesses shorten planning horizons. Communities quietly absorb instability. Workers normalize financial stress. Institutions adapt to distrust. None of this necessarily feels catastrophic. Not at first. That is what makes drift difficult to recognize.

Systems can continue functioning while becoming progressively weaker beneath the surface. A business may still generate revenue while losing operational discipline. A bridge may still stand while structural weakness quietly grows. A relationship may still exist while trust slowly deteriorates. Functioning and healthy are not always the same thing.

Economies are no different. The difficult question is not whether current systems still function. Clearly, they do. The harder question is whether current trajectories remain healthy enough to sustain the kind of stability, participation, opportunity, and resilience societies hope to preserve long term.

That deserves serious reflection. Not panic. Not ideology. And not false certainty. Because this conversation should never imply that alignment is unquestionably right. Or inevitable. Or beyond criticism. It is one framework. One attempt to ask whether healthier incentives might produce healthier long-term outcomes. It may require revision, improvement, adaptation, debate, and pressure testing.

Better ideas layered on top of weaker assumptions. That should be welcomed. But rejecting difficult conversations because outcomes feel uncertain carries its own risk. Especially when existing trajectories already contain uncertainty. That may ultimately be the most important distinction in this entire discussion: *Uncertainty is not unique to change.* Uncertainty already exists. The question is simply where society chooses to place its risk. In intentional improvement, or unmanaged drift.

Because serious systems are not judged only by whether change feels uncomfortable. They are judged by whether continued inaction becomes increasingly expensive to ignore. And if drift is already weakening participation, resilience, confidence, and long-term stability, then asking difficult questions about how to strengthen those things is not recklessness. It is responsibility. Which means the real question is no longer: *Could things go wrong?* Things always can. The better question becomes: *What future becomes more likely if we stop asking whether things could be better and simply accept drift as inevitable?* That question matters. Because healthy systems are not preserved accidentally. They are maintained, adjusted, and improved, before the distance between where things are and where they were intended to go, becomes too large to easily close

Why the Hard Questions Matter

At this point, one thing should feel increasingly clear - the purpose of difficult questions is not to end the conversation. It is to improve it. Because healthy skepticism often gets misunderstood. Sometimes skepticism becomes cynicism. Sometimes criticism becomes dismissal. Sometimes complexity becomes an excuse to avoid uncomfortable conversations entirely.

But serious systems deserve something better than blind confidence and something better than reflexive rejection. They deserve scrutiny. Pressure testing. Honest disagreement. Thoughtful criticism. Revision where revision is necessary. That applies to businesses, governments, institutions, markets, and ideas. Especially ideas attempting to influence how millions of people experience work, stability, opportunity, and participation.

By now, this chapter has asked difficult questions about numerous aspects of our economy. Recession, inflation, capital movement, bad actors, political resistance, participation, failure, unintended consequences, and tradeoffs. Those concerns matter. They should matter. Because healthy systems are not strengthened by pretending weaknesses do not exist. They improve by identifying weaknesses early enough to address them.

That reality is easy to recognize almost everywhere else. Strong businesses stress test assumptions. Pilots train for emergencies. Engineers test systems under pressure. Hospitals prepare for unlikely scenarios. Military leaders plan for failure, not only success. Not because people expect disaster, but because resilience requires preparation.

Economic systems deserve similar seriousness. That distinction is important because one of the easiest mistakes in public conversation is assuming every proposal must be either unquestionably right or completely wrong. Reality rarely works that way.

Most meaningful progress happens imperfectly. Ideas improve through criticism. Weak assumptions get challenged. Blind spots become visible. Better solutions emerge through friction. That should be welcomed. Not feared.

Which means the purpose of this chapter has never been to argue: *"Every concern has been solved."* That would be dishonest. No serious framework solves every concern. The purpose is something more practical: *Can these concerns be answered seriously enough to deserve continued consideration?* That is a different standard. And an important one. Because no society improves by assuming existing systems are beyond criticism. But societies also do not improve by assuming criticism alone creates solutions.

At some point, difficult questions must eventually become constructive ones. Not: *What could go wrong?* But: *What becomes possible if healthier incentives are actually achievable?* Not: *What are the risks of change?* But: *What are the risks of refusing to evolve?* Because every generation inherits systems shaped by the decisions of people before them. Some of those systems deserve preservation. Some deserve refinement. Some deserve deeper scrutiny. And some quietly drift long enough that maintenance becomes unavoidable.

That does not mean every proposed solution is correct. It means serious people remain willing to ask difficult questions before drift grows expensive enough that options become smaller, harder, and more painful. Because healthy systems are not built by avoiding scrutiny. They are built by surviving it. And if alignment deserves continued consideration after difficult questions have been asked, then perhaps the next conversation is no longer whether change feels difficult. But why meaningful change so often struggles to happen at all.

Because difficult questions are not signs an idea has failed. They are signs an idea is finally being treated seriously. Systems worthy of trust should invite scrutiny, remain adaptable, and improve where criticism proves justified. The objective has never been certainty. It has been durability.

And that is where we turn next.

Chapter 13 – Drift, Resistance, and Why Change Is Hard

If healthier systems sound reasonable in theory, an uncomfortable question naturally follows: *Why do systems like this rarely happen?* It is a fair question. Especially because many of the ideas discussed so far are not particularly radical. Stronger participation. Healthier incentives. More stable planning. Greater resilience. Better alignment between contribution, opportunity, and long-term outcomes.

At face value, those goals sound difficult to argue against. So why do societies struggle to move in that direction? Why do systems often remain unchanged even when growing numbers of people quietly feel something is no longer working as well as it once did? The answer is more complicated than politics. More complicated than ideology. And more complicated than disagreement alone. Because systems rarely resist change for only one reason. Habits resist change. Institutions resist change. Incentives resist change. Power resists change. Fear resists change. And perhaps most importantly people adapt to drift long before they decide to confront it.

Drift should not be confused with inevitability. Healthy systems often self-correct. Institutions adapt. Markets respond. Leadership improves. Innovation solves problems unexpectedly. Some periods of pressure eventually reverse. That possibility deserves recognition. The concern is narrower: when enough signs begin pointing in a similar direction, societies benefit from asking whether maintenance has become necessary before correction becomes forced by greater instability later.

This matters because societies rarely wake up one morning and suddenly recognize decline. Most change happens slowly. Quietly. Incrementally.

The things people once tolerated temporarily gradually become normal. Financial pressure. Institutional distrust. Shorter planning horizons. Greater fragility. Lower expectations. The feeling that participation somehow costs more while delivering less certainty in return. Rarely catastrophic. Often survivable. And because adaptation is easier than disruption, people learn to accommodate conditions they once would have questioned.

Businesses do this too. So do institutions. So do governments. Systems continue functioning. Until eventually, functioning gets mistaken for healthy.

That may be one of the hardest truths to recognize about large systems - survival and health are not the same thing. A business can still generate revenue while culture deteriorates. A bridge can still stand while structural weakness quietly grows. A relationship can still exist while trust slowly erodes. Economies are no different. They can function for long periods while underlying resilience weakens beneath the surface. That does not mean collapse becomes inevitable. And it certainly does not mean existing strengths disappear.

Healthy markets still matter. Innovation still matters. Competition still matters. Success still matters. But maintenance matters too. Because systems drift. And drift becomes expensive when ignored for too long. Which means before asking: *How could meaningful change happen?* another question deserves attention first: *Why does meaningful change feel so difficult—even when growing numbers of people sense something should improve?*

This deserves emphasis because strong systems rarely emerge by abandoning everything that already works. Existing institutions contain real strengths. Markets coordinate extraordinary complexity. Businesses create value. Innovation improves lives. Capital allocation matters. Entrepreneurship matters. The purpose of maintenance is not replacement for its own sake. It is preserving strengths while correcting relationships that increasingly struggle to hold.

The Economy Is Not the Problem, Drift Is

By now, an important distinction should feel increasingly clear, the problem is not markets. The problem is not ambition. The problem is not success. And the problem is certainly not capitalism itself. Healthy markets have created extraordinary prosperity. Innovation has improved lives. Competition has created progress. Businesses have expanded opportunity. Entrepreneurs have transformed industries. Workers have created enormous value.

That story matters because this conversation has never been about tearing down what works. Quite the opposite. Healthy systems preserve strengths worth protecting. The harder question is different: *What happens when systems slowly drift away from the outcomes they were originally meant to support?* That question matters because drift rarely feels dramatic. It happens gradually, quietly, almost invisibly at first. A little more instability. A little less purchasing power. A little more fragility. A little less confidence that effort still produces the kind of opportunity people once expected. Rarely catastrophic. Often manageable. At least in the moment.

That is what makes drift difficult to recognize. People adapt. Businesses adapt. Families adapt. Institutions adapt. Workers lower expectations. Businesses shorten planning horizons. Communities absorb instability. Households postpone goals. People become more reactive. Not because they stop caring but because changing conditions quietly reshape what feels rational.

The economy still functions. Stores still open. Paychecks still arrive. Markets still move. But increasingly, people begin asking: *Why does everything feel harder than it should?* That question deserves serious attention. Because healthy systems require maintenance.

No successful business assumes yesterday's systems automatically solve tomorrow's problems. Leaders evaluate, adjust, correct, and adapt. Not because failure already happened, but because drift eventually becomes expensive. Economies are no different.

The difficult question is not whether change feels uncomfortable. Change always feels uncomfortable. The harder question is whether current trajectories feel sustainable enough to preserve the kind of participation, resilience, and opportunity societies hope to maintain long term. This matters because many public conversations unintentionally collapse into false choices. Either: *Everything is working*. Or: *Everything is broken*. Reality rarely works at either extreme. Most systems are neither collapsing nor healthy in equal measure. They are drifting. Strengths remain. Weaknesses grow. Adaptation masks deeper problems. Functioning slowly gets mistaken for flourishing.

That is where serious conversations become necessary. Not because catastrophe is inevitable. And not because current systems lack strengths worth preserving. But because maintenance matters. Healthy systems improve before decline becomes unavoidable. Not after.

That is the spirit of alignment. Not revolution. Not resentment. Not punishment. And not hostility toward success. The objective is not to weaken markets. It is to strengthen participation beneath them. To improve resilience. To reduce unnecessary fragility. To better connect effort, opportunity, stability, and long-term contribution. That may not be the only path forward. And it may not be perfect.

Healthy skepticism still matters. Better ideas should always remain welcome. But dismissing difficult questions does not make drift disappear. Ignoring incentives does not make fragility disappear. And pretending frustration exists only in perception does not make instability feel any less real to the people experiencing it. Because the economy itself is not the enemy. Markets are not the enemy. Success is not the enemy. Drift is. And drift becomes harder to correct the longer people convince themselves maintenance can wait.

Why Systems Drift

Drift rarely begins with bad intentions. That matters. Because one of the easiest ways to misunderstand large systems is to assume decline only happens when people stop caring. Most of the time, the opposite is true. People continue trying. Businesses continue operating. Workers continue contributing. Institutions continue functioning. Governments continue responding. Markets continue adapting. The system still works. At least enough to keep moving.

That is precisely what makes drift difficult to recognize. Because drift rarely announces itself dramatically. It accumulates, quietly, incrementally. One incentive at a time. One adaptation at a time. One compromise at a time. Imagine a successful company.

Early on, leadership remains closely connected to operations. Decision-making feels practical. Customers trust the product. Employees feel invested. Standards remain clear. Over time, pressures emerge. Growth, complexity, cost concerns, leadership changes - short-term priorities begin competing with long-term thinking.

None of the decisions seem catastrophic on their own. One process becomes slightly less effective. One metric becomes more important than another. One compromise feels necessary. One layer of bureaucracy gets added. The business still functions. Until eventually people begin quietly asking: *Why does this place feel different than it used to?*

Economies drift similarly. Rarely through a single failure. More often through accumulated incentives. Short-term fixes replacing long-term thinking. Reactive behavior replacing strategic planning. Fragility quietly increasing while adaptation disguises the cost. Again, none of this necessarily happens maliciously.

In fact, many forms of drift emerge from rational behavior. Businesses optimize for quarterly pressure. Workers adapt to instability. Families become more cautious.

Governments react to political incentives. Institutions prioritize short-term continuity. Each decision makes sense in isolation. That is what makes drift so difficult. No one actor necessarily caused it. No single decision created it. No obvious villain exists. The system simply evolves toward what incentives consistently reward.

That distinction matters because complex systems rarely deteriorate through singular failure. More often, individually rational decisions quietly accumulate into collectively difficult outcomes. Businesses respond to incentives. Families adapt to uncertainty. Governments respond to political pressure. Institutions optimize for continuity. None of those responses are inherently irrational. But systems can still drift when short-term adaptation consistently becomes easier than long-term correction.

This matters because people often imagine systems fail through collapse. Reality tends to look more subtle. Participation weakens gradually. Trust erodes slowly. Planning windows shrink. Long-term thinking becomes harder to sustain. Communities become more fragile. Economic pressure quietly normalizes. People adapt, again and again. Until eventually, adaptation starts getting mistaken for resilience.

But adaptation and resilience are not the same thing. Someone constantly under stress may adapt. A struggling business may adapt. A fragile institution may adapt. But adaptation alone does not necessarily mean health.

Sometimes it simply means people are learning to survive conditions that should have improved. That question deserves reflection: *Are people thriving—or merely adapting?* Because systems often drift when adaptation becomes easier than maintenance.

Maintenance is difficult. It requires honesty. Self-evaluation. Course correction. Sometimes uncomfortable change. Businesses understand this instinctively. Strong leaders review operations before failure becomes unavoidable. They improve systems before fragility compounds. Not because disaster already happened, but because prevention matters.

Healthy economies deserve similar seriousness. That does not mean every sign of drift demands overreaction. Nor does it mean every discomfort signals decline. Healthy systems still experience pressure. Cycles still happen. Tradeoffs still exist. The question is different: *Are incentives reinforcing stronger participation—or gradually weakening it?*

That may ultimately be one of the most important questions societies can ask. Because systems rarely become healthier accidentally. They improve when enough people recognize drift before adaptation quietly becomes permanent decline. And recognizing drift is usually the first step toward correcting it.

Why People Defend Systems They Don't Trust

One of the more difficult realities about large systems is this – people can become deeply frustrated with a system while still defending it. At first glance, that seems contradictory. Why protect something that increasingly feels unstable? Why defend institutions people openly criticize? Why resist alternatives while simultaneously acknowledging growing dissatisfaction? The answer is not usually hypocrisy. It is uncertainty. Because uncertainty changes behavior. Especially at scale.

People may distrust parts of the current system while still fearing the unknown more than the familiar. That instinct is deeply human. And often rational. Most people do not experience economic systems as theories. They experience them through mortgages, paychecks, retirement accounts, healthcare, businesses, children, debt, responsibilities, or just plain daily survival.

When people feel financially exposed, stability, even imperfect stability, can feel safer than experimentation. That matters because many systems survive not only through trust, but through familiarity.

People understand the rules, even when they dislike them. Businesses understand the environment, even when it creates frustration.

Institutions understand how to operate inside existing structures, even when those structures become inefficient. Adaptation creates dependency. Dependency creates caution. Caution creates resistance. Again, none of this necessarily reflects ignorance or bad intentions. Often it reflects risk management.

Resistance is not evidence of failure. It is an expected part of any meaningful transition, which is why implementation must be phased, audited, reviewed, and tested against real-world conditions rather than assumed into existence through optimism alone.

Imagine a company operating on outdated software systems. Employees complain constantly. The systems slow productivity. Processes feel inefficient. Workarounds pile up. Everyone acknowledges problems exist. Yet leadership still hesitates to replace the system. Why? Because transition itself carries risk. Operations could fail during implementation. Training takes time. Unexpected problems emerge. Short-term disruption feels dangerous even when long-term improvement appears necessary.

Economies behave similarly. People often defend systems not because they believe everything works well, but because uncertainty feels expensive. This matters especially because frustration alone rarely creates change. In fact, prolonged instability often creates the opposite effect. People become more defensive. More tribal. More reactive. Less willing to tolerate disruption.

Fear narrows decision-making. That pattern appears repeatedly throughout history. Periods of instability often increase demand for certainty, even imperfect certainty. Not because people stop recognizing problems. Because survival instincts prioritize predictability.

This is one reason meaningful reform becomes difficult precisely when systems begin feeling more fragile. The more pressure people experience, the harder many become willing to risk additional uncertainty. That tension deserves understanding. Not ridicule. Because skepticism toward change is not always resistance to improvement. Sometimes it reflects fear that improvement efforts may unintentionally worsen instability before producing better outcomes. That concern is legitimate. Healthy systems should respect it.

And in many cases, caution reflects wisdom rather than resistance. People carrying mortgages, payrolls, retirement savings, caregiving responsibilities, or business risk often become appropriately skeptical of large promises. They understand something important: transitions create uncertainty too. Serious systems should respect that reality rather than dismiss it. Improvement only becomes durable when people reasonably believe transition risks remain more manageable than continued drift.

Why Big Systems Resist Change

There is another difficult reality worth confronting, even when problems become visible, institutions rarely change quickly. That should not surprise anyone. Because institutions are designed to create stability. Governments, corporations, financial systems, universities, regulatory systems and large organizations of every kind. Their purpose is not speed. Their purpose is continuity.

That does not mean institutions never improve. Many do. Some adapt remarkably well under pressure. Regulatory systems evolve. Businesses reinvent themselves. Public systems modernize. New technologies reshape incentives. The challenge is timing. Institutions often respond after pressure becomes difficult to ignore rather than before strain becomes visible.

Healthy societies depend on institutions strong enough to survive disruption. Strong enough to create consistency. Strong enough to maintain trust. But stability carries a tradeoff. The same systems designed to preserve continuity often become slower to recognize when maintenance is necessary.

That tension matters. Because institutions rarely resist change out of malice. Most resist change because uncertainty feels dangerous. Large systems understand something instinctively, mistakes scale. A poor decision inside a family affects a household. A poor decision inside a company affects employees. A poor decision inside national systems affects millions. That creates caution. Often reasonable caution.

Which means institutions naturally prioritize predictability. Process, incrementalism, consensus, risk reduction. Those instincts make sense. Until they begin protecting continuity more aggressively than health.

Imagine a company with declining culture. Employee turnover increases. Productivity slips. Communication weakens. People quietly disengage. Leadership sees warning signs. But meaningful change feels disruptive. Processes feel entrenched. Incentives feel difficult to untangle.

Short-term stability becomes easier than confronting long-term deterioration. So small fixes replace structural maintenance. Another training program. Another survey. Another temporary adjustment. The business still functions. But underlying problems continue quietly growing.

Large institutions behave similarly. Especially when systems still appear functional. Economic indicators remain positive enough. Markets continue operating. Growth continues unevenly. People continue adapting. Pressure exists, but not enough to force urgency.

That is often where drift becomes difficult to interrupt. Because institutional incentives tend to reward short-term stability more than long-term correction. Political systems prioritize election cycles. Public companies prioritize quarterly pressure. Bureaucracies prioritize continuity. Organizations protect existing structures. Again, not necessarily because people lack good intentions. Because incentives shape behavior.

The same lesson repeated throughout this book appears here too – systems tend to reinforce what they consistently reward. That matters because maintenance often feels politically inconvenient. Operationally difficult. Institutionally uncomfortable. The benefits arrive slowly. The costs appear immediately. Leaders take criticism. Resources shift. Established interests resist. Short-term discomfort increases.

Meanwhile, preserving current systems often feels safer, even when deeper risks quietly accumulate. This is one reason meaningful reform so often arrives later than people expect. Not because no one sees warning signs. Often many people do. But recognition and action are not the same thing. Especially when systems still appear functional enough to postpone difficult decisions.

That dynamic appears everywhere. Bridges receive maintenance after warning signs accumulate. Companies restructure after performance weakens. Families confront problems after trust erodes. Health improves after symptoms become difficult to ignore.

Economies are no different. Societies often delay maintenance until drift becomes expensive enough to command attention. That should create humility. Because resistance to change does not always reflect bad faith. Sometimes it reflects fear. Sometimes caution. Sometimes competing incentives. Sometimes simple institutional inertia. And sometimes genuine uncertainty about what improvement should look like.

This matters because meaningful change rarely happens through accusation alone. Or outrage alone. Or frustration alone. Healthy systems improve when enough people recognize two realities at the same time - the current system still contains strengths worth preserving and maintenance has become necessary. Both things can be true. In fact, they often are.

Which means one of the hardest challenges any society faces is learning how to improve systems before fragility grows large enough that change becomes forced instead of chosen. Because maintenance always feels expensive until drift becomes more expensive still.

Why Change Rarely Starts at the Top

When people imagine major change, they often imagine leadership first. A president. A legislature. A movement. A CEO. A major institution suddenly recognizing a problem and deciding to solve it.

Occasionally, history works that way. More often, it does not. Because meaningful change rarely begins at the top. Usually, it begins much lower – quietly, gradually, through recognition. People noticing something feels increasingly difficult to ignore. Whether it's workers, families, managers, business owners, communities, or operators. People experiencing systems directly before institutions fully recognize what is changing beneath the surface.

That pattern appears repeatedly throughout history. Not because leaders are incapable. Because distance changes perspective. People closest to daily friction often notice problems first. A machine operator notices a process becoming inefficient before leadership sees declining output. A nurse recognizes system strain before reports fully capture the trend. A manager notices morale weakening before turnover appears in the data. A business owner notices customers quietly pulling back before economists begin debating larger patterns. Experience often precedes measurement.

That matters because many forms of drift begin as lived experience long before they become institutional concern. People quietly noticing that housing feels harder or planning feels shorter or savings feel less durable. Effort feels less connected to progress. Opportunity feels more fragile.

That moment matters. Because systems rarely change through frustration alone. They change when recognition becomes collective. When enough people begin seeing similar patterns. Asking similar questions. Experiencing similar pressures. Not necessarily agreeing on solutions but increasingly recognizing the problem deserves attention. That is usually where meaningful conversations begin. Not in certainty. In recognition.

That matters because public conversations often become trapped between extremes – immediate revolution or complete resignation.

Reality tends to move differently. Meaningful change usually emerges slowly. Awareness grows. Conversations deepen. Ideas evolve. Weak assumptions get challenged. Better language develops. Shared understanding expands. Then institutions begin responding. Sometimes reluctantly. Sometimes unevenly. But eventually, that process can feel frustrating. Especially for people experiencing pressure directly. But healthy systems rarely improve through force alone. Durable improvement requires understanding, trust, and shared recognition. Enough consensus that maintenance feels necessary rather than threatening.

Sometimes it also fails. Good ideas arrive too early. Coalitions weaken. Resistance overwhelms momentum. Implementation proves harder than anticipated. Economic conditions change. Public trust collapses. That possibility deserves honesty. Progress is not guaranteed. But neither is stagnation permanent. The point is not certainty. It is remaining willing to continue improving systems where pressure suggests maintenance matters.

This may be one reason alignment matters as a conversation even before it matters as policy. Because meaningful change begins long before implementation. It begins when enough people become willing to ask better questions. Not: *Who should we blame?* but: *What incentives are producing the outcomes we are experiencing?* Not: *Which side is right?* but: *What kind of system better strengthens participation, resilience, and long-term stability?* Those are different questions. More difficult questions. But often more useful ones. Because systems rarely improve through outrage alone. They improve when recognition grows strong enough that maintaining drift begins feeling more expensive than maintaining change.

And recognition almost never begins at the top. It begins with people noticing reality before institutions fully catch up to it.

Recognition alone also guarantees very little. Many periods of pressure produce frustration without meaningful improvement. Conversations fragment. Solutions compete. Fatigue grows. Political incentives interfere. Public trust weakens. Progress stalls. That reality deserves honesty too. Recognition matters because it begins the conversation—not because it guarantees the outcome.

Why Good Ideas Take Time

There is another uncomfortable truth about change, sometimes good ideas arrive before institutions are prepared to act on them. That reality appears repeatedly throughout history. Not because ideas lacked merit. And not because problems were invisible.

Often, the conditions simply were not ready. Public understanding had not matured. Trust had not formed. Institutions had not adapted. The cost of maintaining the current path still felt manageable. That timing matters. Because people often imagine change happening the moment a better solution appears.

Reality tends to work differently. Most meaningful change follows a recognizable pattern: First, people experience friction, then frustration grows, then conversations emerge, then resistance appears, then skepticism, then debate, then gradual recognition.

Only later do institutions begin responding. Usually after enough people quietly conclude: *Continuing the current path feels harder than trying something different.* That process can take years. Sometimes decades. Again, not because people are unintelligent. Because systems are complicated. Trust takes time. Shared understanding takes time. Evidence takes time. And uncertainty naturally slows decision-making.

This is important because one of the easiest ways to become discouraged is expecting immediate change. Especially around large systems. People often imagine a good idea should produce obvious momentum. Quick agreement. Immediate political action. Clear institutional support. But large systems rarely move that way. Healthy skepticism slows movement. Competing interests slow movement. Fear slows movement. Complexity slows movement. That is frustrating. But also understandable.

Imagine introducing a major operational improvement inside a large company. Even if leadership recognizes the benefit immediately, implementation still takes time. People need understanding. Processes need redesign. Concerns need addressing. Resistance appears. Unexpected problems emerge. Trust must develop.

Large-scale change rarely happens simply because an idea sounds compelling in a meeting. Economies are no different. This matters because one of the greatest mistakes reform efforts make is assuming resistance automatically proves failure. Sometimes resistance reflects weakness. But sometimes resistance simply reflects scale. The larger the system, the slower movement often becomes. That does not make change impossible. It makes patience necessary.

At the same time, patience should not become complacency. Because delay carries costs too. Drift continues while debate unfolds. Fragility compounds. Participation weakens. Trust erodes. People adapt to conditions that quietly become harder to sustain.

That tension matters. Move too quickly and systems destabilize. Move too slowly and drift deepens. Healthy societies eventually learn to navigate between those risks. That process rarely feels satisfying in real time. Because meaningful change often feels slower than frustration. And frustration usually arrives before institutions respond.

This may be one reason ideas matter even before implementation. Conversations matter. Shared language matters. Recognition matters. People rarely support what they do not understand. And institutions rarely move toward ideas society has not yet learned how to discuss constructively.

That may ultimately be one reason conversations like this matter. Not certainty. Not immediate solutions. Not ideological persuasion. Something simpler - helping people ask better questions. Creating language for experiences many already feel. Making patterns easier to recognize. And helping conversations mature enough that healthier possibilities eventually become easier to imagine.

Because societies are rarely changed the moment better ideas appear. More often, they change when enough people become ready to hear them. And readiness rarely happens all at once.

Why Suspicion Is Easier Than Participation

There is a reason frustration often turns into sarcasm. Suspicion feels safer. That may sound uncomfortable. But it deserves attention. Because when systems feel increasingly difficult to trust, many people eventually reach a familiar conclusion: *Nothing will change. The system is too broken. Too many interests benefit from the current arrangement. Nothing meaningful ever improves.*

At first glance, that reaction feels understandable. Sometimes even rational. People grow tired. Promises disappoint. Institutions lose credibility. Political conflict becomes exhausting. Economic pressure accumulates. Trust weakens and people adapt, again, and again.

Eventually, hope itself begins feeling risky. This matters because participation requires vulnerability. People invest effort when they believe effort matters. People build when they believe stability is possible. Businesses invest when planning feels rational. Communities strengthen when trust still feels worthwhile.

But when people become more cynical, something subtle begins happening, people stop participating emotionally long before they stop participating practically. They still work. Still pay bills. Still manage responsibilities. Still adapt. But belief weakens. Long-term thinking shrinks. Expectations narrow. The future starts feeling like something to endure rather than something to shape.

That change matters more than it may initially appear. Because healthy systems ultimately depend on something difficult to measure, belief. Not blind optimism. Not naïve confidence. Something more practical. The belief that effort still connects to outcomes. That participation still matters. That institutions remain capable of improvement. That tomorrow can become more stable than today.

Without some version of that belief, people become reactive. Short-term thinking grows. Trust weakens. Participation becomes transactional. Communities fragment. Suspicion spreads. And suspicion is persuasive. Because unlike hope, suspicion rarely risks disappointment.

If people assume improvement is impossible, expectations disappear. Disappointment shrinks. But so does participation. That tradeoff deserves attention. Because suspicion often feels intellectually sophisticated, realistic, and protective. People sometimes mistake pessimism for wisdom. As though expecting less somehow prevents harm.

Occasionally, skepticism protects people. Healthy skepticism matters. But suspicion is different. Skepticism asks questions. Suspicion assumes answers. Skepticism pressure-tests ideas.

Suspicion dismisses possibility before the conversation fully begins. That matters enormously. Especially in large systems. Because societies rarely improve when enough people stop believing improvement remains possible. History repeatedly demonstrates something important. That healthy systems do evolve. Sometimes slowly, sometimes unevenly, sometimes imperfectly, but they evolve because enough people remain willing to ask difficult questions while still believing improvement is worth attempting. That balance matters.

Of course, suspicion sometimes emerges for understandable reasons. Institutions occasionally fail trust. Public promises sometimes disappoint. Poor leadership exists. Systems sometimes create justified frustration. The challenge is not eliminating distrust entirely. It is avoiding the assumption that disappointment automatically makes improvement impossible.

Blind optimism creates fragility. Permanent suspicion creates stagnation. Healthy societies require something harder, clear-eyed realism without surrender. Acknowledging problems without assuming collapse. Recognizing drift without assuming decline is inevitable. Holding skepticism without abandoning participation. That is difficult. Especially during periods of instability. But difficulty does not make it less necessary. Because perhaps one of drift's greatest successes is not instability itself. It is convincing people instability is permanent. That effort no longer matters. That institutions cannot improve. That participation no longer deserves belief.

Once enough people accept those assumptions, meaningful change becomes dramatically harder. Not because better ideas disappeared. Because hope quietly did. That may ultimately be one reason conversations like this matter. Not because books alone change systems. They rarely do. But because healthier futures rarely emerge from populations convinced improvement is impossible.

They emerge when enough people become willing to hold two ideas at the same time - reality deserves honesty and improvement still deserves effort. Because suspicion may feel safer. But participation has always been what moves societies forward.

When Drift Gets Too Expensive to Ignore

There is a pattern large systems tend to follow. People tolerate drift longer than they expect. Longer than outsiders often understand. Longer than frustration alone would seem to justify.

That reality deserves attention. Because one of the most common questions people ask during periods of growing instability is simple: *If so many people feel pressure, why doesn't meaningful change happen sooner?*

The answer is uncomfortable. Because systems usually do not change when problems first appear. They change when the cost of maintaining current conditions begins feeling harder than the uncertainty of trying something different.

At first, drift feels manageable. People adapt. Businesses adjust. Communities compensate. Families delay plans. Workers absorb pressure. Institutions continue functioning. Again, rarely catastrophic. Often survivable. Which makes action easier to postpone. People tell themselves: *Things will improve. Maybe this is temporary. Maybe next year feels better.* And sometimes that instinct proves right.

Healthy systems naturally experience cycles. Pressure comes and goes. Corrections happen. Recovery happens. Not every difficult period signals structural decline. That should be stated clearly. But there is another pattern worth recognizing. Sometimes temporary adaptation quietly becomes permanent accommodation. People normalize conditions that once would have felt unacceptable. Housing instability. Financial fragility. Shrinking purchasing power. Institutional distrust. Shorter planning windows. Greater anxiety surrounding ordinary life. Again, not dramatic but gradual, quiet. Easy to rationalize.

Until eventually, something changes. Not necessarily anger. Recognition. Enough people quietly arriving at the same conclusion: *This no longer feels sustainable.* That moment matters because meaningful change rarely begins with perfect agreement. It begins when enough people recognize maintenance can no longer wait.

Businesses understand this instinctively. A struggling process gets tolerated until operational costs become too expensive. An aging system remains untouched until maintenance delays become riskier than replacement. A weakening culture gets ignored until turnover becomes impossible to dismiss. Then priorities shift. Not because leaders suddenly became wiser. Because pressure became clearer.

Economies are no different. Societies rarely change at the first sign of discomfort. They change when drift becomes visible enough that preserving the current path feels increasingly expensive. Financially, socially, emotionally, and institutionally.

That does not guarantee good decisions. Or perfect outcomes. Fear can distort responses. Politics can distort responses. Frustration can create poor solutions. That risk deserves honesty too. But ignoring pressure rarely eliminates it. And postponing maintenance rarely lowers eventual costs.

That may be one of the hardest truths about drift. The longer systems wait to confront it, the narrower options often become. That does not mean urgency should replace thoughtfulness. Quite the opposite. It means healthy societies become strongest when they recognize maintenance before crisis forces it. Because meaningful change works best when chosen, not when desperation leaves no alternative.

And perhaps that is the deeper question quietly sitting beneath this entire chapter: *How much drift does a society tolerate before maintenance finally feels necessary?*

Because eventually, every system answers that question. The only uncertainty is whether recognition arrives early enough that correction still feels like a choice instead of an emergency.

What Meaningful Change Actually Requires

The next logical question is what does meaningful change actually require? Because we have now established:

- systems drift
- people adapt

- institutions resist maintenance
- suspicion replaces participation
- change happens late

By this point, an important realization should be emerging, meaningful change is harder than frustration makes it seem. That may sound obvious. But it matters. Because people often assume problems alone create momentum. That once enough pressure exists, change naturally follows.

Reality tends to be more complicated. Pressure matters. Frustration matters. Recognition matters. But on their own, they are rarely enough. Because meaningful change requires more than dissatisfaction. It requires direction.

People can agree that something feels wrong while strongly disagreeing on what should happen next. Businesses experience this constantly. A struggling company may recognize performance is slipping. Employees feel pressure. Customers notice problems. Leadership sees warning signs. But recognizing the problem does not automatically solve it. The harder work begins afterward. Diagnosis, prioritization, trust, execution, and finally alignment. The willingness to endure temporary discomfort in service of long-term improvement.

Economies are no different. Societies rarely improve because frustration alone becomes loud enough. They improve when enough people begin sharing something more difficult, a workable understanding of what healthier participation could realistically look like. That process takes time. Language matters. Shared understanding matters. Trust matters.

And trust is difficult. Especially during periods where institutions already feel strained. People reasonably ask: *Can this actually work? Who benefits? What gets disrupted? What are the tradeoffs? Who pays the cost of transition?* Those questions deserve serious answers. Not slogans. Not promises. And not simplistic certainty. Healthy systems improve through realism. Not wishful thinking.

That nuance matters because many conversations about change fail for predictable reasons. Some focus only on problems. Others offer solutions disconnected from operational reality. Some promise too much. Others underestimate resistance. And many assume trust exists where trust has already weakened. That makes people cautious. Again, often reasonably.

Which means meaningful change usually requires several difficult things happening at once. Recognition - enough people seeing similar patterns. Credibility - enough trust that conversations feel serious rather than ideological. Practicality - ideas grounded enough to survive real-world complexity. Patience - enough persistence to survive slow movement. And participation - because systems rarely improve through observation alone.

That may be one of the most uncomfortable truths in this conversation, healthy systems are not spectator projects. People often wish someone else will solve difficult problems. A better politician. A better CEO. A better institution. A better generation. Occasionally leadership matters enormously. But durable improvement almost always requires broader participation from workers, families, business owners, communities, institutions, leaders, citizens, and people willing to engage imperfectly instead of withdrawing completely.

That does not mean agreement becomes universal. It never does. Healthy systems still contain disagreement. Tradeoffs remain. Competing interests remain. But progress becomes possible when enough people begin moving from: *Everything is broken.* to: *What actually improves participation, resilience, and long-term stability?* That is a different question. A harder question. But usually a more productive one.

Because meaningful change rarely begins when frustration peaks. It begins when enough people become willing to trade certainty for seriousness. Blame for maintenance. And resignation for participation. That process rarely feels dramatic. Usually, it feels slower than people want. Messier than people expect. And more imperfect than anyone prefers. But meaningful change rarely arrives fully formed. More often, it emerges through enough people deciding drift no longer deserves passive acceptance and improvement deserves honest effort instead.

Why Waiting Is Still a Decision

One of the more uncomfortable truths about large systems is this, "waiting is still a decision." Even when it does not feel like one. Because conversations about change often frame choices too narrowly. Either: *We change.* or: *We stay the same.*

Reality rarely works that way. Systems never truly stand still. Economies evolve. Communities evolve. Institutions evolve. Markets evolve. Technology changes. Incentives shift. Participation changes. Trust changes. Pressure accumulates. Even without intentional action, systems continue moving.

The real question is usually: *Moving toward what?* That matters because periods of uncertainty often create a powerful temptation, delay. Wait another year. Wait for better conditions. Wait for clearer evidence. Wait for stronger leadership. Wait for greater agreement. Wait until the problem becomes easier to solve.

Sometimes patience is wise. Healthy systems should avoid reckless overreaction. Every period of pressure does not require dramatic intervention. That deserves recognition. But there is another reality worth acknowledging, problems rarely become easier simply because people postpone confronting them.

In some circumstances, slower movement prevents mistakes. Institutions occasionally benefit from caution. Better evidence emerges. Tradeoffs become clearer. Weak assumptions get corrected. Serious systems require enough humility to recognize when timing improves outcomes and when delay quietly compounds cost.

Businesses understand this instinctively. Deferred maintenance grows expensive. Ignored turnover becomes cultural instability. Short-term fixes accumulate hidden costs. Operational weaknesses compound quietly. At first, postponement feels practical. Later, it often feels expensive.

Economies behave similarly. Weakening participation compounds. Distrust compounds. Fragility compounds. Shorter planning windows compound. Financial pressure compounds. Again, usually slowly, quietly, and incrementally.

That is what makes drift dangerous. Rarely dramatic enough to demand immediate attention, but often meaningful enough to quietly reshape expectations. People begin adjusting to conditions that once felt temporary. Businesses normalize shorter planning. Families normalize instability. Communities normalize fragility.

Eventually, adaptation starts resembling acceptance. Because waiting often feels neutral, safe, or even responsible. But waiting carries assumptions too. It assumes current trajectories remain manageable. It assumes present incentives will naturally correct themselves. It assumes fragility will not deepen faster than resilience. Sometimes those assumptions prove correct. Sometimes systems recover naturally. Healthy cycles exist. Pressure eases. Adaptation works. That possibility deserves honesty. But healthy systems also require another kind of honesty, avoiding difficult decisions does not eliminate consequences. And postponing maintenance rarely prevents eventual costs.

That does not mean urgency should replace thoughtfulness. Quite the opposite. Healthy systems require seriousness. Patience where patience helps. Action where maintenance becomes necessary. Humility where uncertainty exists. But one thing should feel increasingly clear by now, that drift does not pause while people debate whether maintenance feels inconvenient. Time continues. Incentives continue. Pressure continues. Adaptation continues. That may ultimately be one of the hardest truths about large systems - eventually, societies still make a choice, even when they believe they are avoiding one. Because preserving current trajectories is still a decision. And every decision quietly shapes the future people eventually inherit.

Which raises a harder question: *What happens if drift continues long enough that today's pressures simply become tomorrow's normal?*

None of this guarantees agreement. Or success. Or immediate momentum. Serious systems remain complicated. Tradeoffs remain real. Resistance remains normal. But once enough people begin recognizing similar patterns, a different kind of question quietly emerges—not whether change feels difficult, but whether maintaining drift feels increasingly difficult too.

And that is where we turn next.

Chapter 14 – How Change Actually Happens

By now, an uncomfortable reality should feel increasingly clear, meaningful change is difficult. Not because people are incapable. Not because institutions are universally broken. And not because good ideas never exist. Change is difficult because systems develop gravity. Habits form. Incentives reinforce themselves.

Institutions stabilize around what already exists. People adapt. Businesses adapt. Governments adapt. Entire societies gradually organize themselves around assumptions that once may have been temporary, but eventually begin feeling permanent.

None of this guarantees improvement. Some systems resist maintenance far longer than expected. Some periods of pressure deepen without producing meaningful reform. Some societies normalize drift rather than confronting it. That possibility deserves honesty too. The point is not inevitability. It is understanding the conditions under which healthier change becomes more possible—and the reasons it so often arrives later than people hope.

That reality matters. Because one of the easiest mistakes people make when thinking about large systems is assuming meaningful change happens suddenly. A new law. A new leader. A new movement. A breakthrough idea. And overnight, everything shifts. History rarely works that way.

More often, meaningful change happens slowly. Awareness grows. Pressure accumulates. Frustration becomes shared. Language develops. New ideas emerge. Old assumptions begin weakening. Recognition spreads. Then, gradually, institutions begin moving. Sometimes reluctantly. Sometimes imperfectly. But eventually. That process can feel frustrating. Especially for people experiencing pressure directly. Because when instability feels personal, patience often feels expensive.

Recognition should also not be confused with agreement. Shared pressure often increases debate before consensus. Different explanations compete. Priorities conflict. Ideologies sharpen. Institutions hesitate. Progress stalls and resumes unevenly. That complexity deserves honesty because serious systems rarely move forward cleanly. Recognition matters because it creates room for better questions—not because it automatically resolves disagreement.

And yet large systems rarely improve through force alone. They improve through trust. Shared understanding. Practicality. Enough confidence that change begins feeling less dangerous than drift.

This matters because healthy systems are rarely built through destruction. More often, they emerge through maintenance. Through adaptation. Through recognizing what still works, preserving it, and improving what no longer does. That is especially true in economies. No serious person rebuilds an airplane while it is flying. No responsible leader intentionally destabilizes the systems millions of people depend on.

That is precisely why responsible transitions are built in stages. Complex systems are not replaced all at once. They are measured, tested, reviewed, and implemented through deliberate phases designed to preserve continuity while exposing weaknesses before they become failures.

The Alignment Economy follows the same principle. New mechanisms are introduced gradually, tested against real-world conditions, coordinated across institutions, and evaluated before broader obligations change. Parallel operation, independent review, administrative coordination, and continuity protections exist for the same reason engineers test critical systems before relying upon them: stability is easier to preserve than it is to restore after disruption.

The objective is not speed. The objective is confidence. Large-scale change becomes possible when implementation is structured, transparent, and capable of demonstrating that it works before people are asked to depend upon it.

Meaningful change, if it happens, must account for reality. Mortgages still exist. Businesses still operate. Paychecks still matter. Markets still function. People still need stability while systems evolve. That may be one reason conversations about change often feel so unsatisfying. People tend to imagine only extremes: *Tear everything down.* or: *Leave everything exactly as it is.*

Reality usually lives somewhere harder. Between disruption and denial. Between complacency and revolution. Between preserving what works and repairing what no longer does. That middle ground is rarely exciting. But it is often where durable change actually happens. Which raises an important question: *If meaningful change rarely happens all at once... how does it begin?*

That is where we turn next.

Change Begins Before Policy

Most people imagine change beginning with policy - a bill, a law, an election, a speech, maybe a new administration suddenly deciding to move in a different direction. Occasionally, history remembers moments that way.

Reality is usually quieter. Because meaningful change almost never begins with policy. Policy tends to formalize change after something deeper has already shifted. How people think. How people talk. What people notice. What people tolerate. What people no longer believe should remain normal.

That distinction deserves precision. Policy still matters enormously. Large systems require laws, institutions, accountability, administration, and public legitimacy. The point is sequencing. Durable policy tends to scale relationships people increasingly recognize as workable rather than creating trust through declaration alone. Evidence builds confidence. Confidence expands participation. Policy helps stabilize what society increasingly recognizes as worth preserving.

This matters because one of the easiest mistakes societies make is assuming institutions create movements entirely on their own. Most of the time, institutions respond to pressures already building beneath the surface. Workers feeling strain. Businesses experiencing friction. Families quietly adapting. Communities recognizing instability. People beginning to notice patterns that once felt isolated. Again, this rarely happens all at once. More often, it begins quietly. A growing sense that something feels harder than it should. A realization that effort no longer produces the same confidence it once did.

Questions people once dismissed slowly becoming harder to ignore. At first, those concerns often remain private. Personal. People assume: *Maybe it is just me. Maybe costs simply rose. Maybe expectations changed. Maybe everyone else somehow figured out something they did not.* But eventually recognition becomes shared. Conversations begin. Patterns emerge. People realize: *This feels familiar to other people too.*

That moment matters because change rarely begins with certainty. It usually begins with recognition. Enough people quietly noticing the same tension. Enough people becoming willing to ask better questions. Not: *Who failed?* but: *What incentives created these outcomes?* Not: *Who should we blame?* but: *What structure would better support participation, stability, and long-term resilience?*

Those questions matter because healthier systems rarely emerge from outrage alone. Outrage can attract attention. Frustration can create urgency. But durable change usually requires something harder, shared understanding. Enough trust that people become willing to examine assumptions they once accepted automatically. Enough confidence that better possibilities feel worth discussing seriously.

That process takes time. Especially in large systems. Businesses understand this instinctively.

Before major transformation happens, organizations first recognize a problem. People discuss it. Data confirms it. Language develops around it. Trust forms. Then strategy emerges. Only afterward does implementation begin.

Economies are no different. Which means if healthier systems ever become possible, change will likely begin long before policy appears. It begins when enough people become willing to ask difficult questions seriously. When enough people stop mistaking adaptation for health. When enough people decide drift deserves attention before crisis forces it. That may feel slower than frustration prefers. But healthy systems are rarely built overnight. They are built when recognition becomes strong enough that maintenance finally feels necessary. And recognition almost always arrives before reform does.

Change Requires Trust Before Agreement

One of the more difficult truths about meaningful change is that people rarely agree first. That may sound obvious. But it matters. Because one of the easiest ways to become discouraged about large systems is assuming progress requires universal consensus. History rarely works that way. People disagree. Sometimes deeply. About priorities, tradeoffs, timing, risk, responsibility, and what improvement should even look like.

Economies are especially difficult because they touch nearly every part of life including work, business, housing, retirement, healthcare, education, opportunity, risk, and stability. People experience the same system differently. Which means disagreement should be expected. Not feared.

That matters because meaningful change rarely begins when everyone suddenly agrees. Usually, it begins when enough people become willing to agree on something smaller: *The current trajectory deserves serious attention.* That is a different threshold. And a more realistic one. People may disagree about causes. Disagree about solutions. Disagree about timing. Yet still recognize: *Something feels increasingly difficult to ignore.*

That recognition creates room for conversation. And conversation matters because trust almost always arrives before agreement. People rarely support ideas they do not trust. Especially during periods of uncertainty. Trust does not require certainty. But it does require seriousness, honesty, willingness to confront difficult questions, and a humility about tradeoffs.

Trust also develops unevenly. Some communities remain skeptical longer. Some industries adapt more quickly. Different generations, businesses, and institutions may respond differently to similar pressures. Trust grows through repeated experience, not singular persuasion. Setbacks happen. Confidence weakens and rebuilds. That unevenness should be expected rather than mistaken for failure

That matters because trust has weakened in many institutions like governments, markets, media, corporations, and expert systems. For many people, skepticism no longer feels exceptional. It feels rational. That reality should not be dismissed.

Healthy systems should expect scrutiny. Earn confidence. Survive difficult questions. Not demand automatic belief. Which means if healthier systems ever emerge, trust will likely matter more than persuasion. Not: *How do we convince everyone?* but: *How do we build enough confidence that people remain willing to participate in difficult conversations?*

That distinction changes things because people rarely trust perfection. Perfection sounds artificial. People tend to trust honesty. Acknowledged tradeoffs. Clear limitations. Good-faith effort. The willingness to say: *Here is what works. Here is what does not. Here is what still needs refinement.*

Businesses understand this instinctively. Strong leadership does not emerge because every employee agrees. It emerges because enough trust exists that people remain willing to move together despite uncertainty.

Healthy societies often work similarly. Trust creates room for disagreement without collapse. Room for experimentation without panic. Room for improvement without assuming disruption automatically means danger. That does not make change easy. And it certainly does not remove conflict. But it makes movement possible. Because meaningful change rarely begins with agreement. More often, it begins with enough trust that people become willing to stay in the conversation long enough for better ideas to mature.

And perhaps that matters more than certainty ever could.

Change Becomes Real When Participation Feels Possible

There is another difficult truth about meaningful change, that people rarely move toward systems they believe they cannot realistically participate in. That matters because one of the easiest mistakes conversations about change make is assuming people resist improvement simply because they dislike new ideas.

Possible should not be confused with automatic. Many people remain cautious after long periods of instability. Financial pressure narrows imagination. Disappointment weakens trust. Survival habits take time to unwind. Participation often returns gradually, unevenly, and imperfectly. The important shift is smaller, but meaningful: people slowly begin believing effort may once again produce outcomes worth investing in.

Often, resistance is more practical than that. People are busy, tired, financially stretched, and focused on responsibilities directly in front of them like mortgages, rent, children, healthcare, work, and debt. Survival leaves limited room for abstraction. That reality deserves respect. Especially because many people experiencing the greatest pressure are often the same people with the least flexibility to absorb uncertainty.

Which means meaningful change cannot depend entirely on idealism. Or outrage. Or hope alone. Healthy systems become possible when participation itself begins feeling realistic. People participate when effort feels connected to outcomes. Workers invest in themselves when advancement feels achievable. Businesses invest when planning feels stable enough to justify risk. Communities strengthen when trust begins feeling worthwhile again.

People engage when participation feels capable of producing something durable. Without that connection, withdrawal becomes rational. Not because people stop caring. Because survival changes priorities. Short-term thinking expands. Risk feels dangerous. Planning shrinks. Trust becomes harder to sustain. People adapt quietly, often without realizing how much survival has narrowed what feels possible. Until eventually many stop asking: *How do I simply get through this?*

That shift matters more than it may initially appear. Because healthy societies ultimately depend on participation. Not perfect participation. And not universal agreement. Something simpler, those people who remain unwilling to invest effort into the future. Into work. Into business. Into family. Into communities. Into institutions. Into each other. That investment becomes difficult when too many people quietly conclude: *The effort no longer feels worth the risk.*

This may be one reason systems drift longer than they should. People experiencing the greatest strain are often too busy adapting to imagine alternatives. Meanwhile, people with more stability may not fully experience the pressures building underneath the surface. The result is distance, misunderstanding, frustration, and eventually suspicion. That pattern matters because meaningful change often becomes possible only when enough people begin believing participation could realistically matter again. Not perfectly. Not immediately. But meaningfully.

Enough confidence that effort feels worth reinvesting. Enough trust that planning feels rational. Enough stability that risk begins feeling productive instead of dangerous. Businesses understand this instinctively. People commit to difficult transformations when success feels difficult, but still possible.

Economies are no different. Which means healthier systems likely begin not when everyone suddenly agrees, but when enough people begin believing improvement no longer feels impossible. Because participation rarely grows from certainty. More often, it grows from possibility. And possibility tends to expand only when people can realistically imagine themselves inside the future being discussed.

Change Requires Something to Move Toward

There is a reason frustration alone rarely creates durable change. Frustration can attract attention. It can create urgency. Sometimes it can even force difficult conversations. But frustration, by itself, rarely builds anything. Because one of the easiest mistakes societies make during periods of pressure is assuming dissatisfaction automatically creates direction. History rarely works that way. People can agree something feels increasingly difficult while strongly disagreeing about what should happen next.

Businesses understand this instinctively. Recognizing a problem does not automatically create a solution. A struggling company may acknowledge declining performance. Employees feel strain. Customers notice friction. Leadership recognizes warning signs. Yet confusion still remains: *What exactly are we trying to build instead?* That question matters because uncertainty creates hesitation. Especially when people already feel exposed.

The same dynamic appears in larger systems. People experiencing instability often recognize pressure long before they trust alternatives. And understandably so. Most people do not want disruption for its own sake. They want stability. Predictability. A future that feels possible enough to plan toward.

That means meaningful change requires more than criticism. It requires direction. Not perfection. Not certainty. Something simpler, a future people can realistically imagine themselves inside. That may ultimately be one reason some ideas struggle even when frustration is widespread. People rarely move toward abstraction. They move toward something they can picture. Something that feels practical enough to believe in. Work that feels worthwhile. Businesses stable enough to plan. Communities capable of growing again. Risk that feels productive instead of dangerous. Effort that feels connected to outcomes. Participation that feels capable of producing something more durable than survival.

That vision matters. Not because it guarantees agreement. And not because everyone imagines the future the same way. Healthy societies still contain disagreement. Tradeoffs remain. Different priorities remain. But movement becomes easier when enough people begin asking: *Could something healthier realistically exist?* That question matters more than it may initially appear because possibility changes behavior. People plan differently when tomorrow feels buildable. Businesses invest differently when stability feels more predictable. Communities strengthen when confidence begins returning. Participation expands when effort feels worth reinvesting.

Without some version of that belief, frustration often collapses inward. People disengage, withdraw, adapt, lower expectations, and eventually stop imagining improvement altogether. That is often where drift becomes most dangerous. Not when people become angry. When they stop believing anything better is possible.

This may be one reason meaningful change often depends on imagination as much as policy. Not fantasy. Not idealism. Practical imagination. The ability to picture something imperfect, but healthier. Something difficult, but achievable. Something realistic enough that participation begins feeling worthwhile again. Because healthy systems rarely emerge from dissatisfaction alone. They emerge when enough people begin moving toward something they believe might actually hold. And belief, however imperfect, often begins before certainty ever arrives.

Change Must Feel Safe Enough to Try

There is a reason that large systems often resist change even when pressure becomes difficult to ignore. People fear making things worse. That fear deserves respect. Because most people are not experiencing the economy as theory. They are experiencing it through responsibilities. Through their mortgages, their rent. With their children or in their businesses. They worry about their healthcare, their retirement, or debt. They remained concerned about ordinary life. And ordinary life leaves limited room for unnecessary risk.

That reality matters. Especially because one of the easiest mistakes conversations about change make is assuming resistance automatically reflects selfishness, ignorance, or fear of improvement. Often, resistance reflects something simpler: People cannot afford instability. Not emotionally. Not financially. And certainly not when the systems surrounding them already feel fragile.

That concern becomes even more understandable when large institutions are involved. Governments make mistakes. Markets make mistakes. Businesses make mistakes. Policies sometimes create consequences no one intended. People know this. Which means skepticism toward change is not only understandable, it is often rational.

That matters because meaningful change rarely becomes possible when people believe they are being asked to gamble everything they depend on. Healthy systems understand this instinctively. Strong businesses do not transform by abandoning everything overnight. Hospitals do not redesign critical systems without safeguards. Engineers do not remove structural supports before testing alternatives. Responsible leaders preserve continuity while improvement takes shape. Economies deserve similar seriousness.

That does not mean avoiding change indefinitely. It means recognizing that healthy change often succeeds when people feel protected enough to participate in it. Businesses still need continuity. Workers still need income. Families still need predictability. Communities still need stability.

The future cannot require people to sacrifice survival in order to believe in improvement. That is one reason meaningful change often happens incrementally. Not because urgency lacks importance. But because trust grows when people see evidence. Small improvements. Predictable outcomes. Demonstrated stability. Proof that disruption is not the objective. Maintenance is. This matters because conversations about reform often collapse into extremes. Either: *Change everything immediately*. or: *Change nothing at all.*

Reality usually lives somewhere harder. Safer, more practical. Improvement that preserves stability while reducing fragility. Progress that allows participation instead of demanding sacrifice. Systems that evolve without forcing unnecessary chaos onto the people already carrying enough uncertainty. That approach may feel slower than frustration prefers. But durable change usually does. Because healthy systems are not strengthened by forcing people into fear. They improve when enough people begin believing: *Maybe improvement no longer feels more dangerous than staying where we are.*

Even then, uncertainty remains. Tradeoffs remain. Mistakes remain possible. Serious transitions still create friction. Some efforts fail. Some unintended consequences emerge. The relevant question is not whether risk disappears. It is whether maintaining current trajectories increasingly begins feeling riskier than thoughtful improvement.

That may ultimately be one of the quiet thresholds where meaningful change becomes possible. Not certainty. Not perfection. Just enough confidence that trying begins feeling safer than drifting.

Change Rarely Comes from One Place

One of the easiest mistakes people make when thinking about meaningful change is assuming it arrives from a single source. Either from a president, a law, a movement, a company, or a generation. One moment where everything suddenly shifts. History occasionally remembers change that way.

History also deserves humility. Some societies improve substantially. Others repeat mistakes. Some reforms strengthen resilience. Others create unintended consequences. Progress rarely follows a straight line. That complexity matters because meaningful change deserves seriousness rather than certainty.

Reality is usually more complicated. Because meaningful change rarely comes from one place. More often, it emerges through accumulation. Through conversations and pressure and leadership. From institutions, communities and businesses. By people making decisions differently long before history recognizes something larger has shifted.

That matters because one of the easiest ways to feel powerless is assuming improvement depends entirely on someone else acting first. A better politician. A stronger institution. A more responsible corporation. A different generation.

Occasionally leadership matters enormously. But healthy systems rarely improve through leadership alone. They improve when participation expands. Businesses adapt. Communities organize. Workers ask better questions. Leaders respond. Institutions slowly evolve. Pressure builds from multiple directions at once. That process matters because even strong ideas struggle when people feel excluded from them. Change rarely lasts when it feels imposed. People support difficult transitions when they understand them, trust them, and can realistically imagine themselves participating in them.

Businesses understand this instinctively. Successful transformation rarely happens because one executive gives a speech. Culture changes when expectations change. When incentives change. When trust develops. When people throughout the organization begin moving in similar directions.

Large systems work similarly. Meaningful change tends to happen when enough parts of a system begin recognizing the same pressure at the same time. Workers recognizing instability. Business leaders recognizing unsustainable strain. Communities recognizing growing fragility. Policymakers recognizing rising distrust. Institutions recognizing maintenance can no longer wait. Rarely perfect alignment. Rarely unanimous agreement. But enough recognition that momentum begins forming.

Momentum rarely moves cleanly forward. Progress pauses. Resistance returns. Political incentives shift. Economic conditions change. Coalitions weaken. Public trust fluctuates. Some periods advance quickly while others stall unexpectedly. That reality deserves honesty because durability matters more than speed.

That process may feel messier than people prefer. Slower than frustration wants. And more imperfect than anyone imagines. But perhaps that is exactly what makes durable change possible. Because healthy systems rarely improve through force alone. Or ideology alone. Or outrage alone. They improve when enough people across enough parts of society begin asking similar questions: *What still works? What no longer does? What deserves preservation? What deserves maintenance?*

That matters because one of the most damaging assumptions people carry is this: *Nothing changes unless someone powerful decides to change it*. Power matters. Leadership matters. Institutions matter. But large systems rarely move without participation beneath them. That participation may look ordinary. Small conversations. New expectations. Different assumptions. Businesses adapting differently. Communities rebuilding trust. People becoming willing to imagine alternatives without immediately dismissing them. Rarely dramatic. Often quiet. But meaningful.

This may be one reason change often feels invisible until suddenly it does not. The groundwork usually begins long before outcomes become visible. Long before institutions formally respond. Long before policy catches up. Because healthy systems rarely improve all at once. They improve when enough people across enough places slowly begin moving in the same direction. And meaningful movement rarely begins from one place alone.

Why Change Still Feels Unlikely Until It Doesn't

There is another reality worth acknowledging, meaningful change often feels unlikely right up until the moment it begins happening. That is not idealism. It is pattern recognition. Because one of the easiest things to underestimate while living inside large systems is how permanent the present can feel. Conditions normalize. Institutions stabilize. People adapt.

Even difficult realities begin feeling strangely familiar over time. Which makes alternatives difficult to imagine. That instinct is understandable. Most people are not historians. They are participants. Busy living inside the pressures directly in front of them. Their work, their bills and responsibilities. And their business pressures and family obligations. Survival rarely leaves much time for imagining large structural change. Which means the present often feels more permanent than history suggests it actually is.

Businesses understand this instinctively. A struggling organization can appear impossible to repair until leadership changes. Or incentives change. Or pressure becomes impossible to ignore. Then what once felt immovable begins shifting surprisingly quickly. Not effortlessly. Not perfectly. But noticeably.

Large systems often work similarly. For long periods, change appears distant, unrealistic, even naïve. People assume: *This is simply how things are now.* or: *Nothing meaningful ever changes.* Sometimes frustration deepens into resignation. Sometimes suspicion hardens into withdrawal.

People stop expecting improvement. And that may be one of the quietest dangers drift creates. Not instability itself. But shrinking imagination. The gradual belief that healthier alternatives no longer feel realistic enough to seriously discuss. That matters because societies rarely improve when enough people quietly conclude: *Nothing better is possible.*

At the same time, realism matters. Not every frustration signals transformation. Not every difficult period produces meaningful reform. Some pressures ease naturally. Some systems correct themselves. Some moments pass. That deserves honesty too. But history also suggests something else, conditions people once accepted as permanent often become negotiable once enough pressure, recognition, and participation begin moving together. Rarely overnight. Rarely cleanly. And rarely without disagreement. But eventually.

That may be one reason meaningful change often feels invisible while it is beginning. The earliest stages rarely look dramatic. They look like conversations or questions or recognition. New expectations. People becoming willing to challenge assumptions that once felt untouchable. Trust growing slowly. Participation expanding gradually. Momentum forming quietly. Until eventually what once felt unrealistic begins feeling increasingly reasonable.

And perhaps that is one of the hardest things about living inside periods of drift, the future often looks impossible, right up until people begin building it. That does not guarantee success. And it certainly does not remove uncertainty. But healthy systems have always depended on something difficult to measure; people remaining willing to believe improvement still deserves serious effort. Even before proof fully arrives. Because meaningful change often feels unlikely until suddenly it no longer does.

What Happens Next Depends on Participation

At this point, one thing should feel increasingly clear, meaningful change is difficult. Not because people do not care. And not because better ideas never exist. Change is difficult because large systems are complex. People disagree. Institutions resist movement. Trust takes time. Pressure accumulates unevenly. And ordinary life rarely pauses long enough for large questions to feel urgent.

That reality deserves honesty because one of the easiest mistakes people make when thinking about the future is assuming outcomes arrive automatically. Either: *Things eventually get better.* or: *Things inevitably get worse.* Reality is usually more complicated. Systems respond to incentives. To participation, trust, pressure, and recognition. To the countless small decisions people make about what deserves attention, investment, patience, skepticism, or effort. That matters because drift is not inevitable. But neither is improvement.

Healthy systems rarely sustain themselves automatically. Businesses understand this instinctively. Strong cultures require maintenance. Good leadership requires reinforcement. Trust requires consistency. Performance requires participation. The moment people stop investing in those things, deterioration quietly begins.

Economies are no different. The future rarely arrives fully formed. More often, it emerges through accumulation. One decision. One conversation. One expectation. One business investing. One worker planning further ahead. One community rebuilding trust. One institution becoming willing to question assumptions that no longer seem sustainable. Again, rarely dramatic. Often invisible at first. But meaningful.

That is significant because one of the quiet temptations during difficult periods is withdrawal. People become exhausted. Suspicion grows. Disappointment accumulates. And eventually many begin assuming: *Nothing changes anyway*. That instinct is understandable. But it may also be one of the most expensive assumptions societies can quietly normalize. Because participation matters, even when progress feels slow. Questions matter. Conversations matter. Pressure matters. Good faith matters.

That does not mean every individual carries equal responsibility for structural outcomes. Circumstances differ. Capacity differs. Periods of life differ. Some people are surviving more than participating. That reality deserves compassion. The argument is narrower: healthier systems become more possible when enough people, institutions, and communities remain willing to engage honestly rather than withdraw completely.

The willingness to imagine healthier systems matters. Not because any single person changes everything. But because large systems rarely improve without enough people remaining willing to participate in improvement at all. That does not require perfect optimism. Or blind trust. Healthy skepticism still matters. Difficult questions still matter. Accountability still matters. But perhaps the harder question sitting beneath all of this is simpler: *What happens when enough people stop believing better outcomes are worth trying for?* Because every society eventually answers that question. Quietly, through action, or inaction. Through participation. Or withdrawal. Through maintenance. Or drift.

And perhaps that is where this conversation ultimately leads: not toward certainty, but responsibility. The recognition that healthier systems rarely emerge on their own. They emerge when enough people decide the future still deserves effort—even before outcomes feel guaranteed. Because what happens next has never depended entirely on policy. It has always depended, at least in part, on participation.

None of this guarantees outcomes. Serious systems remain difficult. Trust remains fragile. Tradeoffs remain real. But history repeatedly suggests something worth remembering: healthier futures become more possible when enough people remain willing to ask difficult questions while still believing improvement deserves effort.

Why this Still Matters

At this point, a reasonable question may still remain: *Why does any of this matter so much?* After all, economies change. Pressure comes and goes. History moves in cycles. People adapt. And in many ways, life continues. That is true. But it is only part of the story. Because while systems may feel abstract, their consequences rarely are.

Economic systems eventually become lived experiences. A family deciding whether they can afford another child. A worker postponing retirement. A small business owner delaying hiring. A young adult wondering whether stability still feels realistic. Parents quietly worrying whether their children will have it harder than they did. Communities shrinking. Trust weakening. Planning becoming shorter. Hope becoming more cautious. Again, rarely dramatic.

Often gradual. Quiet enough that people simply adapt. Until eventually adaptation begins feeling normal.

That reality matters because societies are shaped by what people quietly stop expecting. Stable housing. Upward mobility. Predictable opportunity. The belief that effort meaningfully improves life over time. Not perfection. Not guarantees. Something simpler, confidence that participation still feels worthwhile. That confidence matters more than it may initially appear. Because healthy economies are not ultimately sustained by spreadsheets. Or headlines. Or quarterly reports. They are sustained through ordinary people remaining willing to believe the future deserves investment. Workers investing effort. Families investing trust. Businesses investing risk. Communities investing patience. People investing belief that tomorrow can become more stable than today.

When that confidence weakens long enough, systems become harder to sustain. Not because people stop caring. But because survival naturally narrows horizons. Shorter planning. Smaller expectations. Lower trust. Less participation. And eventually, quieter forms of resignation. That may ultimately be one reason conversations like this matter. Not because one book changes systems. Books rarely do. But because meaningful change almost always begins the same way:

People becoming willing to see something differently. To question assumptions that once felt permanent. To recognize patterns that previously felt isolated. To ask whether drift deserves attention before fragility becomes normalized. And perhaps most importantly: To ask whether healthier outcomes still feel worth trying to build. Because behind every economic chart, every policy debate, every headline about inflation, growth, labor, or instability, there are people. Ordinary people. Trying to build ordinary lives. And perhaps that is what makes this conversation worth having. Not because better systems guarantee better outcomes. But because healthier systems increase the possibility that effort, participation, and responsibility once again feel connected to something more durable than survival - a future people can realistically believe in.

Chapter 15 – The Choice

At this point, one thing should feel increasingly clear, this conversation was never really about economics alone. Economics may have been the language. The mechanism. The structure underneath the discussion. But underneath all of that, something more human has always been sitting quietly at the center, how people experience life together. Whether effort still feels connected to stability. Whether responsibility still feels capable of producing security. Whether participation still feels worthwhile. Whether ordinary people can realistically imagine a future that feels more buildable than fragile.

Those questions matter because economies eventually become lived experiences. Not charts. Not headlines. Not political arguments. Lived experiences. A parent deciding whether they can afford another child. A young adult wondering whether stability still feels realistic. A worker postponing retirement. A small business owner delaying hiring. Communities adapting to pressures they never expected to normalize. People quietly lowering expectations, not because they stopped caring, but because caring began feeling expensive.

That reality deserves reflection because one of the easiest mistakes people make when discussing systems is forgetting who systems are ultimately supposed to serve. Growth matters. Markets matter. Innovation matters. Business matters. Competition matters. Success matters.

This book has argued that repeatedly for a reason. Healthy societies require those things. But eventually another question emerges: *What are healthy systems supposed to produce?* Not perfection. Not equal outcomes. Not lives free from hardship. Something more practical. A society where effort still feels meaningful. Where participation still feels worthwhile. Where stability feels achievable often enough that people remain willing to plan, risk, build, invest, and hope.

None of this should be mistaken for simplicity. Healthy systems remain difficult. Tradeoffs remain unavoidable. Good intentions still fail sometimes. Institutions still make mistakes. Markets still misprice risk. Businesses still struggle. Families still experience hardship. The argument throughout this book has never been that difficulty disappears. Only that healthy systems should make participation feel more capable of producing durable outcomes than fragility.

That may sound simple. It is not. Healthy systems are difficult, messy, and imperfect. They require maintenance, adjustment, and humility. The willingness to confront drift before instability quietly becomes normal. And perhaps that is where this conversation has always been leading. Not toward certainty. Not toward ideology. Not toward a single perfect answer. Something harder. Responsibility.

No system remains permanently solved. Conditions evolve. Incentives shift. Technologies reshape work. Demographics change. New pressures emerge. Healthy systems survive not because they become perfect, but because they remain willing to adapt honestly as reality changes around them.

The recognition that large systems do not become healthier automatically. They improve when enough people remain willing to ask difficult questions seriously. When enough people remain willing to participate. When enough people remain willing to believe better outcomes still deserve effort, even when guarantees do not exist. Because ultimately, every generation inherits systems it did not fully build. And every generation leaves something behind.

The harder question is whether we leave behind systems stronger than the ones we inherited or simply ask the next generation to adapt to the drift we chose not to confront. That question matters because the future, however distant it feels, has a way of arriving quietly. Often long before people realize they were shaping it. And perhaps that is where we begin.

What Healthy Systems Are Supposed to Do

After long conversations about systems, incentives, productivity, markets, institutions, and drift, it may be worth returning to a simpler question: *What are healthy systems actually supposed to do?* That question matters. Because over time, people can become so focused on managing problems that they quietly stop asking what success was supposed to feel like in the first place. Especially during long periods of adaptation. People adjust. Expectations shift. Pressure becomes familiar. Things once considered temporary begin feeling permanent. And slowly, often without realizing it, people begin measuring success differently. Not: *Can ordinary people build stable lives?* But: *Can people survive what increasingly feels normal?*

This matters because healthy systems were never supposed to eliminate hardship. Life will always contain uncertainty, risk, failure, illness, economic cycles, and unfairness. No serious system promises otherwise. Healthy systems are not measured by perfection. They are measured by function. Whether participation still feels worthwhile.

Whether effort still feels meaningfully connected to outcomes. Whether workers, businesses, families, and communities can realistically imagine stability often enough to plan toward it. Not guaranteed stability. Achievable stability.

That difference matters. Healthy systems create conditions where responsibility remains meaningful. Where hard work still improves odds. Where risk feels productive instead of punishing. Where businesses can grow. Innovation can thrive. Competition can reward execution. And success remains worth pursuing.

This book has argued repeatedly that these things matter because prosperity matters. Growth matters. Business matters. Healthy markets matter. But eventually another truth emerges - healthy systems should translate success into durability. Not perfectly. And not equally. But broadly enough that participation remains worth reinvesting in.

That may ultimately be one of the quiet tensions many people feel today. Growth exists. Innovation exists. Extraordinary success exists. Yet confidence often feels weaker than the numbers suggest it should. Planning feels shorter. Pressure feels heavier. Stability feels harder to trust. Again, not collapse. Something quieter. A growing question about whether systems still feel aligned closely enough to produce what people reasonably believed participation once made possible.

That question deserves seriousness. Not nostalgia. And not resentment. Seriousness. Because every generation eventually faces some version of the same responsibility, to ask whether the systems surrounding them still produce the outcomes they were intended to support. And if not whether maintenance deserves attention before adaptation quietly becomes expectation. That question is rarely easy. But healthy systems have always depended on people remaining willing to ask it honestly. Because before systems can improve, people first have to remember what healthy systems were supposed to make possible at all.

What Happens When People Stop Believing

One of the quieter risks facing any society is not disagreement. Healthy societies have always contained disagreement. Different priorities. Different beliefs. Different visions of what improvement should look like. That part is normal. The deeper risk appears when enough people begin quietly losing confidence that participation still matters.

Disagreement itself is not failure. Healthy societies argue. Compete. Reconsider priorities. Debate tradeoffs. Test assumptions. Different communities value different outcomes. Different generations see risk differently. The objective is not uniformity. It is preserving enough trust that disagreement remains productive rather than corrosive.

This matters, because societies are held together through more than laws. Or markets. Or institutions. They are also held together through belief. The belief that effort matters. That responsibility improves outcomes. That participation still feels worthwhile. That tomorrow can realistically become more stable than today. Not guaranteed. But possible. That belief matters more than it may initially appear. Because when people trust systems—even imperfect systems—they tend to invest in the future. Workers pursue skills. Families plan further ahead. Businesses invest. Communities strengthen. People remain willing to tolerate setbacks because progress still feels believable. Again, not perfect systems. Trusted enough systems.

But when confidence weakens long enough, behavior changes. Quietly, gradually, people stop planning as far ahead. Risk feels less worthwhile. Trust becomes harder to sustain. Communities thin. Institutions feel distant. Short-term thinking expands. Not because people become irresponsible. Because instability changes what feels rational. People adapt again and again. Until eventually many stop asking: *How do I build something better?* and begin asking: *How do I simply protect what I still have?*

That shift matters. Because healthy systems ultimately depend on people remaining willing to participate in them. Not perfectly. But consistently. Participation in work. In business. In communities. In institutions. In the future itself. That investment becomes fragile when enough people quietly stop believing participation changes outcomes. That may sound abstract. It is not. That reality deserves seriousness. Not fear. And not blame. Seriousness. Because one of the hardest things societies eventually confront is this confidence, once weakened long enough, becomes difficult to rebuild.

Trust takes time. Participation takes reinforcement. And belief, once replaced by resignation, rarely returns automatically. That may ultimately be why conversations about drift matter. Not because every period of pressure becomes crisis. But because healthy systems depend on maintaining something easy to overlook while it still exists, the quiet belief that participation remains worth the effort. And perhaps that belief is more fragile, and more valuable, than many societies realize while they still have it.

What We Leave Behind

Every generation inherits systems it did not fully build. Roads, institutions, laws, markets, schools, businesses, communities, norms, and frankly, expectations. Ways of thinking about responsibility, work, risk, stability, and opportunity.

Some inherited systems create resilience. Others create fragility. Most contain some version of both. That reality matters because one of the easiest mistakes societies make is assuming inheritance only moves in one direction, backward. What we received. What previous generations built. What earlier decisions created. But inheritance moves forward too. Quietly, constantly, and through the systems people strengthen and ignore and repair or postpone maintaining.

This matters because every generation leaves something behind. Not only wealth. Or debt. Or infrastructure. Something harder to measure, conditions. The environment future people inherit when they begin trying to build lives of their own. Will participation feel worthwhile? Will stability feel achievable? Will hard work still feel meaningfully connected to outcomes? Will planning feel rational? Will trust feel easier to sustain or harder? Those questions matter because people rarely experience inherited systems immediately.

At first, systems simply feel normal. The economy someone grows up inside often feels inevitable. Housing costs feel inevitable. Work expectations feel inevitable. Risk feels inevitable. Opportunity feels inevitable. Pressure feels inevitable. People adapt to what surrounds them. Until eventually someone asks: *Did things always feel this way?* That question matters. Because drift rarely announces itself. It accumulates. Quietly, one adaptation at a time. One postponed correction at a time. One accepted fragility at a time.

And eventually the conditions surrounding ordinary life begin changing enough that future generations quietly inherit pressures previous generations never intended. Not through malice. And rarely through neglect alone. More often through accumulated postponement. The assumption that maintenance can always happen later. That future people will somehow adapt. And people do adapt. Often remarkably well. But adaptation should not be confused with health.

This matters because one of the quiet responsibilities healthy societies eventually confront is this future generations deserve more than instructions for survival. They deserve systems healthy enough that effort still feels capable of producing stability. Not guarantees, not perfection, possibility. The possibility that work still matters. Planning still matters. Responsibility still matters. Participation still matters. That possibility deserves protection. Not because the future owes anyone comfort. But because healthy societies have always depended on people believing tomorrow remains worth building toward.

Trust and participation also rarely return evenly. Some communities recover confidence faster than others. Some people remain cautious much longer. Periods of instability often leave emotional and institutional scars that take time to rebuild. That reality deserves patience rather than frustration. Meaningful participation usually returns gradually, reinforced through repeated experience rather than promises alone.

That may ultimately be what this conversation has always been about. Not whether systems are perfect. Not whether every problem disappears. Something simpler. Whether the people who come after us inherit conditions strong enough that participation still feels worth the effort. Because eventually every generation leaves something behind.

The harder question is whether future people inherit stronger foundations or simply better explanations for why drift became normal.

And fairness matters here too. No generation solves every problem. Every generation inherits pressures it did not fully create while trying to respond to conditions it only partially controls. Most inherited systems contain strengths worth preserving alongside weaknesses worth improving. Responsibility matters—not blame.

What Responsibility Looks Like

By now, another question may naturally begin emerging: *If any of this is true, what responsibility do ordinary people actually have?* That question deserves care. Because one of the easiest ways difficult conversations lose people is by quietly implying responsibility belongs entirely to someone else. Governments, corporations, markets, institutions, leaders, and experts. And to be fair, those things matter enormously.

Leadership matters. Policy matters. Business decisions matter. Institutional choices matter. Large systems influence millions of lives. That should never be minimized. But healthy societies rarely improve through leadership alone. They improve when responsibility becomes distributed. Quietly, practically, and imperfectly.

That matters because responsibility does not always look dramatic. Often it looks ordinary. Asking harder questions. Participating in conversations without surrendering curiosity to cynicism. Building businesses that treat people seriously. Leading organizations responsibly. Investing in communities. Remaining willing to challenge assumptions that no longer seem sustainable. Staying engaged even when certainty feels unavailable. That may sound small. Sometimes frustratingly small. Especially when problems feel large. But businesses understand this instinctively.

Healthy cultures rarely emerge because someone announces: *Things are different now.* Culture changes through repetition. Through expectations. Through accountability. And through participation. Enough people reinforcing healthier behavior consistently over time.

Large systems tend to work similarly. Which means responsibility rarely belongs entirely to institutions. Or entirely to individuals. Usually it exists somewhere harder: In between. Leaders have responsibilities. Businesses have responsibilities. Communities have responsibilities. Citizens have responsibilities. And none of those responsibilities require perfect agreement. That matters because one of the quieter temptations during difficult periods is disengagement. Suspicion grows. Fatigue grows. People begin assuming: *Nothing I do really matters anyway.*

That instinct is understandable. But perhaps also dangerous. Because healthy systems are rarely maintained through perfection. They are maintained through participation. The willingness to remain engaged even when outcomes feel uncertain. The willingness to ask difficult questions without surrendering to resignation. The willingness to believe improvement deserves effort even when guarantees do not exist.

That does not mean everyone must become an activist. Or policymaker. Or economist. Responsibility looks different for different people. Sometimes it looks like building responsibly. Sometimes leading responsibly. Sometimes staying curious. Sometimes refusing to normalize fragility too quickly. Sometimes simply remaining willing to participate in conversations that feel difficult but necessary.

That may ultimately be one of the hardest truths about healthy societies. That responsibility rarely feels convenient. But systems rarely improve when enough people quietly decide responsibility belongs only to someone else. Because eventually, drift becomes everyone's problem. And maintenance, however imperfect, eventually becomes everyone's responsibility too.

Why Hope Still Matters

By now, one thing should feel increasingly clear, none of this is simple. Healthy systems are difficult. Tradeoffs exist. Mistakes happen. Pressure accumulates. Drift happens. And no serious person should pretend meaningful change arrives without friction because one of the easiest ways difficult conversations lose credibility is by promising certainty where none exists.

Certainty sounds reassuring. Reality rarely works that way. Especially in large systems. Which may raise another reasonable question: *Why remain hopeful at all?*

- If change feels difficult...
- If institutions move slowly...

- If pressure often compounds before correction happens...

Why believe healthier outcomes remain possible? That question deserves attention. Because skepticism often feels rational. Many people have watched promises fail. Institutions disappoint. Leaders overpromise. Systems drift. Trust weaken. Adaptation replace progress. People learn caution. And sometimes caution becomes suspicion. That instinct is understandable. But there is an important distinction worth making, skepticism and hopelessness are not the same thing. Skepticism asks hard questions. Hopelessness stops asking. Skepticism still participates. Hopelessness withdraws. Skepticism demands seriousness. Hopelessness quietly assumes seriousness no longer matters.

This matters because healthy systems rarely improve through blind optimism. People are right to ask difficult questions. Right to challenge assumptions. Right to demand better thinking. Right to remain careful about large promises. But healthy systems also depend on something harder to sustain, the willingness to believe improvement remains possible—even before proof fully arrives. Not guaranteed improvement. Possible improvement. That difference matters.

Businesses understand this instinctively. Turnarounds happen because enough people continue believing difficult things remain achievable. Not easy, not certain, but achievable. Communities rebuild because enough people remain willing to invest effort before outcomes feel obvious. Families plan because tomorrow still feels worth preparing for. People continue building because possibility still feels stronger than resignation. Large systems often work similarly. That does not mean optimism should replace realism. Quite the opposite. Healthy hope tends to be grounded, measured, and practical. It recognizes constraints. Acknowledges uncertainty. And still asks: *Could something healthier realistically exist?*

That question matters. Because one of the quietest dangers drift creates is not instability itself. It is shrinking imagination. The gradual belief that improvement feels unrealistic enough to stop discussing seriously. And perhaps that is what makes hope more important than it initially appears. Not because hope guarantees outcomes. But because people rarely build toward futures they no longer believe deserve effort. Healthy skepticism matters. Difficult questions matter. Accountability matters. But perhaps hope matters too. Not as certainty, but as permission to continue participating before guarantees exist. Because healthier systems have never emerged from resignation alone. They begin when enough people remain willing to believe: *Maybe better is still worth trying for.*

Hope should not be confused with certainty. Serious systems still fail sometimes. Good ideas still struggle. Tradeoffs remain real. Conditions change. Some efforts disappoint. But healthy skepticism and cautious hope are not opposites. In many ways, they work best together. Skepticism sharpens ideas. Hope keeps people willing to continue participating long enough for better ones to emerge.

Remembering Ronnie

Somewhere along the way, this conversation stopped being entirely theoretical. It became personal. Not only for me. Likely for many readers too. Because after enough pages, enough examples, enough conversations about incentives, systems, drift, participation, and stability, most people quietly begin seeing someone. A parent, a coworker, a friend, a business owner, a neighbor, or even someone who worked hard. Did the right things. Carried responsibility seriously. And still somehow found stability becoming harder to hold than it felt like it should have been.

For me, that person was Ronnie. Not because Ronnie represented failure. Quite the opposite. Ronnie represented effort, responsibility, persistence, and the belief that hard work was still supposed to mean something. And yet over time, something changed. Not all at once, but slowly, quietly. The kind of drift difficult to notice while living inside it. Work still happened. Responsibilities still existed. Life still moved forward. But stability became harder. Pressure became heavier. Confidence became more difficult to sustain. Again, not collapse. Something quieter. Something many people increasingly recognize.

That matters because Ronnie was never really the point. The point was what Ronnie represented. Ordinary people trying to build ordinary lives. People not asking for perfection. Or guarantees. Or lives free from hardship. Something simpler. A fair chance. The belief that effort still matters. That responsibility still improves outcomes often enough to make participation feel worthwhile. That tomorrow still feels buildable.

Ronnie's story was never meant to suggest everyone experiences pressure the same way. Many people are doing well. Some industries remain strong. Some families feel stable. Many businesses continue thriving. The point was never universality. The point was visibility. Ronnie represented something increasingly familiar: people carrying responsibility seriously while quietly wondering why stability feels harder to sustain than expected.

This book has never argued that hardship should disappear. Or that healthy systems guarantee success. Life will always remain difficult sometimes. Failure will still exist. Risk will still exist. Tradeoffs will still exist. But healthy systems should make effort feel connected to possibility. Not perfectly. But meaningfully.

That matters because somewhere right now there are still people like Ronnie. People carrying responsibilities seriously. Showing up to work. Running businesses. Raising families. Trying, often quietly and without recognition. And many of them are still asking some version of the same question: *Why does this feel harder than it should?*

That question deserves consideration. Not dismissal. And perhaps that is ultimately why conversations like this matter. Not because one framework solves everything. And not because one book changes systems. But because ordinary people deserve systems healthy enough that effort still feels capable of producing something durable like stability, opportunity, dignity, and participation. The possibility that tomorrow still feels worth building toward.

Ronnie mattered because millions of people quietly carry some version of that same story. And perhaps the real question was never: *What happened to Ronnie?* The harder question may be: *How many more people quietly begin feeling the same way before societies decide drift deserves maintenance?* Because eventually, every system answers that question. The only uncertainty is when. And how many people quietly carry the cost while waiting.

The Conversation We Still Need to Have

If there is one hope sitting quietly underneath everything in this book, perhaps it is this, that the conversation does not end here. Not because this book contains every answer. It does not. And certainly not because one framework deserves unquestioned agreement. Healthy systems should always survive skepticism. Difficult questions matter. Counterarguments matter. Tradeoffs matter. No serious conversation about something this important should ask people to suspend critical thinking. Quite the opposite. The questions should become harder from here. Not easier.

Because by now, the conversation may no longer simply be: *What is wrong with the economy?* Perhaps the harder questions begin emerging instead: *What are healthy systems actually supposed to produce? What relationship should exist between effort and stability? How much drift should societies tolerate before maintenance becomes necessary? What responsibilities do institutions, businesses, communities, and individuals owe one another? What conditions make participation feel worthwhile again?* And perhaps most importantly: *What kind of future still feels worth building toward?* Those questions matter because large systems rarely improve through silence. Or slogans. Or outrage alone.

That incompleteness matters. Serious systems improve because difficult questions continue long after first frameworks emerge. Better assumptions appear. Weaknesses become visible. Tradeoffs sharpen. Institutions learn. Conversations mature. If anything, responsible thinking should become more demanding—not less—as possibilities become more real.

Healthy systems improve through serious conversations. Difficult conversations. Conversations capable of surviving disagreement without collapsing into hostility. Conversations where skepticism sharpens ideas instead of ending them. That kind of seriousness matters. Especially now. Because one thing should feel increasingly clear, the pressures many people experience are not imaginary. The frustration is not imaginary. The instability is not imaginary. And the growing feeling that something increasingly feels harder than it should deserves better than dismissal. But difficult realities deserve something else too Careful thinking humility, and patience. The willingness to challenge assumptions without pretending easy answers exist.

This book has argued repeatedly that the economy itself is not the enemy. Markets are not the enemy. Business is not the enemy. Success is not the enemy. Drift is. Misalignment is. The quiet accumulation of incentives no longer producing the outcomes people reasonably believed participation once made possible. That conversation is important. Not because agreement already exists. But because the stakes matter. Families matter. Communities matter. Businesses matter. Opportunity matters. The future matters. And perhaps healthier systems become possible only when enough people remain willing to ask difficult questions without surrendering either curiosity or responsibility.

If this book succeeds at anything, perhaps success is simple. Not agreement. Not persuasion. Just a conversation serious enough that people remain willing to keep asking: *Could something healthier still be possible?* Because meaningful change has always begun with questions people finally decide are worth asking seriously.

And perhaps that is where this conversation truly begins. Because the future has a way of arriving long before societies feel ready for the questions shaping it.

The Future Arrives Quietly

One of the stranger things about history is that major transitions rarely feel historic while people are living inside them. Most days simply feel ordinary. People go to work. Businesses try to stay open. Families navigate responsibilities. Bills arrive. Communities adapt. Life continues – quietly.

Futures also remain unpredictable. New technologies emerge. Unexpected crises appear. Assumptions fail. Progress accelerates in some places while slowing elsewhere. Conditions shift faster than anyone expects. That uncertainty matters because healthier systems are rarely those that perfectly predict the future. They are the ones flexible enough to remain resilient when reality changes unexpectedly.

That matters because one of the easiest mistakes people make when imagining the future is assuming meaningful change announces itself dramatically. Sometimes it does. More often, it accumulates. One decision at a time. One policy at a time. One business investment. One changed expectation. One adaptation. One conversation. One generation inheriting conditions slightly different than the one before it. Again, drift rarely announces itself. But healthier futures rarely announce themselves either. They are built. Often imperfectly and often without recognition at first.

That distinction matters because every generation eventually finds itself living inside questions previous generations postponed. Questions about affordability and opportunity and trust and participation, and responsibility, and ultimately, about stability. Questions that once felt distant eventually become ordinary. And eventually someone asks: *How did things end up this way?*

That question matters. Because systems are rarely shaped through single moments alone. More often, they are shaped through accumulation. Small choices repeated long enough that they begin feeling inevitable, again and again. Until eventually people forget those choices were ever choices at all. But history suggests something else too, that healthier futures often begin the same way. Not perfectly. And rarely all at once. People ask harder questions. Businesses adapt. Communities strengthen. Institutions slowly evolve. Conversations mature. Assumptions change. Participation expands.

Enough people begin deciding maintenance deserves effort before fragility becomes expectation. Rarely dramatic. Often frustratingly slow. But meaningful. That may ultimately be one of the harder truths about responsibility, that the future is rarely something people suddenly arrive inside. More often, it is something people quietly shape while believing they are simply responding to the present. That can feel overwhelming. But perhaps it should also feel empowering. Because if drift accumulates, improvement can accumulate too. Trust can accumulate. Better incentives can accumulate. Participation can accumulate. Healthier expectations can accumulate. Again, not perfectly, but meaningfully. And perhaps that matters because the future has a way of arriving whether people intentionally shape it or not.

Responsibility should also not be confused with blame. Circumstances differ. Capacity differs. Some people are surviving more than participating. That reality deserves compassion. Responsibility matters because systems rarely improve when everyone quietly assumes someone else must carry the burden alone.

The only real question is: *What exactly are we building while we wait for it to arrive?* Because eventually, quietly, and often sooner than expected the future becomes the present someone else has to live inside.

The Question We Leave Behind

After everything in this book, the questions about drift, incentives, participation, stability, responsibility, business, trust, and change; perhaps one final question quietly remains. Not a technical question. Not a political question. A human one. *What kind of future are we leaving behind?* That question matters because economies are never really about numbers alone. Numbers matter. Growth matters. Markets matter. Business matters. Productivity matters.

Healthy societies require all of those things. But eventually every system produces something deeper than outputs. It produces lived conditions. What ordinary life feels like. How difficult stability becomes. Whether effort still feels connected to outcomes. Whether planning feels rational. Whether participation still feels worthwhile. Whether tomorrow feels more buildable than fragile. Again, not perfection. No serious system promises perfection.

Life will always remain difficult sometimes. Setbacks will still happen. Risk will still exist. Failure will still exist. Healthy systems do not eliminate hardship. They make resilience more realistic.

That matters because somewhere right now there are parents quietly wondering whether life will feel harder for their children. Workers trying to understand why effort no longer stretches the way it once seemed to.

Business owners delaying decisions because uncertainty feels increasingly difficult to price.

Young adults questioning whether stability still feels realistic enough to plan toward.

People adapting, quietly, again and again. Trying, often harder than anyone realizes. That effort deserves seriousness. Not resentment. Not dismissal. But seriousness. Because perhaps the deeper responsibility of healthy societies has always been simple, not guaranteeing outcomes, but protecting possibility. The possibility that participation still matters. That work still matters. That responsibility still matters.

That tomorrow still feels worth preparing for. And perhaps that is where this conversation ultimately leaves us. Not with answers fully finished. But with responsibility. The responsibility to ask harder questions. To remain curious. To stay serious. To resist surrendering difficult conversations to outrage, resignation, or cynicism. And perhaps most importantly, to remain willing to believe healthier futures still deserve effort, even when certainty feels unavailable.

None of this guarantees agreement. Or success. Or easy answers. Serious systems remain difficult. Honest people will disagree. Tradeoffs remain unavoidable. But perhaps difficult futures deserve the same seriousness people already bring to difficult businesses, difficult families, and difficult communities: care, patience, responsibility, and a willingness to keep improving what matters.

Because the future, whether people notice it or not, is already arriving. Quietly. Through the systems being reinforced. The incentives being accepted. The questions being ignored. The conversations being avoided. Or the work people remain willing to begin. And perhaps the final question is not whether healthier systems are possible. Perhaps the harder question is simpler: What kind of future still feels worth building toward—and what responsibilities quietly come with leaving something stronger behind than we inherited? Because, eventually someone else has to live inside whatever we choose to leave behind.

If this work has done its job, it has not asked you to agree with every conclusion. It has asked you to consider the possibility that many of the challenges we experience are not isolated failures, but the predictable result of systems operating according to the incentives and measurements they were built to follow.

Whether the Alignment Economy ultimately succeeds or fails should not be determined by rhetoric, optimism, or ideology. It should be determined by whether its assumptions survive scrutiny, whether its mechanisms function as intended, and whether its outcomes can be demonstrated in practice.

That is why this manuscript does not stand alone. The companion technical appendices exist to examine the mathematics, implementation requirements, operational constraints, and administrative realities behind the ideas presented here. The legislative framework exists to explore the legal authority, institutional safeguards, and execution architecture required to translate those ideas into practice.

The purpose of this book is to make the structure visible. The purpose of the companion documents is to test whether that structure can withstand examination. Together, they provide a framework that can be understood, challenged, refined, and evaluated on its merits.

The question is no longer whether a different system can be imagined.

The question is whether a more aligned one can be built.

Purpose of the Correlation Table

The Alignment Economy was intentionally designed as a three-document ecosystem.

The manuscript explains the problem, makes the structure visible, and explores why the relationship between effort, participation, productivity, and stability has weakened over time.

The Alignment Economy Act provides the statutory framework necessary to authorize, govern, and constrain the system in law.

The Technical Appendices provide the operational architecture, implementation mechanisms, validation models, stress testing, and administrative requirements necessary to determine whether the framework can function in practice.

Each document serves a different purpose.

The manuscript creates belief.

The legislative framework creates authority.

The technical appendices create execution.

Because these documents were developed together, every material claim presented within the manuscript should be traceable to both a governing legal authority and a corresponding implementation mechanism. The purpose of this correlation table is to make that relationship visible.

This table serves three functions.

First, it allows readers to move directly from a concept introduced in the manuscript to the specific statutory provisions and technical sections supporting that concept.

Second, it provides a verification tool for researchers, reviewers, policymakers, economists, journalists, and other readers who wish to evaluate whether the framework is internally consistent across all three documents.

Third, it demonstrates a core design principle of the project itself: claims should not exist without implementation, implementation should not exist without authority, and authority should not exist without a clearly defined purpose.

The objective is not to ask readers to accept ideas on trust.

The objective is to provide a transparent path from concept, to law, to execution so each element can be independently examined, challenged, tested, and evaluated on its merits.

Taken together, the manuscript, the legislative framework, and the technical appendices form a single integrated system. This correlation table exists to make those connections visible.

Manuscript → Legislation → Appendix Correlation Table

Section 1 — The National Productivity Unit (NPU)

Manuscript Claim	Legislation	Appendix
The NPU is a single calculated unit connecting what the economy produces to what it costs to live (Ch1, Ch3)	Title I — §1.01 (Why NPU Must Exist), §1.02 (What NPU Measures), §1.03 (Construction of NPU)	A.1.1 (Operational Definition), A.1.21 (What NPU Represents)
NPU formula: NPU = (α × GDP per capita) + (β × EEBV) (Ch1, Ch3)	Title I — §1.03 (Construction), §1.04 (Calibration), §1.04.1 (Annual Calculation)	A.1.1 (Formula), E.2.1 (NPU Calculation System Operational Form), E.2.2 (Data Inputs and Validation Pipeline)
The weighting is fixed at 50/50 between productivity and participation cost; changes require Congress (Ch1, Ch15)	Title I — §1.03 (Construction), §1.04.7 (Congressional Review Authority)	A.1.22.4 (Why 50/50 Weighting — full justification), A.1.22.7 (What Prevents Political Manipulation)

Manuscript Claim	Legislation	Appendix
The EEBV comprises six categories: housing, food, healthcare, transportation, utilities, and basic communication (Ch1, Ch3)	Title I — §1.02 (EEBV definition), §1.03 (Construction)	A.1.1, E.2.3 (Essential Economic Basket Construction — six-category build)
NPU adjusts automatically as economic conditions change; it is calculated, not set politically (Ch1, Ch3)	Title I — §1.04.1 (Annual Calculation), §1.04.3 (Published NPU), §1.04.4 (Economic Alignment Increment), §0.18.1 (Formula-Driven Administration Rule)	A.1.4 (Calibration), A.1.15–A.1.16 (Failure Modes and Calibration Scenarios), E.2.4 (NPU Publication Cycle)
NPU is smoothed to prevent single-year volatility from whipsawing wages (Ch3, Ch6)	Title I — §1.04.2 (Smoothed Raw NPU), §1.04.3 (Published NPU), §1.04.6 (Convergence Period Administration)	A.5.2 (Annual Adjustment Constraint), A.5.3 (Multi-Year Smoothing Mechanism)

Manuscript Claim	Legislation	Appendix
During recession, NPU does not decrease even if inputs fall (Ch9, Ch12)	Title I — §1.04.6.1 (Extraordinary Economic Contraction and Effective NPU Continuity Protection)	A.1.22.9 (What Happens During Recession), C.1.0.6 (Recessionary Non-Decrease Constraint)
NPU transparency: inputs are known, relationships are defined, outcomes can be verified (Ch6)	Title I — §1.04.8 (Publication and Transparency Requirements), §0.06 (Role of Government)	E.2.8 (Audit and Verification Framework), E.2.5 (Mid-Cycle Monitoring)
The "illustrative" $20/hour NPU example; 1.0 NPU × 1,500 hours = $30,000 (Ch1)	Title I — §1.03.x (NPU construction produces the dollar value); example is illustrative per Ch15 disclaimer	A.1.17.1–A.1.17.5 (Low/Middle/High-Income Household and Employer Examples)
1.0 NPU = essential participation. 1.25 NPU = livable buffer. 2.0 NPU = skilled trades. 5.0 NPU = executive (Ch1, Ch3, Ch10)	Title I — §1.06 (Redefinition of Compensation Through NPU), §1.07 (Interpretive Application of NPU)	A.2.2 (Wage Bands / Observed Distribution Anchors), A.2.3 (Worker-Level Examples Cross-Sector)

Manuscript Claim	Legislation	Appendix
NPUX: book's shorthand for expressing any economic value as a multiple of NPU; does not replace negotiation (Ch4)	Title I — §1.05 (Economic Identity of NPU), §1.06; NPUX is the book's explanatory label for NPU multiples, not a separate statutory term	A.1.21 (What NPU Represents), A.2.1 (Wage Determination Framework)

Section 2 — Wages, Compensation, and Labor

Manuscript Claim	Legislation	Appendix
Wages are anchored to NPU; the relationship between contribution and output is no longer indirect (Ch3, Ch4)	Title I — §1.06, §1.07; Title VI — §6.01–§6.04 (Corporate Alignment and Productivity)	A.2.1 (Wage Determination Framework), A.2.4 (Wage Distribution Effects)
Workers still negotiate compensation; what changes is the reference point, not the act of	Title VI — §6.05 (construction clause: preserves "lawful enterprise discretion in compensation determination")	A.2.1 (Wage Determination Framework), A.2.9 (Labor Market Equilibrium Effects)

Manuscript Claim	Legislation	Appendix
negotiation (Ch4, Ch7)		
Employers who pay below 1.25 NPU (the Average Compensation Level threshold) contribute to the Stability Fund (Ch4, Ch9)	Title VI — §6.05 (Wage Alignment Contribution Adjustment — ACL threshold, δ-bounded formula)	B.4.5 (Employer Wage Alignment Contribution Mechanics), B.4.5.1 (Multi-Employer Attribution)
Multi-employer fragmentation is addressed: each employer's obligation is calculated on its own compensation and hours (Ch2, Ch4)	Title VI — §6.05.1 (Multi-Employer Wage Alignment Attribution)	B.4.5.1 (Multi-Employer Wage Alignment Attribution, anti-fragmentation)
Small businesses get transition protection — costs are not shock-absorbed all at once (Ch7, Ch9, Ch11)	Title V — §5.x (Transition and Phased Implementation); Title VI — §6.05(b) (δ phase-down)	A.2.8 (Small Business Case — Critical Edge Case), A.3.6 (Small Business Transition Path), A.2.6.1 (Sectoral Transition Safeguards)

Manuscript Claim	Legislation	Appendix
Turnover improves because workers are no longer reactive to small wage differences when underlying stability holds (Ch11)	Title I — §1.06, §1.07; Title VI — §6.05	A.2.4 (Wage Distribution Effects), A.2.11.1–A.2.11.5 (Worker and Household Scenarios)
Non-reduction transition rule: wages do not fall during transition (Ch6, Ch8)	Title V — Transition protections; Title VI — §6.05(b) δ convergence clause	A.3.7 (Non-Reduction Transition Rule — Binding Constraint), A.3.7.1 (Contraction Scenario Clarification)
Income is anchored to output and scales with system productivity growth (Ch4, Ch10)	Title I — §1.08 (Automatic Adjustment, Smoothing, Convergence)	A.1.20 (System Behavior Before and After NPU), A.2.4 (Wage Distribution Effects)

Section 3 — Taxation

Manuscript Claim	Legislation	Appendix
Tax system is anchored to NPU;	Title II — NPU-aligned tax	A.4.3 (Tax Bracket Structure NPU-

Manuscript Claim	Legislation	Appendix
brackets scale automatically with the unit rather than requiring political renegotiation (Ch4, Ch11)	system; §0.18.1 (Formula-Driven Administration Rule)	Based), A.4.3.1 (Definition of Baseline for Scaled Bracket Thresholds), B.3.4.1 (Annual Liability Schedule NPU-Based Participation Brackets)
Payroll withholding is real-time and cumulative across employers; no end-of-year surprise adjustments (Ch4, Ch11)	Title II — withholding provisions; §0.06.1 (Express Congressional Authorization for Implementation Systems)	A.4.5 (Payroll Withholding System), B.2.3 (Cumulative Participation Ledger / CPL), B.2.4 (Atomic Transaction and Reservation Engine / ATRE), B.2.7 (Multi-Payor Synchronization)
Capital gains and investment income are integrated into the same NPU-based system (Ch11)	Title II — capital gains provisions; Title IX — Financial System Integration	A.4.6 (Capital Gains and Investment Income), B.1.3.2 (Labor Versus Capital Attribution Rule)
Tax brackets eliminate gaming	Title II — §0.19 (Anti-	B.2.12 (Anti-Avoidance

Manuscript Claim	Legislation	Appendix
through NPU-denominated thresholds that adjust automatically (Ch6, Ch12)	Circumvention), §0.18.1 (Formula-Driven Administration)	Structural Controls), B.1.11 (Anti-Avoidance Controls and Economic Substance Safeguards)
Tax rates, brackets, and implementation thresholds in this book are illustrative; the weighting structure is not (Ch15)	Title I — §1.04.7 (Congressional Review Authority); Title II — amendable by Congress	A.4.8 (Criticism Handling), F.1.2 (Static vs Dynamic Scoring), F.1.10 (Interpretation Guidelines)

Section 4 — The Stability Fund

Manuscript Claim	Legislation	Appendix
The Stability Fund is not a reserve pool — it is a continuous, permanent part of the system's operation (Ch4, Ch5)	Title IV (Stability Fund Operational Stabilization / Resilience Mechanics); Title X (Funding, Solvency, Reserve Architecture)	A.5.1 (Core Stability Principle); A.6.9.9 (Stability Fund Interaction); F.1.6 (Stability Fund Modeling Approach)

Manuscript Claim	Legislation	Appendix
The Stability Fund is automatically triggered by conditions, not by political decision (Ch5, Ch6)	Title IV — automatic governor mechanisms; Title X — §10.09 (reserve targets per §4.08)	A.5.1 ("automatically triggered and automatically resolved... not discretionary, not political")
During stable periods the system builds Stability Fund capacity; during stress it deploys that capacity (Ch5)	Title IV — operational stabilization mechanics; Title X — funding and reserve architecture	A.5.2 (Annual Adjustment Constraint), F.1.6 (Stability Fund Modeling Approach), F.2.0.3 (Stability Fund Revenue Routing and Stream Character)
The Stability Fund distributes structurally — rule-governed, not arbitrarily or by discretion (Ch4, Ch5)	Title IV — rule-based draw triggers; Title X — reserve ratio and solvency architecture	A.6.9.9 ("governed by rules, not decisions... permanent, rules-based national economic stabilizer")
Existing programs (support, social insurance) are not immediately eliminated — they	Title V — §5.x (Transition, parallel operation, continuity); Title X — transition	A.3.3 (Dual System Operation Years 1–3), D.1.0 (Governing Transition

Manuscript Claim	Legislation	Appendix
run in parallel while the Stability Fund proves its capacity (Ch6, Ch8)	funding mechanisms	Continuity Architecture), D.2.3 (Phase III – Active System Shift)
Over time, as the Stability Fund proves sustained capacity, future retirement participation may transition; existing beneficiaries are protected throughout (Ch4)	Title V – Transition protections; §0.20 (Transition, Continuity, and Implementation Protection)	D.4.0 (Governing Household Transition Behavior), D.3.7 (Automatic Pause Mechanism)
Stability Fund contributions come from individual participation, business output, and system-level economic activity (Ch4, Ch5)	Title IV – contribution sources; Title X – funding architecture	F.2.0 (Governing Revenue Modeling Architecture), F.3.4 (Corporate Contribution Model), F.3.6 (Supplemental Revenue Mechanisms)

Section 5 — Corporate Participation, Extraction, and Capital

Manuscript Claim	Legislation	Appendix
Corporations participate proportionally to system output, labor utilization, and system integration level (Ch4, Ch9)	Title VI — §6.01–§6.04 (Corporate Alignment, Productivity, Capital Discipline), §0.07 (Role of Corporations)	B.4.1 (Covered Entities), B.4.2 (Core Principle — Productivity-Linked Contribution), B.4.4 (Contribution Categories)
Extraction: when economic participation becomes disconnected from productive circulation, allowing value to accumulate outside the system that produced it (Ch11)	Title II — Extraction Participation Levy: "extraction shall mean the sustained retention or allocation of materially elevated participation in a manner materially disconnected from productive circulation"	A.6.9 (Systemic Capital Participation Assessment / SCPA), A.6.9.1 (Core Principle)
Extraction is not success, wealth,	Title II — extraction	A.6.9.7.5 (Economic

Manuscript Claim	Legislation	Appendix
entrepreneurship, or hard work — it is disconnection from productive circulation (Ch11)	definition expressly excludes investment, R&D, wages, and productive deployment	Substance and Continuity Principle)
Businesses operating in the system are rewarded for productivity and penalized for excessive disconnection, not punished for success (Ch4, Ch9, Ch11)	Title VI — §6.01–§6.14; Title II — EPL structure preserves productive investment	A.6.9.7 (Anti-Avoidance Constraint), C.2.6 (Profit Model Reconfiguration), C.2.7 (Adversarial Firm Behavior)
Automation displacement generates a contribution obligation proportional to the labor it replaces (Ch4, implied Ch11)	Title VI — §6.13 (Automation Participation and Continuity Contribution)	B.4.6 (Automation Displacement Contribution / ADC)
Offshore capital remains connected through graduated	Title VI — §6.15 (Offshore Productivity	A.6.9.7.4 (Synthetic and Substitute

Manuscript Claim	Legislation	Appendix
alignment incentives; increasing disconnection receives progressively adjusted participation treatment (Ch4)	Participation); Title VII (Global Alignment, Trade Discipline, External Enforcement)	Economic Exposure), B.2.13 (Cross-Border Income Controls)
Capital flight concern: businesses optimize for predictability, labor stability, and demand — not only for marginal tax differences (Ch12)	Title VII — Global Alignment framework; Title VI — §6.15 offshore participation	H.0.6 (External Pressure — Global Trade, Capital Movement), A.1.22.3 (Why not alternative tax structures)
No cap on success — high NPUX positions (2.0, 5.0, higher) remain fully rewarded within the system (Ch1, Ch3, Ch4, Ch10)	Title I — §1.06, §1.07; Title II — progressive bracket structure preserves high-earner participation	A.2.2 (Wage Bands), A.4.4 (Progressive Tax Calculation Full Walkthrough), A.4.9 (Human Tax Perception Comparison)
Market Stability Assessment: financial-market participation	Title IX — Financial System, Banking,	A.6.8 (Market Participation Contributions / MSA), A.6.8.1–

Manuscript Claim	Legislation	Appendix
contributes to system stability (not in manuscript by name, but referenced as financial system integration)	Capital Flow Integration	A.6.8.9 (full MSA mechanics)

Section 6 — Transition Architecture

Manuscript Claim	Legislation	Appendix
Nothing is taken away first — the system begins by stabilizing conditions before replacing anything (Ch7, Ch8)	Title V — §5.x (Transition, Implementation, System Adoption); §0.20 (Transition, Continuity, Implementation Protection)	A.3.1 (Transition Objectives), A.3.3 (Dual System Operation), D.1.0 (Governing Transition Continuity Architecture)
Transition occurs in phases: the Stability Fund first demonstrates capacity, then integration occurs, then	Title V — phased implementation; §0.20	D.2.1–D.2.4 (Phase I through IV), D.3.0 (Governing Phased Implementation Architecture)

Manuscript Claim	Legislation	Appendix
consolidation (Ch6, Ch7, Ch8)		
Adoption spreads through demonstrated function, not forced replacement (Ch7)	Title V — voluntary adoption and incentive structures; §0.04 (Philosophy of Alignment)	D.2.0.3 (Transition Trigger Conditions), D.3.7 (Automatic Pause Mechanism)
Wage Alignment Contribution (δ) is temporary — it phases down as wages converge toward the 1.25 NPU threshold (Ch4, Ch8)	Title VI — §6.05(b)(4): δ bounded ≤ 1.0, must phase toward ordinary treatment	B.4.5 (Employer Wage Alignment Contribution Mechanics — δ phase-down)
The system has a tipping point: once enough participation moves through aligned structures, operating outside becomes the harder choice (Ch7)	Title V — convergence mechanics; §0.21 (Long-Term Preservation and Continuity)	D.2.4 (Phase IV — Full Alignment), D.2.6 (Governing Conclusion)

Manuscript Claim	Legislation	Appendix
Transition metrics are defined and publicly verifiable — the system does not advance until it earns the right to (Ch8)	Title V — phase advancement conditions; §0.16 (Administrative Construction and Limitation)	D.3.1–D.3.10 (Core Transition Metrics Framework through Transparency and Public Verification), D.3.7 (Automatic Pause Mechanism)

Section 7 — System Resilience and Stress Response

Manuscript Claim	Legislation	Appendix
An aligned economy does not prevent recession — it improves recession durability (Ch9, Ch12)	Title IV — Stability Fund resilience mechanics; Title I — §1.04.6.1 (Contraction Protection)	A.1.22.9 (What Happens During Recession), H.0.3 (Output Disruption), D.1.9 (Governing Conclusion)
When participation slows, the system responds automatically	Title IV — automatic stabilization triggers; Title I — §1.04.6 (Convergence	A.5.1 (Core Stability Principle), H.0.1 (Stress Event Categories), H.0.8 (System Response Mechanisms)

Manuscript Claim	Legislation	Appendix
— not after the fact (Ch5, Ch9)	Period Administration)	
Inflation: the system strengthens productive resilience, making inflation easier to manage — not eliminating it (Ch12)	Title IV — Stability Fund countercyclical function; Title I — NPU smoothing	A.5.4 (Wage-Price Feedback Control), A.5.5 (Full System Walkthrough: Wage→Price→Demand Loop), A.5.6 (High Inflation Stress Case), A.5.7 (Failure Mode: True Wage-Price Spiral)
Bad actors: healthy systems plan for imperfection; exploitation becomes harder to sustain than productive participation (Ch12)	§0.19 (Anti-Circumvention, Functional Equivalence, Preservation of Statutory Effect); Title VIII — Governance and Enforcement	B.2.12 (Anti-Avoidance Structural Controls), B.1.11 (Anti-Avoidance Controls), C.3 (Adversarial Actor Classes and Strategies), H.0.5 (Behavioral Distortion)
The system resists incremental	§0.19 (Anti-Circumvention); §0.21 (Long-	A.1.19 (Failure Mode: Political Manipulation), A.1.22.7 (What Prevents

Manuscript Claim	Legislation	Appendix
erosion — small changes cannot shift the foundation, only the inputs (Ch6)	Term Preservation); §0.22 (Governing Rule of Interpretation)	Political Manipulation), H.1.0.3 (Congressional Amendment and Methodology Lock)

Section 8 — Governance and Independence

Manuscript Claim	Legislation	Appendix
NPU governance is independent of short-term political cycles, institutional incentives, and market pressure (Ch6)	§0.06 (Role of Government), §0.16 (Administrative Construction), §0.22 (Governing Rule of Interpretation); Title VIII — Governance and System Integrity	A.1.22.7 (What Prevents Political Manipulation), H.1.0.1 (Ministerial Implementation Requirement), H.1.0.2 (Judicial Construction and Review Boundary)
No single entity controls all inputs to NPU calculation — natural constraint against	§0.16, §0.19; Title VIII — multi-agency verification	E.2.2 (Data Inputs and Validation Pipeline), E.3.1 (Core Design Principle), B.2.17 (Privacy, Data

Manuscript Claim	Legislation	Appendix
manipulation (Ch6)		Minimization, System Firewalls)
Government enables structure; it does not dictate outcomes (Ch6, Ch14)	§0.06 (Role of Government), §0.06.1 (Express Congressional Authorization), §0.04 (Philosophy of Alignment)	E.1.0 (Governing Institutional Implementation Architecture), E.1.1 (National Productivity Authority), E.1.2 (Treasury Execution Authority)
Congress retains authority to amend; the weighting structure is deliberately bounded against routine adjustment (Ch15)	Title I — §1.04.7 (Congressional Review Authority); §0.18.1 (Formula-Driven Administration)	A.1.22.7, H.1.0.3 (Congressional Amendment and Methodology Lock)

Section 9 — Specific Structural Claims Verified Against Both Documents

Manuscript Claim	Legislation	Appendix
The Stability Fund's draw is rule-governed and automatic, not discretionary or political (Ch4, Ch5)	Title IV — statutory draw triggers and governor conditions; Title X — reserve ratio per §4.08	A.6.9.9 ("governed by rules, not decisions"), A.5.1 ("automatically triggered and automatically resolved") — **W2 CONFIRMED CLOSED**
Offshore profits remain connected through graduated participation incentives; disconnection is progressively adjusted, not binary-penalized (Ch4) — W3	Title VI — §6.15; Title VII — Global Alignment	B.2.13 (Cross-Border Income Controls), A.6.9.7.4 (Synthetic and Substitute Economic Exposure) — **W3 CONFIRMED CLOSED**
Capital-flight deterrence rests on predictability and productive stability, not solely tax structure (Ch12) — W4	Title VII; Title VI — §6.15	H.0.6 (External Pressure), A.1.22.3 — **W4 CONFIRMED CLOSED**

Manuscript Claim	Legislation	Appendix
The NPU weighting structure is a structural design choice distinct from illustrative parameters; Congress can modify it but it is bounded against routine adjustment (Ch15) — W5	Title I — §1.04.7; §0.18.1	A.1.22.4, A.1.22.7 — W5 Confirmed Closed

Section 10 — Messaging and Communication Consistency

Manuscript Claim	Legislation	Appendix
This is not redistribution — it is structural reconnection of contribution to output (Ch3, Ch4, Ch11)	§0.04 (Philosophy of Alignment); §0.07 (Role of Corporations); Title I — §1.01	G.1.6 (The "What It Is NOT" Clarification), G.2.7 (Managing Perceived Trade-Offs), G.3.1.5 (The "Why It Feels Fair" Explanation)
This is not central planning — markets still price, businesses still	§0.06 (Role of Government), §0.04; Title VI	G.1.6, G.2.9 (Common Messaging Mistakes to Avoid), I.1.3

Manuscript Claim	Legislation	Appendix
compete, workers still negotiate (Ch4, Ch7, Ch12)	construction clause	(Perceived Unfairness)
This is not a cap on success — rewards still exist for skill, risk, contribution, and innovation (Ch1, Ch4, Ch10, Ch11)	Title I — §1.06, §1.07; Title II — progressive bracket structure	G.2.4 (Business Leaders / Employers), G.2.3 (workers), A.4.9 (Human Tax Perception Comparison)
Extraction is not morally framed — it is a structural condition, not an accusation (Ch11)	Title II — extraction defined as a measurable condition, not a moral judgment	G.1.6, G.2.9, G.3.1.5
The system strengthens competition by reducing survival-pressure fragility, not by eliminating competitive outcomes (Ch11, Ch12)	§0.07 (Role of Corporations); §0.04	C.2.6 (Profit Model Reconfiguration), C.2.12 (Long-Term Equilibrium)

About This Work

This book was written to make the structure visible. Its purpose is not to answer every technical question, model every fiscal assumption, or reproduce the full legislative framework required to implement a system of this scale.

Those questions matter. But they serve a different purpose.

The Alignment Economy exists to explain:

- why the current system behaves the way it does;
- why instability continues despite productivity and growth;
- what structural misalignment looks like;
- and what an alternative could realistically become.

Understanding must come before implementation. A system cannot be seriously evaluated until it can first be clearly seen.

That is the purpose of this manuscript.

For readers seeking deeper technical detail, this work is supported by companion materials designed for different forms of scrutiny.

Technical Framework & Implementation Appendices

provide deeper operational detail regarding system mechanics, execution pathways, modeling assumptions, and implementation structure.

The Alignment Economy Act

contains the legislative framework necessary to operationalize the system in statutory form.

These documents are intentionally different. Not because one matters more than another, but because serious ideas must survive different kinds of scrutiny.

Some questions are philosophical. Some are technical. Some are legislative. And some are practical.

This book begins with understanding.

The rest exists for those who want to test what understanding reveals.

The full technical appendices and legislative framework are made publicly available for low or no cost at https://The-Alignment-Economy.com because serious ideas deserve serious scrutiny. Email requestmoreinfo@the-alignment-economy.com for more information.

A Note on Initiative

Thirty years ago, I walked into a shipbuilding operation and started talking about levels of initiative. I've been giving some version of that speech ever since.

The framework wasn't mine originally. William Oncken Jr. and Donald Wass described five levels of initiative in a 1974 Harvard Business Review article later popularized by Ken Blanchard. Stephen Covey expanded it to six levels in Principle Centered Leadership. I adapted it for the shop floor and have been using it in operations ever since.

Here's how I explain it:

Level One — Wait to be told.
This level should be reserved for toddlers. When a two-year-old needs to be told to pick up their toys, that's appropriate. Nobody in a functioning workplace should be here.

Level Two — Be told, then report back.
We expect this of early grade school children — someone tells them to do something and they come back on their own to confirm it's done. Some adults operate here. That's a culture problem, not a capability problem. It can be grown.

Level Three — Do it, report back, and suggest what comes next.
This is where middle schoolers start to operate. It's also the minimum expectation for every hourly worker in any operation I have ever run. Every day. In all work-related activities. Not occasionally. Not just when it's convenient.

Level Four — Identify problems and ask what to do.
This is where every lead person and frontline supervisor

should be executing regularly. The shift from level three to level four is significant — you're no longer waiting for problems to be handed to you. You're finding them.

Level Five — Identify problems, build solutions, and ask to implement.
Every manager and above should operate here at minimum. The solution comes with the problem. You're not bringing me a question. You're bringing me a recommendation.

Level Six — Fix the problem and report what you have done.
This is the goal of operational excellence. Every person responsible for leading people should aspire to this level in everything they do. You saw it, you solved it, you executed it, and you closed the loop.

Level Seven — Just fix it.
No report required. Full autonomy. Full accountability.

Here's what I tell every workforce I've ever addressed:

"Every single one of you is already at level seven before you walk through that door. You're living your lives — mowing your lawns, paying your bills, raising your children, running your entire personal operation — at level seven. It's ludicrous to believe we should accept anything less from ourselves at work."

I wrote this book at level six.

I identified a problem that has been visible for forty-five years but rarely described as a single system. I built a solution. I created the implementation path. I am reporting what I've done.

The work of level seven belongs to the American people and the representatives they elect to act on their behalf.

That's not a limitation of this book. That's how large systems are supposed to change.

Oncken, William Jr. and Donald L. Wass. "Management Time: Who's Got the Monkey?" *Harvard Business Review*, November-December 1974.
Covey, Stephen R. *Principle Centered Leadership.* Simon & Schuster, 1990.

A Note on the Numbers

The Alignment Economy is a structural proposal. Its value lies in the architecture — the relationship between wages, productivity, cost of living, and taxation — not in any specific parameter within it. The specific tax rates, Essential Economic Basket components, implementation thresholds, and other policy parameters presented throughout this work are illustrative and appropriately subject to legislative debate, empirical refinement, and democratic negotiation.

The National Productivity Unit weighting structure is different. The framework is intentionally built around a fixed 50/50 balance between productive output and participation cost. That balance is a structural design choice rather than a policy preference. It exists to ensure that neither productivity nor participation can dominate the measurement system over time.

While Congress retains the authority to modify any statutory framework, the weighting structure is deliberately bounded because allowing routine political or administrative adjustment of those coefficients would gradually reintroduce the same measurement distortions the system is designed to solve.

Legislative adoption, if it comes, will be messy. It should be. The specific numbers in this proposal are the appropriate subject of democratic negotiation — between legislators, economists, labor representatives, and the public. What should not be negotiated away is the principle: that wages, taxation, and the cost of essential participation in the economy must be anchored to the same reference point and move together.

A change to the weighting of the NPU formula does not break the system. A change to the tax brackets does not break the system. The system breaks only if the anchor itself is removed — if wages, taxes, and costs are once again allowed to drift independently of one another. That is the line this work asks legislators not to cross, regardless of what they do with the numbers on either side of it.

Nothing in this work should be interpreted as legal, financial, or investment advice. The projections and modeling contained herein are illustrative and intended to demonstrate structural relationships rather than predict future outcomes

www.ingramcontent.com/pod-product-compliance
Lightning Source LLC
LaVergne TN
LVHW040517210926
848480LV00007BA/1486
9798995922100